To Sonny

TRUTH
AND
JUSTICE
FOR FUN
AND
PROFIT

Best

MICHAEL HEATON

TRUTH AND JUSTICE FOR FUN AND PROFIT

GRAY & COMPANY, PUBLISHERS · CLEVELAND

Gray & Company, Publishers
www.grayco.com

Library of Congress Cataloging-in-Publication Data
Heaton, Michael, 1956-
Truth and justice for fun and profit: collected reporting / Michael Heaton.
    p. cm.
ISBN-13: 978-1-59851-039-3 (hardcover)
1. United States–Social conditions—1980-   I. Title.
HN59.2.H43 2007
306.0973'09045—dc22   2007025669

Printed in the United States of America
10 9 8 7 6 5 4 3 2 1

*This book is dedicated with love to
Nancy, Madison, Zoey and Sidney.
Always and forever.*

CONTENTS

FOREWORD

Michael Heaton is my favorite Cleveland columnist. Not only because of his title—to be "Minister of Culture" in Cleveland is a wild and wacky oxymoron . . . (*Minister of Culture?* In our boozy, brawling, burping, wife-beater-clad town?)—but because Michael Heaton tells the truth in a perceptive, sometimes provocative, usually funny way. He swings for a fence every time while his columnist colleagues too often are too proud of bunting their way to first base.

He isn't afraid to stick the old bloody pin in, either, as I myself discovered when he was discussing *Basic Instinct.* (I stood him up for a drink as payback and as payback for *that*, he presented me with a remedial primer about screenwriting). I forgave him, of course, not only because of his charm and blarney but also because he has proven that he is not afraid to stick the old bloody pin into himself, either. He once wrote a column listing all his observations and prognostications that the passage of time revealed to be stupid.

Before I tell you about this book, I want to tell you about its author. He once had hair; now he doesn't. He once was lean; now he isn't. He loves John Prine and Tom Waits and Elmore Leonard and the blues and reggae, which defines him I think as an FDIT: Fuddy-duddy in training. Yes, he's a writer and a good one, but there is nothing ascetic or abstract that I can detect about him. His face looks now like the face of a guy sitting down at the end of the bar with his third boilermaker, loudly and obscenely bitching about how you can't find good weed on the West Side anymore. While he likes going out to L.A. to see his sister (who, thankfully doesn't look like him), he loves Cleveland.

Get this: Michael Heaton left some of the primo hip cities of the world (New York, San Francisco) *to come back to Cleveland.* Yup, he's nuts; blessed by God with the usual writerly (and Irish) madness. (I know all about it; I, too, am blessed in my Hunky way.)

To sum him up: he tells truths, he loves bars, he loves Cleveland, he loves his family, he's a great dad, and he tries his best (don't we all?) to be a good husband. And he's nuts (but only a little).

Now a few things about his book: If Michael Heaton's columns are poems (they aren't) then the stories in this book read like short stories (they don't). Well, you know, *sort of.* These stories are journalism, after all, but at their best they approach the layered impact of a good short story. To a great extent that's because Michael Heaton isn't afraid to illuminate the dark side, but also because he *likes* people and sees the jewel inside every person he writes about and, I suspect, every person he meets. He understands humanity because he doesn't deny his own. While he shows skill and intelligence in the form of journalism, where dispassionate objectivity rules, he is unafraid to show his own heart as he tells us what makes the people he writes about tick.

His canvas is broad. The people he writes about, the people he is fascinated by, the people he writes about to understand himself (as all good writers do) are like characters out of a novel.

These are some of the people in this book: A mob guy turned FBI informant who puts his best friend in jail; a cop who hunts pedophiles; a local photographer who becomes part of Manhattan's art world; another local photographer who suddenly finds himself in the line of fire; the men of Fire Engine Company 41; a war hero who becomes part of the Nixon White House and then a drug dealer.

There are legendary Clevelanders here, too: Robert Manry, whose feat of sailing the Atlantic Ocean took a tragic toll upon his children; comic graphic novelist Harvey Pekar; Browns legend Gary Collins; sportcaster Casey Coleman, who bravely fought to live; and Mayor Frank Jackson, who declared war on drug dealers and prostitutes.

What unites all the people in this book is their connection to Cleveland. Does Michael Heaton love *Clevelanders* as much as he loves Cleveland? Yes, he does (as I do). Why? Because, as I said earlier, he's a little nuts (as am I).

But we chose to live here. *We are Clevelanders,* and our constant bitching about the city is the best indication of how much we love this damn, rusty, polluted, God-forsaken place.

Michael Heaton is one whiz-bang lollapalooza of a talented writer. He is always fun to read, but this book is a celebration of the human spirit. It sings and zings!

—Joe Eszterhas

THE FUNNEST THING EVER

People will tell you that journalism is about doing good, fighting for the oppressed, seeking truth and justice, and changing the world.

Sometimes it is.

But what they never tell you is how much *fun* it is.

This business is so much excruciating, frustrating and thrilling fun.

Many brave journalists have given their lives in search of The Story, for the good of others and the world. But even those heroes were first drawn in by a DNA-driven desire to see things, ask questions, write about and explain the world.

Is there any other line of work where being an impertinent, inquisitive, self-involved son of a bitch is considered a virtue?

This profession allows me to have a daily, active, if minor role in what Ambrose Bierce called The Passing Show. I have been able to splash in this world's public pond for almost 30 years. And it is a blast.

In this business, if you do it right, you get close enough to people to smell them. You meet the politicians, soldiers, cops, criminals, artists, musicians, movie stars, doctors, lawyers, scientists, priests, prophets and kings.

That stew gives off a heady scent.

But most importantly, this job puts a lucky schmoe like me next to the proverbial one-legged man pushing a three-wheeled shopping cart full of Diet Dr Pepper cans who swears you owe his ex-wife, the Eskimo, twelve bucks. (The best part of that scenario is that the man is not deranged or lying. The Eskimo woman did in fact give you that money—for a waiting cab—the night the crystal-nosed gangbangers at the bar thought you were asking way too many questions, even though you explained earlier in the evening that's exactly what you were there to do. Crystal champagne and home-rocked crack can bring on sudden, potentially lethal mood changes in people. These are things you don't learn in most accredited colleges. Hence my ongoing employment in this business.)

The two things that most prepared me for journalism were hitchhiking and sneaking into rock concerts. Both misdemeanors. (I'm a little criminal; God forgive me.)

I hitchhiked to high school and around college for eight years. It taught me how to talk to complete strangers. There's no training like getting in a car with someone and starting a conversation from road tar. I had rides that lasted eight minutes and eight hours. I met saints and sinners. Most importantly I learned that everyone has a story, and they are all aching to tell it. This single fact keeps all newspapers and magazines in business today.

Sneaking into concerts in the 1970s was a hobby that became a habit. Now, when told that "Press" isn't invited to some public event, I make it my business to not only get in, but bring six of my friends, and then get backstage for an exclusive interview and dried-out turkey sandwiches from the deli tray. Access is everything.

Talk these days of the death of old-fashioned journalism on paper abounds. Guess where? The Internet. But newspaper and magazine journalism still gets big stories in a way that other mediums don't: close up, on the ground, in the first person. Internet content doesn't appear by magic. Most often the magic starts with ink-stained, flat footed, question-asking, note-taking guys and gals like, well . . . us.

My rules of journalism are as these:

1. ABC, Always Be Curious.
2. Read everything.
3. Always ask questions.
4. Never take no for an answer.
5. Don't talk, LISTEN.
6. Pray. There's no such thing as luck.
7. Think of the re-write as a second chance. Everybody deserves one.
8. A good editor is a gift from God.
9. Live to write another day.
10. Be kind. It's the gift you leave your colleagues.

I didn't get into this business to change the world. I got into it to discover it. With a corporate credit card.

Professionally, I did it all backwards. New York, San Francisco, Cleveland. According to high-priced career counselors, it should have been the other way around. But no complaints. I made stops in El Salvador, Paris and Bali along the way. And man, I know how lucky I am to be doing this.

I'd like to believe my writing is important. That some of my work changed the world. Some lives? Even a little? Maybe?

The truth is I've had more fun than any honest working person should ever admit.

I enjoyed writing these stories. And if the Lord is willing and illiteracy don't rise, I intend to keep writing them.

—Michael Heaton

CRIME AND PUNISHMENT

FBI UNDERCOVER

*Battle-scarred and disillusioned, FBI agent
Ted Domine calls it quits after 15 years.*

Cleveland racketeer Sal Del Vecchio swaggered into the lounge of the JFK Airport Marriott to talk with two Gambino crime family associates about a $3 million American Express counterfeit check scam and to offer some long-promised phony car titles to the mobsters.

The wise guys, Mike Zampana, a tall, dark and massively built New York City sanitation worker, and the sawed-off Charlie Schiavo, a mobbed-up, one-man crime wave, sat down with Del Vecchio, ordered drinks and began discussing "business."

Suddenly, urgently and inexplicably, Zampana insisted they move the meeting to Del Vecchio's hotel room. Something was bad wrong. Once in the room, Zampana threw Del Vecchio up against a wall, put the snub-nosed barrel of a nickel-plated .38-caliber pistol in his ear and cocked the hammer.

Del Vecchio swore violently. There'd been a prior agreement about no guns. But Del Vecchio knew Zampana was crazy. Only the day before, Del Vecchio noticed blood and gray matter on the wall of the garage where they were cutting up stolen cars to sell for parts. Zampana told him he had just whacked a guy who'd been holding out.

But the real problem at the Marriott was that Sal Del Vecchio wasn't who he claimed to be. He was Cleveland FBI agent Ted Domine. And he was wearing a wire. Once Zampana began to frisk the agent, he *knew* he was done for.

Undercover work is a game of percentages and Domine had been pushing his luck for years. On that day in 1994, Domine swore that if he survived, he would get out from undercover. This was one close call too many. He had to cut back. However long it took, he had to get out.

• • •

Ted Domine's law-enforcement career spanned 27 years. During that time, he assumed a half-dozen identities, developing cases that resulted in hundreds of arrests involving murder, drugs, organized crime, counterfeiting, corruption and millions in stolen goods. No FBI agent in Cleveland history has "made" the number of cases Domine initiated and executed. Colleagues say only a handful of agents in the country can match the number of arrests and the commendations he received from the Bureau for resourcefulness, dedication and enterprise.

"He made a lot of bosses look good over the years," says John B. Gibons, a prosecutor in the U.S. Attorney's office in Cleveland from 1985 to 1989 who handled some of the cases that Domine developed.

FBI officials in the Cleveland office didn't respond to requests for interviews regarding Domine. However, by all other accounts, in an organization that lives and breathes on agent-generated statistics indicating the number of convictions, Domine was a prized employee.

"He always brought in airtight, prosecutable cases," says Gibbons. Domine was noted for initiating his own operations and for cutting through the dense, often maddening government bureaucracy to make them happen.

On the street he slipped in and out of character, playing Sal Del Vecchio. Vinnie Spinoza or Tony Amatangelo. His courage was offset by a raucous sense of humor that served him well in the most dangerous situations. He was an equal opportunity undercover guy. He'd arrest anybody: Italians, African Americans, South Americans, truck thieves, drug dealers, outlaw bikers. Not to mention police captains and suburban majors. Some could even laugh about it afterwards. Cops and politicians excepted.

Domine has a foot-thick photo album full of newspaper clippings of his exploits and awards, letters of commendation and appreciation from supervisors, executives and a congressman. He has certificates of achievement from three FBI directors. There's even a photograph of Domine and a young man standing together in the FBI office sharing a laugh for the camera. They look like old friends. It's Tom Foster, a bank robber Domine apprehended earlier that afternoon.

Domine has a classic love/hate relationship with the Bureau and undercover work. The problem with an undercover career, says

Domine, is the long-term effects. The work all but consumed him. His devotion to, and talent for, the job cut two ways. He excelled at undercover work, but it almost destroyed his personal life. He now believes he stayed undercover too long. He was *allowed* to work undercover much longer than was healthy for him and was fair to his parents, wife and child.

He believes the Bureau should have seen that happening and intervened.

"They used me like a whore," he says of the FBI. "But I let them. Nobody forced me to do this. Undercover work became an addiction for me. It got out of hand."

Domine says the physical and psychological rush of closing a case is beyond description. His eyes are wide and his face goes Fourth of July when describing the euphoria. The bigger the bust, the greater the risk he was willing to take. From operation to operation, Domine kept flying closer to the flame.

Over time, the job began to eclipse his personal life. While undercover he couldn't make plans at home. He was on standby 24 hours a day. The average criminal enterprise is not a 9-to-5 job. It's 2 a.m. phone calls. Weekends away. He regularly missed holidays, family birthdays and anniversaries. His life was not his own.

Ten years into his undercover work Domine began to exhibit behavior twelve-step counselors call "isolating." He was uncomfortable at home, and didn't trust his family. Domine distinctly remembers in 1988 being antsy and anxious at his daughter's sixth birthday party at a roller skating rink. He didn't want to be there. He wanted to be out on the street.

He lost interest in his hobbies of scuba diving and golf. His undercover life became more real than his real life. In the end, it all added up to one thing: He'd been under too long.

This summer, Ted Domine put the job he loved behind him. He wept when he called his mother in Pennsylvania to tell her his law-enforcement career was over.

As might be expected from someone with an uncanny talent for undercover work, Ted Domine has a complex personality shot through with contradiction. He's Ted the agent, Ted the wise guy, Ted the suburban husband and dad.

On a recent drive to visit his mother, he's Ted the dutiful son, revisiting his past. Domine, 48, is the only child of Ted Sr., a retired electrical finisher who died last year, and Josephine, who still lives in the house where Domine grew up in southwest Pennsylvania. The last name was originally Domineo. Sicilian.

He drives through the geography of his youth: Canonsburg, Pennsylvania, population 10,000, is the birthplace of both Perry Como and Bobby Vinton. The former mining town is home to Futchie's Pool Hall and storefronts such as Hair's Looking At You beauty parlor and Shorty's Diner, a booth-lined dive that has served its famous chili dogs since the Thirties.

Domine's emotions whipsaw back and forth. This is where he grew up, swam in the creeks, caddied at the public golf course and set pins at the bowling alley.

This is where he first learned and practiced law enforcement. His mood swings from fondly nostalgic, thinking about his childhood, to profoundly sad that he's looking back on his career. He grimaces with revulsion at some of the police-work memories, the bodies that surface in his mind as he drives along the small towns of Charleroi, Magic City, Donora and the rolling hills that surround them.

In 1974, on Domine's first day as a detective in the tough, gritty mill town of Monessen, Pennsylvania, he saw a well-known numbers racketeer walking down Main Street, blatantly making his rounds from the barbershop to the diner to the tavern with cash in hand and gambling receipts hanging out of his pocket.

Domine put him in the squad car and drove two blocks to the station house. He had the man fingerprinted and was taking him over to a cell when he ran into Chief Bruce Pezzelle. The chief grabbed the fingerprint cards out of Domine's hand, ripped them up and threw them on the floor.

"Boy, don't you *ever* arrest a gambler in my town again," Pezzelle barked at the rookie.

"Yes, sir," said Domine respectfully. And he didn't.

Domine served four years on the elite eight-detective Mon Valley Regional Police Department Investigative Division, which covered five cities and handled the heavier cases of homicide, robbery and burglary.

Driving north, Domine stops the car at a steel span bridge that crosses the Monongahela River. In a trancelike monotone he describes getting a radio call that five men just robbed a nearby appliance store at gunpoint. As he was listening to the call, he could see them driving toward him. He turned his car sideways, got out, drew his gun and hollered for the car to halt. The car smoked its tires stopping, the suspects piled out, and all ran in the other direction except for one. Gun in hand, he drew down on Domine.

"I shot him right through the neck with a .357," says Domine, "And the guy *lived*."

Small, poor river towns in southwest Pennsylvania were racket controlled. Pezzelle, says Domine, liked to say to his colleagues there was something seriously *wrong* with a chief who couldn't double his salary in these parts. Even the leader of Domine's detective squad had a scam going. Once a week, Chief Detective William Verno had a couple of detectives, including Domine, round up piles of that day's newspaper from local stores and deliver them to his wife at home. She clipped the grocery coupons from hundreds of papers, which he passed on to grocery store managers to turn into manufacturers for reimbursement in a small-time fraud scheme. The corruption was systemic, from the chief on down. At Christmas, the local mob even threw the cops a party at the FOP Hall.

(Verno died last October. Pezzelle calls Domine's allegations "asinine.")

Domine felt he couldn't get away from it. Which is why he signed up for the FBI in 1978. Surely the squeaky-clean Bureau was above reproach. The grueling 16-week course of academics, physical training and firearms was tough for the out-of-shape small town cop. Halfway through the course, Domine broke his foot. He was told he could go home, heal and repeat the 16-week course with the next class. Domine couldn't face starting all over again.

Instead, after signing a release absolving the Bureau of all responsibility, Domine tore off his cast using a ball-point pen to stab away the plaster and completed the two-mile run. In 12 minutes 49 seconds. The feat earned him the nickname "Blood and Guts Domine."

The boy who grew up watching *The Untouchables* and *The FBI* on TV graduated from the FBI Academy in 1978.

"The day he graduated from the FBI, the first thing he did was come over and thank his father and me," says Josephine Domine, tearing up at the memory. "That's the kind of son he is."

Domine's first undercover case for the Bureau was a huge investment of time whose greatest return was the lesson it taught him. Taking a tip from another agent, Domine became a bartender to crack a loan-sharking case. But there was a problem: No loan-sharking operation existed. From then on, Domine promised himself to develop his own leads. He kept the vow religiously.

During his 22-year government tenure, he orchestrated a record number of sting operations, including one that broke up a ring of construction equipment hijackers and heroin dealers and another involving the 1984 arrest of Cleveland Police Captain John Madison, the highest-ranking Cleveland police officer convicted for corruption. Domine also initiated a sting that resulted in 47 arrests for grand theft auto, and recovered 98 cars worth $860,000. He brought down the sheriff of Jasper County, South Carolina, in a national sting operation on conspiracy and extortion charges. He infiltrated Cleveland's outlaw North Coast Motorcycle Club, and later found out that club members had taken out a contract on his life. He confiscated $20 million in stolen property and obtained 53 indictments against the long-haul tractor-trailer thieves. And, he arrested a Cleveland Police sergeant for illegally trafficking in $15,000 worth of food stamps.

Those are just the *big* cases he worked on.

While posing as various nefarious types over the years. Domine had other FBI responsibilities as well. He performed his share of meat-and-potatoes crime-solving. In '96, he picked up bank robber Daniel Sagister the old-fashioned way. Like the gumshoes of yore, he canvassed all the gin joints on West 25th and showed Sagister's picture to every bartender and barmaid he met, spreading word of reward money. Domine got a call the next day from a barmaid. Sagister was there. After the arrest she refused to take a dime, Domine notes with admiration. Said it was her civic duty.

Most traditional FBI operations are textbook jobs characterized by a high degree of intelligence information, methodical preparation and team execution. Undercover work is the opposite of all that.

"The street is unpredictable," Domine says.

He was constantly required to make life-and-death split-second decisions. Anything can go wrong. Especially when 90 percent of the people you're hanging around are stupid, crazy on drugs or armed. Or all of the above.

A single afternoon during Operation Scoop in 1979 shows how fast and deadly simple events can turn. The operation involved drug dealer-turned-informant Frank Sumpter. Domine and a partner posing as local mob guys, were meeting with two groups of high-powered South American drug dealers at Sumpter's Hough Avenue store.

An interpreter was there to help the dealers communicate with Sumpter and Domine. But the interpreter wasn't very good. For reasons never determined, guns came out all around the room and the air was suddenly heavy with hot lead. Domine and his partner made for the nearest door, never looking back.

The next morning at 2, Domine got a call at home from Sumpter. One drug dealer returned to the store and stabbed him in the leg. Domine asked, "What happened to the drug dealer?" That's what Sumpter called about. He had pulled out his .38 and shot the dealer through the heart. The guy was lying there dead on the floor of Sumpter's store.

"I told him to call the police," Domine says, recalling the incident with a mixture of humor and horror.

Some of those same South Americans introduced Domine to Rosa Darvella, a drug dealer who offered the agent ten kilos of cocaine from Miami at $20,000 apiece.

The Bureau couldn't afford that much "buy money," so Domine had to turn her down. He did, however, tell the Drug Enforcement Agency where Darvella would be collecting the package in South Miami and they promptly arrested and arraigned her.

In court she pleaded guilty, unaware that Domine had turned her in. She called Domine from the courthouse pay phone to tell him she had two remaining kilos of coke and did he want to buy them. She needed the money to pay her lawyer.

"She brought two kilos of cocaine to her sentencing," says Domine, laughing in disbelief. He told her he'd take them off her hands and she put her husband on the next flight to Cleveland Hopkins with the drugs. Domine and a partner picked him up at the airport in a blue Monte Carlo.

"I put a gun to his head and said, 'FBI, you're under arrest.' He started crying. Rosa got 20 years," Domine says.

Some colleagues say the key to Domine's success was his gift for engaging people from both sides of the street—criminals and other law-enforcement.

Tom Del Regno, commander of the Medina County Sheriff's Office detective bureau, worked with Domine when Del Regno was with the Cleveland Police Department's auto theft unit in the mid-Eighties.

Del Regno says Domine was the opposite of the FBI image. Despite a bachelor's degree in criminal justice and a master's in business administration, both from the University of Pittsburgh, he wasn't one of the white shirt and tie guys with a tendency to talk down to you. Domine had a reputation for putting intra-agency politics aside. And unlike most agents, he shared information. Domine's experience as a street cop in Pennsylvania helped him immensely.

The 1985 job they worked together. Operation Snow Wheels targeting car thieves, was a textbook illustration of Domine's talent for the art of deception. Domine and a partner set up shop at a garage in Warrensville Heights called Sonny's Motors. They had a budget of $160,000 to buy stolen cars. They put the word out to organized car thieves that they were open for business. Within weeks, bad guys were literally lined up around the block with hot cars. Business eventually became so brisk Domine had to turn people away. What the thieves didn't know is that they were all being secretly video- and audio-taped.

Domine and his partners had fun in the process. Some of these guys were like the Keystone Crooks.

"We wouldn't do business with them unless they stopped at Mama Guciardo's restaurant and picked us up some veal cutlet sandwiches. I'd say, 'And don't forget the pepperocinis, you #!@%*, or you're not getting your title,'" he says, laughing.

Domine could have called the operation America's Stupidest Criminals. To ID the thieves, he would accuse them of being cops, then demand to see their driver's licenses. Claiming to have a friend in the police department, he'd call the FBI and read the vital information to a waiting clerk.

"Or I'd say, 'How old are you?' And the guy would tell me his age and I'd say, 'Bullshit, you're not 25. Let me see your license.' And they would," howls Domine.

Every day at Sonny's was different, says Domine. Big Dick Williams, a bad guy from Detroit, showed up once with a stolen truck. He didn't know it was a Defense Department truck—or that there was a $50,000 anti-ballistic cruise missile computer in the back. "He was so anxious to get rid of it. I offered him gas money to get back to Detroit and he took it," says Domine.

But there were also people at Sonny's who weren't very funny. Like Fat Gerald Peyton who, angry that Domine declined to buy his car, fired two rounds from a .45 into the shop, nearly hitting Domine, his partner and a customer. Or the time organized crime figure August Palladino, who had been up all night partying, wandered into the shop while Domine was in the back room changing the tape in the hidden video camera. Palladino found a loaded gun while rummaging in a desk drawer. When Domine came out of the back room, the two startled each other. The gun went off and the round sailed over Domine's head, almost hitting him.

There was more ugliness.

One afternoon, Fat Gerald pulled up with his girlfriend, Stephanie, in the back seat of his car. He had a pistol in his waistband and asked Domine if he had given Stephanie the money for a car he asked her to deliver. Stephanie was looking at Domine and shaking her head "no." But Domine *had* given her the money. And he said as much to Gerald. He couldn't blow his cover.

"Do you know the sound of a big, wet fish being dropped on cement? It has a kind of wet slap and thud," says Domine. "That's what it sounded like when he was beating her. It was sickening. He beat her viciously and there was nothing I could do about it.

"I still feel bad about that."

Some of Domine's best reviews come from the people he put away. Organized crime associate Anthony Delmonti was arrested for auto theft, among other things, during the operation. He recently finished his twelve-year sentence, six in jail, six on probation, for racketeering, drugs, grand theft auto and fraud. He says he *still* doesn't believe Domine's an agent.

"He talked the language, knew about cocaine, he knew his Italian stuff, the gambling. He knew what was going on and was very natural," says Delmonti.

Of all Domine's cases, his favorite is the gambling sting operation that nabbed Jasper County, South Carolina, Sheriff Clifford Brantley. Brantley was interested in establishing a local gambling spot. Domine posed as a Cleveland mob guy named Ted Spinoza. For their first meeting, Brantley put Domine in a Jasper County jail cell and told him to drop his pants so he could frisk him. The sheriff missed the wire and the two worked out a deal.

Domine rented a defunct lounge and called it Bernie's Silver Fox. He agreed to pay the sheriff $500 a month for protection. One weekend a month, undercover FBI agents from all over the United

States flew into Hilton Head to patronize Bernie's Silver Fox and make it look like a big-time gambling operation.

Once the club was up and rolling, Brantley looked for ways to diversify the business. Domine, as Ted Spinoza, was happy to oblige.

"Off the top of my head I came up with this idea about the Chili Bordello. I told him guys like chili and they like prostitutes, so we could have the prostitutes serve the chili on one floor and gambling on another. He liked that idea a lot," Domine says, grinning as if he still can't believe it. "Chili Bordello."

Brantley was charged with conspiracy, extortion and accepting a total of $2,300 before being indicted. He was sentenced to five years in prison.

Beneath the danger, deception and the dual life, undercover work is built on paper—reams and reams of paper. To procure government money for a sting operation, an agent must submit a detailed blueprint of the plan: How much it will cost, who the primary targets are, what their criminal history is, how long the operation will take and what the ultimate results will be. The standards for approval are stringent. But according to colleagues, Domine had a gift for getting the green light.

"Ted's paperwork was meticulous," says Dan Gordon as if describing a piece of music or work of art. Gordon was Domine's supervisor at the Bureau from 1979 to 1989. It wasn't uncommon for an undercover proposal to run 50 pages.

Among his colleagues, Domine had a reputation as a hot dog and a hothead. Domine instigated more than one fistfight with other agents. He was known for speaking his mind. Loudly at times. It didn't always win him friends.

"Did he piss people off? Yes. Did I have to settle disputes caused by Ted? Yes," says Gordon. "But I don't think any single FBI agent has Ted's statistics. He made me look good every year he worked for me.

"Before I retired in '89, I recommended Ted transfer to over to 'Applicants.' Undercover is tough. I thought he should get out for a while. But he did even *more* dangerous work after I left."

That dangerous work led Domine to the hotel room at the JFK Marriott. And East Coast Gambino enforcer Mike Zampana sticking a loaded gun in his ear. The incident and its aftermath haunt him to this day.

"My life flashed before my eyes," Domine says. "You hear that, but it's really true. It was like zzzziiiiip. I was outside my body watching the whole scene unfold from above. Everything I had ever done in law enforcement, every pressure, every fear, everything that had ever taken a toll on me psychologically, collapsed in on me at that moment."

But as quickly as the frisk started, it ended. And miraculously, Zampana never found the recorder. He even apologized, explaining the gun was necessary because he wanted to talk about a deal involving 100 kilos (more than 200 pounds) of heroin, worth millions.

The deal never went down. But Domine was able to put Mike Zampana, Charlie Schiavo, and a third partner in crime, Joey Randazzo, away for sentences ranging from six to ten years on the stolen cars and counterfeit checks charges. But he could never quite shake how close he came that day to taking a bullet in the head in an airport hotel room in Queens, New York. He remembered his promise. It was time to start getting out. Out from undercover. He'd had enough.

After the operation in New York, Domine applied for two positions outside the Undercover Unit at the Bureau. Domine hoped he might get preference considering the work he'd done and the sacrifices he made. But nothing materialized. Eventually, he drifted back to what he knew best: Undercover work. And the case of Cleveland Police Sergeant Arthur Armstrong. It would be Domine's last.

"If I've learned one thing in all my years in undercover, it's this: 'Don't mess with an Italian's cannolis,'" says Domine with a smile. "That's what brought down Arthur Armstrong."

Fifth District Police Sergeant Arthur Armstrong always made it a point to stop at Presti's doughnut shop on Murray Hill for the occasional free doughnut and coffee the place accorded local cops. But Armstrong's occasional free doughnuts and coffee became daily free doughnuts and coffee. At first, the woman subletting the business from Presti's didn't mind. Armstrong was a friendly, talkative type.

Soon, however, Armstrong was taking a dozen free doughnuts each visit. He told the woman they were for the boys back at the precinct house. The shopkeeper began to get annoyed.

It was about this time that Domine began stopping by the doughnut shop. He'd been trying to recruit the woman as an FBI informant to get a line on organized crime activities in the area. The woman hadn't said anything about Armstrong to Domine. She wasn't sure about turning the policeman in.

Then one day Armstrong made the fateful mistake of copping some free cannolis. That was this woman's line in the sand. Cannolis were sacred, something you didn't mess with. She called Domine.

"She was so mad," Domine recalls. "I remember her saying, 'Those cannolis cost me a dollar twenty-five apiece!'" She finally agreed to "do" Armstrong by mentioning that her cousin "Sal" was a guy who had access to food stamps. Armstrong went for the bait. He said he could move food stamps.

Between July and January of 1998. Armstrong illegally acquired $15,025 in food stamps, reselling them for 65 cents on the dollar. He then split the proceeds with the informant, who has since left Presti's. Armstrong later pleaded guilty as part of a plea agreement and was given six months in federal prison. He also was required to return $10,180 to the Department of Agriculture, which issues food stamps.

Ted Domine officially retired from federal rolls June 2 after 22 years with the FBI. He took early retirement after a job-related car accident last year hospitalized him with back and neck injuries. While Domine is disillusioned and disappointed, he still cherishes his "creds," his mounted FBI badge and credentials. They have come to symbolize all that's left of his career.

"I feel like the taxpayers got their money's worth," Domine says today, assessing his career. He still believes undercover work is an invaluable tool. He just doesn't think it's wise to have one agent do so much of it.

Most of the people Domine sent to jail are back on the streets now. Sheriff Brantley won an election by 2,500 votes *after* he was indicted in the Hilton Head case. Domine says it doesn't bother him.

"I tried never to concern myself with what happened to people once they got to court. My job was done at that point. From there it was somebody else's responsibility," he says. "I also think that once someone's paid their debt to society they should be given another chance. I never wanted to destroy anyone's life. I may have changed some people's plans for a few years," he says.

Ted Domine has a lot to show for his 27 years in law enforcement. Besides the raises and awards, he's blind in one eye and has severe hearing loss in one ear. The car accident left him with seven fused vertebrae and a 12-inch titanium plate in his neck with 14 stainless-steel screws, two in each vertebrae. He also has nerve damage that allows his hands only four sensations: Burning, tingling, numbness and pain. He has only partial mobility in his left hand and limited movement in his neck. An operation is scheduled for later this summer that, if successful, will help block the burning sensation.

"The bear definitely got more of me than I got of the bear," Domine says. You get the feeling he could easily substitute the word "Bureau" for "bear."

When asked what he would do if he could go back to the beginning and start over, Domine pauses, considering his unparalleled law-enforcement career.

"Knowing what I know now, I'd choose another line of work."

June 18, 2000

THE FBI'S 'MADE' MAN

Brains, bravado turned Clevelander
into agency's top informant

Cleveland mobster Anthony Delmonti couldn't believe what he was hearing.

In the summer of 1999, he was winding down a meeting in a hotel room with Rochester, N.Y., mob boss Tommy Marotta about laundering money and moving some cocaine. Delmonti also had a line on some contraband food stamps. They were planning some golf for later . . . then Marotta became curiously quiet.

He suggested "making" Delmonti on the spot.

Delmonti was floored. Get "straightened out" right here, right now? Marotta just stared, tightening his steel-blue eyes. He was the boss, he said. He could do whatever he wanted.

There had been discussions about officially making Delmonti a member of the Mafia. He had been a good "earner" for the Rochester arm of New York City's Bonanno family. Marotta had permission from Delmonti's Cleveland mob boss to make him. But what about the ceremony? Delmonti asked. The sponsor? Burning the holy card? The speeches in Sicilian?

Marotta waved it off. He was still on probation and not supposed to associate with any of the guys. The ceremony was unnecessary. Made guy Joe T. would be the sponsor. He explained to Delmonti what being "made" entailed, its privileges and responsibilities.

This family comes first. Even before Delmonti's own family. No other member could kill him without permission from Marotta. Delmonti would turn over all his earnings to Marotta. He would be getting a share of whatever the family was bringing in. No fooling with drugs. Delmonti was never to mess with the wives or girlfriends of any other made guys. That was sacred. No made guys would ever mess with Delmonti's wife or girlfriend.

Delmonti was in shock. Marotta was a legend. An old-school

wiseguy. He did nine years on a racketeering violation in 1987 and survived two different attempts on his life in 1983. He caught eight bullets from a .22 and was still walking around scaring the hell out of people.

And now he was officially bringing Delmonti into the family. Emotionally, Delmonti was all over the map. He was awed and humbled. It was something he never expected to happen. It was a wiseguy's dream come true.

Marotta got up from his chair and embraced Delmonti, kissing him on both cheeks. It was done. Marotta said there would be a reception later. Told him to bring his appetite. Pressed for time, Marotta said he had another appointment and left the room.

Delmonti sat dazed for a minute. He went to unlock the door that opened to the adjoining room. He paused, savoring what had just happened. He took a breath, opening the door wide.

"That's riiiiigght!" he said to the five FBI agents who were there with the video equipment. "I'm the big boss now. You saw it."

The agents cheered and high-fived Delmonti. They jokingly kissed his ring and laughed. He was already an outstanding informant. But this was unprecedented. An FBI informant being "made" by a mob boss. And it was all on tape. It was one of the undercover coups of all time. Delmonti was pumped.

An hour later, back in his own hotel room, Delmonti called his girlfriend in Cleveland. As he explained what happened, she covered her mouth and cried. She knew that his friend and mentor Tommy Marotta was as good as in jail. And Delmonti had put him there. He hung up the phone. Then he cried, too.

UNDERCOVER

Thomas Marotta is currently serving a nine-year prison sentence for cocaine trafficking. He was one of many people whose lives were changed by Anthony Delmonti.

The Cleveland career criminal worked as an FBI informant from July 1998 to July of this year. He aided federal agents in arresting people all across the country for crimes ranging from murder to selling drugs to money laundering, food-stamp fraud, auto theft and weapons violations.

According to law-enforcement sources, Delmonti made more than 500 audio tapes and videotapes for the FBI, contributing to the arrest of more than 50 people with more still pending. He was responsible for the recovery of more than $250,000 in stolen vehicles, the seizure of $80,000 in illicit drug money and $100,000 in illegal gambling money.

Delmonti also orchestrated one of the largest gambling busts in Cleveland history, leading to the arrest this month of Cleveland numbers kingpin Virgil Ogletree and five associates. Ogletree had run the numbers racket here for more than 50 years.

"Tony was the best informant I ever worked with in 21 years in law enforcement," said former FBI agent John Ligato, who worked with Delmonti on several cases.

"He's a legitimate wiseguy. He has both balls and brains. If you don't have the brains, you don't live too long. If you don't have the guts, nothing gets done. Tony is a mob guy from central casting. He has the swagger and underlying menace. But he's also very likable. He's fun to be around. He was extremely productive undercover. As operatives go, it doesn't get any better than Tony."

In exchange for Delmonti's services, the government dismissed the last $154,000 of a fine he owned for his 1988 cocaine distribution conviction, paid his living expenses for five years and gave him an undisclosed lump-sum payment. He is not in the government's witness protection program.

Delmonti, 57, now lives far away from Cleveland, but at 6 feet, 250 pounds, he remains a larger-than-life character who carries his mob persona with pride. He wears designer tinted glasses, gold jewelry and favors big, fancy cars. He fractures the English language with gusto, swears like Tony Soprano and tells uproarious stories about his underworld exploits. But when asked about the risk he is taking as an informant, he becomes serious.

"I'm in danger. In front of my girlfriend, I say, 'I'm not.' But I am. These guys in New York, these are not children I'm playing with. My guys in Cleveland, I don't feel too threatened by them. But these Buffalo and Rochester guys? That's a lot of guys going to jail, and they have family. They kill people. I believe if the Bonanno family found where I was at, they would kill me. I'm a convicted felon. I can't carry a weapon. I'm dead," he said.

MOB LIFE

Delmonti says he wasn't predisposed to a life of crime other than the fact that his father, Anthony Delmonti Sr., was a small-time bookmaker. His family lived on Royal Road in Collinwood.

"I grew up in a rough neighborhood, but we were the richest family in it. I was a rich kid who went bad. My mother thought I could do no wrong. She always blamed everyone else. Bad companions," said Delmonti.

After getting a football scholarship and flunking out of two colleges, Delmonti found ways to generate his own money. He learned the collection business from neighborhood pal and mobster Eugene "The Animal" Ciasullo.

"I used to send guys wheelchairs with a note that said, 'You're gonna need a case of aspirin for the beating we're gonna give you,'" Delmonti said.

In 1969, an opportunity of the criminal variety came to Delmonti. The Cleveland Heights Police Department hired him as a dispatcher. He used the job to expand his criminal activities. He describes 1969 as "the year we robbed the whole town."

Delmonti's life of crime carried on unabated for the next five years until 1974, when he was arrested on charges of aggravated burglary. He served three years at the state prison at Marion. When Delmonti got out in 1978, he became serious about his criminal career. He put together a crew from the old Collinwood neighborhood.

They bought kilos of cocaine for $12,000, selling them for $20,000. Soon he was flush again. He also started using cocaine. It wasn't long before Delmonti was out of control. It led to his second stint in jail in 1987.

"That's when I met Vinny Bada-Bing, the undercover FBI agent," Delmonti said referring to retired agent Ted Domine. Domine, posing as a car thief with a chop shop, busted Delmonti for racketeering, drugs and stolen cars.

Delmonti spent the next six years in prisons in Michigan, Indiana and Pennsylvania, giving him the opportunity to meet gangsters from all over the country. Domine, a master recruiter, realized Delmonti would be an ideal informant. The agent did some personal favors, looking out for Delmonti's family. A relationship developed.

After Delmonti got out of jail in 1993, Domine stayed in touch. In November 1996, Delmonti opened The Drip Stick coffee shop on West Sixth Street in downtown Cleveland. Domine convinced Delmonti that working for the FBI was his smartest option. Too many thugs were telling cops they had evidence on Delmonti. Most of the crooks didn't even know Delmonti. They saw him as a walking get-out-of-jail-free card.

"I did enough prison time in my life for other people. I was ratted on in both cases. I thought this time I'm going to the table," said Delmonti.

Delmonti went back and forth on the decision to work for Domine. Some of Domine's colleagues questioned Delmonti's commitment and resolve. But he convinced everybody in 1998 when he went after his former cohort, Ronnie Lucarelli.

Delmonti's first case for the FBI illustrates the crazy bravado and street smarts that served him so well. Lucarelli was extremely cautious and tough to get. He wouldn't go see Delmonti to pick up the ounce of coke. He made Delmonti come to him in Collinwood, where there was a lookout on every block and a stranger stuck out like a pineapple pizza.

Delmonti had to make sure an agent witnessed the transaction. The bureau sent a woman. Delmonti told Lucarelli she was the pastry chef from his coffee shop. Lucarelli conducted the exchange indoors and insisted the woman stay in the car. Delmonti outfoxed him. He stuffed the ounce of cocaine in his shirt and made sure it fell out on the ground in plain sight as he returned to the car.

This didn't sit well with Lucarelli's crew. They were suspicious and vocal about it. Who was the broad in the car?

Delmonti didn't flinch. He said she was a lesbian. And that she often participated in three-way trysts with him and a girlfriend. He described their activity graphically. Suddenly, nobody was worried about Delmonti's loyalty anymore. They just wanted to hear more about his sexual adventures.

Lucarelli is now doing 10 years in federal prison on drug charges.

In 1999, Delmonti began the operation on Virgil Ogletree.

"Virgil came to me because he needed a partner. He had worked before with mob guys like [Anthony] Liberatore before so it was no big deal. The dangerous part is that an old guy like Virgil knows a lot of people. Very connected. Every day when I would drive over there I'm thinking, 'Is this the day somebody called Virgil and told him about me?' That's always on your mind. Because when that day comes, you're dead," said Delmonti.

Delmonti's role was to provide an infusion of cash and staunch the flow of losses.

"So I bring an agent in saying this person knows about numbers and can help the operation. The agent has a hidden camera. As I introduce the agent around the room, I'm saying, 'This is Virgil, and Marvin. Hi, Mary, here's someone I want you to meet.' Meanwhile the feds can look at the tape and ID everyone when they are ready to go in. That was a little nerve-racking."

Those tapes were used as evidence when Ogletree was arrested this month.

That same year, Delmonti had a close call in a Cleveland bank where he had convinced a bank officer to help him launder money. During the meeting, an undercover agent was with him posing as a mobster.

"The agent got recognized by a friend of the bank guy. He knows the agent from another undercover thing. He comes to the bank officer hysterical. He says that guy you met was an FBI agent! I made up a story that he wasn't that guy. I said he just looked like that guy," Delmonti said.

"Then I got this same guy going around town telling people I'm in the FBI. So I catch him in the bathroom at a restaurant in Mayfield Heights. They had a pay phone in there, and I grabbed the hand part and cracked him on the head so many times you could play ring toss with the lumps on his head. I was able to overcome those kinds of mistakes because I'm me. Anybody else would have gotten killed."

Delmonti's days as an informant were hectic. There was always one more person to see, one more place to go, one more call to make. He says the frantic pace became the norm during those first three years.

"I'd drive five hours up to Rochester and check into the hotel. One time the lady at the hotel desk says, 'Oh, your friends are already here.' Meaning the agents in the next room! What if I had been standing there with the boss or a wiseguy? That's exactly the kind of slip that could get you killed."

Only now is Delmonti feeling the cumulative effect of five years of living the double life. It's not something he recommends.

"This is the hardest thing I've ever done. So many things could have happened. They had me running crazy. It got to me. That's why I got sick. I was in Hillcrest Hospital [in Mayfield Heights] for three months with pneumonia in 2001. My body couldn't take it anymore," he said.

•   •   •

CLOSE CALL

One of Delmonti's last cases was his most serious and celebrated. And the only one during which he was present for the bust.

On Dec. 29, 2000, the targets were prominent Rochester defense attorney Anthony Leonardo Jr. and hit man Albert Ranieri. Delmonti had gotten them both on tape admitting to murder and a $10 million armored-car robbery. He lured them both to a hotel in Brighton, N.Y., where he was to receive a payment of $100,000 for 10 kilos of cocaine. There was a heavily armed SWAT team in the next room and agents all over the lobby and parking lot.

Delmonti thought the feds were overdoing it. He knew the unwritten rule among mob guys. You never bring a gun to a meeting. It's not protocol. The takedown would be easy, he thought.

"So I'm in there talking away. They're [Leonardo and Ranieri] telling me more and more stuff they've done. Almost an hour went by. We're planning an armored-car thing in Cleveland, when . . . BAM! . . . that door explodes open, and the place is full of these hooded ninjas [the SWAT team] with guns that look like if they hit you, you'd disappear. I've seen a lot of scary stuff, but this was amazing. I saw the split-second look on Leonardo's face. The color went away. He was saying goodbye to his life. They cuffed me, too, and hustled me out. The SWAT guys tell me later, both of them had guns. They were gonna kill me.

"Then the phone rings. It's two other guys looking to buy cocaine. They said, 'Why not?' The ninjas got dressed, we put the room back together, and 20 minutes later we did it all over again. I coulda slept for a week when that was all over," he said.

Leonardo is currently serving 12 years and Ranieri 30 to life in federal prisons.

UNCERTAIN FUTURE

Today, Delmonti is in hiding, his life is different and almost everything familiar—people, places and routines—has vanished.

"Right now I'm up in the air. It's not a good feeling. I was born and raised in Cleveland. My family's there. I left everybody. It's like living out of a bag. You do the best you can. I feel like a gypsy."

Delmonti says his mob days are over, despite his lingering nostalgia.

"I miss the guys. I don't know why. I don't think they miss me. There was a closeness there. But I also know it was a false closeness. Now if I want that kind of camaraderie, I have to watch *The Sopranos*. People are ratting on each other right and left. It wasn't real except in my mind and memory. There's no honor anymore like the old days. The FBI and mob are exactly the same. They both lost their honor around the same time," he said.

Though Delmonti's future is uncertain, there are times when he doesn't seem too worried. He sees himself as being resourceful. And careful.

"I can adapt to anything. I did a lot of time in jail, I worked for the police, I'm a mob guy, I'm a social director. I wear a lot of hats," he said. "I try not to think each day might be my last, but I'm always aware of it. When I pull out of the driveway I'm always looking to see if anybody's following me. I'm always in that rearview mirror."

Delmonti wears a large gold crucifix on a chain around his neck. It was a gift from his Bonanno family boss, Tommy Marotta.

What would Jesus think of him wearing that crucifix?

"I think he'd understand," Delmonti said, pausing, turning the idea over in his mind. "Jesus had a crew."

Then comes the afterthought.

"He even had a rat in his crew," he said, laughing.

August 31, 2003

SMACK IS BACK

Heroin rears its deadly head in the suburbs

Heroin is the world's greatest pain reliever. It provides a euphoria unsurpassed by any other drug.

Users describe the high in sexual and religious terms. They refer to it as "a full, two-minute body orgasm," "feeling the hand of God on your head," "kissing Jesus on the lips" and "floating down a river of melted butter on a warm piece of toast."

They say it delivers them from pain and anxiety and encompasses them from head to toe in a deep, glowing feeling of supernatural well-being.

Heroin also is the most addictive and the fastest acting of all the opiate drugs.

And it's closer to your front door than you think.

On the night of Sunday, February 6, a Westlake narcotics officer with an uncanny eye for suspicious vehicles drives through the parking lot of a motel. A 1986 gold Chevy Cavalier catches his eye.

He runs the plates and finds the owner's driver's license has been suspended. The woman also has some drug arrests. He checks with the front desk of the motel and discovers the owner is registered. The officer "sits" on the car.

When four people, including a young boy, get in the car the next afternoon and turn onto I-90 east, the officer pulls them over. None of the adults in the car has a valid driver's license. The officer finds 180 packets of heroin, heroin in bulk, drug paraphernalia—kitchen scales, grinders, sifters, plastic bags and rubber bands, used to package the heroin for street sale—and a semi-automatic handgun in the car's back seat.

The packaged and bulk heroin together comes to about two ounces, worth about $50,000 on the street. Edmismer Arango, a 24-year-old Cuban national who failed to show up at the Justice

Center in November for a three-year jail sentence for selling heroin, 24-year-old Maria Montanez and 19-year-old Maria Rossy are charged with drug possession and drug preparation for sale, which are second- and third-degree felonies. Arango is being held under $500,000 bond and the women are being held under $300,000 bond in the Cuyahoga County Jail.

A Westlake policeman asks the 5-year-old boy, whose nickname, "Kay-Kay Jr.," is tattooed on the neck of his mother, Montanez, if he knows what his mom and her friends are packaging.

"Bad stuff," he tells the cop disdainfully.

The "bad stuff" is here, making inroads into communities not normally associated with hard drug use.

"People out here have the money and resources to keep a drug habit private," Westlake Police Captain Guy Turner says. "You might be surprised to find out how many heroin users there are."

"The numbers don't lie. Crack is still king in Cleveland. Judging by our seizures, and by the arrests our detectives are making, heroin use is not on the rise in Cleveland proper," says Lieutenant Don Duman, head of narcotics for the Cleveland Police Department.

Despite state and federal statistics, and the demand for beds at Cleveland-area treatment centers, Cleveland police insist they aren't seeing an increase in heroin use. "There may be a regional problem," concedes Duman. "Maybe it's more of a problem in the outlying suburbs."

There's no doubt a problem exists in Greater Cleveland, and the number of treatment centers proves it. Under the category of "dubious achievement," Northeast Ohio qualified for a federal HIDTA grant last June. HIDTA stands for High Intensity Drug Trafficking Area, and Cleveland falls in with Akron, Toledo, Canton and Youngstown.

"In this five-county area, crack and coke use have increased, as have heroin-related deaths," says John B. Sommer, executive director of the Ohio HIDTA. "The program began in the early Nineties, focusing on source cities like New York and Miami. Now we've moved to what we call the consumer cities."

"Crack can be king, but that doesn't mean that heroin isn't coming on strong," says Robert Fiatal, supervisory special agent at the Cleveland office of the FBI.

"Obviously, we don't do the street-corner stuff; we concentrate on conspiracy to distribute. The whole market has opened up in the last five years."

The three men in the meeting room at Freedom House, a half-way house for drug and alcohol addicts on Cleveland's West Side, have agreed to talk anonymously about their heroin addiction. If they were characters from an updated *Snow White*, they'd be Dopey, Queasy and Grumpy.

Dopey, his eyes at half-mast, his manner subdued, is 17 years old and from Toledo. He has been treated for heroin addiction seven times during the last two years. He was addicted the first time he snorted the drug at 15. It helps him "not think," he says. He enjoys the sedation.

Queasy, a 42-year-old Cleveland resident who is going through heroin withdrawal, had eight years of sobriety and was working in the recovery field before relapsing. He blames himself. His dentist prescribed pain pills and Queasy neglected to mention his history of drug addiction. He took the pills and his sobriety became history.

Grumpy is in his late 50s and from Cleveland. He doesn't really want to be at Freedom House. The 12-Step meetings bore him. He began shooting heroin more than 20 years ago. Grumpy has been in and out of the drug life but says his lack of health insurance keeps him from getting private treatment. He has become a master thief to feed his habit, estimating his shoplifting during the last five years has cost Ohioans half a million dollars in prosecution, court costs and jail time.

Each of these men, decades apart in age, has a different story and different reasons for using heroin. What all three share is the opinion that the drug is back in a big way. It is cheap, pure and readily available in Northeast Ohio.

Cleveland is cresting the wave of a national heroin epidemic that has many health and law-enforcement officials concerned. According to the local FBI and Drug Enforcement Administration (DEA) offices, South American drug cartels are using their established cocaine trade routes to flood the United States with heroin.

People from all demographic stratas are trying the drug for the first time, and statistics show that one out of every two people who try heroin becomes addicted. Middle-aged couples from the suburbs and college kids are experimenting by snorting the drug. Former addicts who haven't touched the drug in 20 years are returning to their poison of choice for the purity and the bargain.

"Everything changed in March of 1993," says Jane Loisdaughter, director of intake and community education at the Free Medical Clinic of Greater Cleveland.

"The price of heroin went down and the purity went up," Loisdaughter says. "Ten years earlier, street heroin was 3 percent to 5 percent pure. The heroin out there now is far more potent. We're seeing 30 percent to 70 percent purity.

"Nobody sets out to become an addict," Loisdaughter adds. "People begin experimenting with this exquisite, intense pleasure, and before they know it they're a slave to a filthy, dirty drug."

Last year, the U.S. government reported the number of Americans seeking treatment for heroin addiction surpassed those seeking help for cocaine use. From 1992 to 1997, the estimated number of heroin users nationwide rose 28 percent, from 180,000 to 232,000. In the same time period, cocaine declined 17 percent, from 267,000 to 222,000. (Privately funded treatment centers were not included in the study.)

Locally, bottomed-out heroin addicts in record numbers are seeking beds at treatment centers. Heroin addicts can expect to wait five to 10 days for a detox bed at local clinics. Drug-treatment professionals are overwhelmed, says Dr. Gregory Collins, a psychiatrist who founded the Cleveland Clinic's Alcohol and Drug Recovery Center 20 years ago.

"There is definitely an epidemic," he says. "In the Eighties, I didn't see 10 heroin addicts in the whole decade. Today, I get 10 people a week looking for treatment.

"It's not a ghetto drug anymore," he says matter-of-factly. "I see all kinds of people. Lawyers, doctors, nurses, self-employed entrepreneurs, people in construction, blue-collar workers and a whole new wave of young people: white suburban kids.

"It's a big story, and a real bad thing. Up close and personal, it's ugly and tragic," says Collins. "On average, every addict touches the lives of five other people. The despair and misery spreads exponentially."

Death certificate records from the Ohio Department of Health reveal that heroin overdose deaths statewide have almost doubled in the last decade, from 54 in 1988 to 93 in 1998. And while those numbers may not seem staggering compared to handgun homicides, which run between 300 and 400 annually in Ohio, they are only the tip of the iceberg. A lethal overdose is only one indicator of heroin use.

"There are a lot of ways to die when you're a heroin addict. You can OD, crash your car, get AIDS, hepatitis, pneumonia, get murdered," says Collins grimly. "I don't know of a single addict who didn't at one time or another seriously consider suicide."

Statewide statistics show that 3,500 heroin addicts came in for treatment in 1998. Last year, that number rose to 4,100—28.5 percent (or 1,170) of those people were from Cuyahoga County. Health officials estimate that every person in treatment represents nine more still actively using heroin.

Private and publicly funded rehabilitation centers in Cleveland have been blindsided by the crush of heroin addicts seeking help.

Margaret Roche is the executive director at Stella Maris, a 50-year-old Cleveland alcohol and drug treatment center. Stella Maris' original mission was battling alcoholism. In the Eighties, however, counselors saw a rise in the number of clients with cocaine problems. Today, 80 percent of the center's clients are heroin addicts.

"I get five calls a day from heroin addicts looking for a bed here," Roche says. "The numbers of heroin users and the depth of their addiction caught us off-guard. It's been an education for us."

But numbers don't tell the full stories of lives destroyed, or the toll on families and society. Collins has seen the damage.

"Heroin addiction turns decent citizens into professional criminals. People become thieves and prostitutes. They start fencing and dealing. I've seen embezzlement and bank fraud.

"It's amazing what the drug does to people. They lose their reputation and self-respect because of disgusting activity they get into to get the drug," notes Collins, who says people from all walks of life are affected.

"Smarts don't matter. Lots of smart, affluent people get addicted. They get seduced," Collins explains. "They compare it to falling in love. And love is blind. The chemical is powerful and it distorts people."

Collins offers his own estimates fro heroin use in this area. He says there are anywhere from 3,000 to 5,000 hard-core heroin addicts in Northeast Ohio and perhaps 15,000 to 20,000 recreational users. He believes that if the problem isn't dealt with, it will become even more pervasive.

"It's more ominous than people think. . . . It will affect everybody eventually. This issue isn't compelling to people until it's their kid who gets addicted." Collins Says.

Mary (not her real name) is a graduate of the Cleveland Clinic recovery center. Formerly of Rocky River, Mary, now 23 and living out of state, agreed to talk by phone about her heroin addiction. She first experimented with drugs and alcohol in high school.

"I was 17 when I tried heroin. I snorted it. I knew I had a problem right away. It was so euphoric.

"I used to snort it here or there. I knew who had it and would hang around them. At first you tell yourself, 'Only on weekends.' Then it's twice a week. Then every day. Then you realize that using a needle is more economical. I was one of these needle-phobic people. Within six months [of trying heroin], I was shooting," she says.

Mary hid her full-blown habit for two years. When her parents intervened, she was in her fourth year at Ohio State, majoring in criminal justice and working 32 hours a week at a clothing store.

"At the end, I was spending $200 a day," she says. "I lost my job because I was spending the whole shift in the bathroom. I was OD'ing all the time. My roommate finally called my mother and told her. I was so skinny [during the time I was using], my mom thought I had an eating disorder. My parents came down to Columbus and pulled me out of school."

Mary completed a week of detox at the Cleveland Clinic and four months of outpatient treatment in another state. She removed herself from the familiar haunts and former friends that could trigger a relapse. She started her life over.

But, like the majority of heroin addicts, Mary did not stay clean. She relapsed five months after treatment.

"Mentally, I had never really committed to the idea that I could never use anything ever again," she says. "I thought that I could put the heroin behind me, but it would be OK to smoke a joint or to have an occasional glass of wine. One night I went out and had four beers. The next morning I was downtown buying heroin. It was like I had never quit."

Mary hopes to celebrate her first year of sobriety this month.

She's pleased with her progress, but now knows—after having learned the hard way—that she can't run from her problem. "It's everywhere," Mary says of the heroin scene. "I've never seen anything like it."

Less than 10 percent of heroin addicts get clean on their first rehab attempt, says Dr. Chris Adelman, who works at St. Vincent Charity Hospital's Rosary Hall, the alcohol and drug treatment center. "There's a whole new generation that hasn't gotten the message on heroin," he says. "It's not a drug you can do recreationally."

"All the treatment centers are swamped with people looking for heroin detox. The problem has been building steadily for the last three years or so," explains Adelman. "I thought for a time it was peaking, but it just continues to grow. I wouldn't say we're at a panic level yet, but I don't see this thing going away anytime soon."

Betty Piche has been the behavioral intake coordinator at Rosary Hall for 11 years. She says she has seen the heroin problem escalate over the last five.

"It's the drug that steals your soul," she says. "We have more demands daily than beds. Heroin addicts have the highest relapse record of any group."

Piche has seen addicts use treatment centers like a revolving door. She wonders about he effectiveness of treatment programs when some addicts use what they call a "spin dry," or quickie detox, to begin enjoying heroin's high again.

"People come in trying to change. They beg for detox," she says. "But the follow-up is rarely there. You want to detox those who ask, but when they call back six months later and want to detox again, I wonder, what's going to be different this time? They lie to themselves and then they lie to others. At some point you become the enabler."

Recently Piche has seen her share of young people walk blindly into a lifelong battle with addiction.

"I see sweet girls with names like Heather and Sarah in their mid-20s who started with pot and Ecstasy and they all wind up saying the same thing. They don't know how they got here," she says.

"Life closes in on you with heroin. You run out of money and fall back on survival tactics. You steal a purse, then a car. It will make you do things you could never imagine," says Piche sadly.

Her phone rings and Piche answers it.

"When were you last here, dear?" she asks a potential client. "What's going to be different this time?"

Tom Pazdernik, the director of rehabilitation at Freedom House, a halfway house on Cleveland's West Side, is at his desk in his office. The top, a huge slab of pine-green marble with "Harley-Davidson" inscribed in gold, was a gift from former clients. The lower right-hand side of the top reads "Paz," and underneath, "October 11, 1993."

It's not Paz's birthday. It's his sobriety date.

"When I die, they can just stick it in the ground and use it as my tombstone," he says and laughs. The 44-year-old Pazdernik is not only a Freedom House manager, he's also a former client. In fact, he's a lot of former stuff. When it comes to drugs, he's done them all. More amazing, he's lived to tell about it. He's a poster boy for drug-and-alcohol recovery.

Raised virtually unsupervised by his grandmother in Parma, Pazdernik spent his youth working on cars, smoking pot, drinking and doing speed in the form of diet pills. He had his first drug-induced heart attack at 18. After dropping out of high school, he worked several menial jobs until he found his calling: selling pot. At 19, a deal went bad and Pazdernik was robbed of several pounds of marijuana. During the heist he was shot in the chest with a 12-gauge shotgun.

At the hospital, after surgery, he was introduced to the opiate painkiller Demerol, which he was given every three hours for three months. When he was released, he had to rely on friends for street drugs to dull his pain and keep him high. Heroin soon became his drug of choice.

Over the next three years, Pazdernik was treated for various addictions seven times. Eventually, he had a stroke from shooting cocaine and was paralyzed from the neck down on his left side for 10 months. After his recovery, he went back to his three favorite pastimes: shooting heroin, smoking pot and drinking Wild Irish Rose.

Pazdernik continued to sell drugs. He used to hang "Open" and "Sorry, We're Closed" signs in the front window of his house for the benefit of his drug customers. In 1991, Pazdernik became the first person to be arrested for dealing drugs under a new Ohio law that allowed the county to confiscate and sell his Parma home because it was used in the commission of a drug offense.

Pazdernik was expecting a two-year stint at the Lorain Correctional Institution. He was relieved. It was a chance for him to get away from the vicious cycle of drugs that had been consuming his life. But the judge gave him probation. Heartbroken and homeless, he borrowed $5 from a cop, bought a bottle of wine and a pack of cigarettes, and hit the streets, resuming his life of use and abuse.

Two years later, on October 11, 1993, Pazdernik hit bottom. On that day he prayed for God to change his life and had the "moment of clarity" so many recovering addicts describe. Pazdernik says he became instantly and effortlessly sober. With nowhere else to go, and with just $2.50 in his pocket, he walked into Freedom House, hoping for a place to stay. Two months later, he was named a counselor. He has since dedicated his life to helping other addicts.

"Every morning I ask God to help me be the best person I can be and every night I thank him for keeping me alive one more day," Pazdernik says. "You see a lot of tragedy here. A lot of these guys are emotional junkyards."

One component of the new heroin epidemic is the influx of new young users. Statistics from the Office of the National Drug Control Policy in Washington, D.C., show that the average Ohio heroin addict is 40 years old. But treatment centers are reporting much younger clients.

Some experts blame the spread of heroin use among the young on a fashion trend called "heroin chic." The term was coined in 1997 in a *New York Times* story about fashion photographer David Sorrenti, whose photographs popularized the thin, pale, glassy-eyed look that model Kate Moss and others made famous. Ironically, Sorrenti died of a heroin overdose that same year.

"Somewhere along the line heroin lost the stigma it used to have 10 years ago," says Jim Hummel, resident agent in charge of the Cleveland office of the DEA.

"Now you hear about all these Hollywood movie stars doing heroin," Hummel says. "There's a lot more around. It's become popular. Crack was the focus the last five year. Now the Colombians have introduced a new product line into their marketing chain. And they're flooding the market with heroin.

In the late Eighties and into the Nineties, movies such as *Drugstore Cowboy*, *Pulp Fiction* and *Trainspotting* all dealt graphically with heroin addiction. During the same period several popular rock stars died from overdoses. So did actor River Phoenix. Actor Robert Downey Jr. is serving a three-year prison sentence for violating his probation on a charge of heroin possession.

All of these events have sent a mixed message: Despite its deadly effects, heroin has gained popularity as a "glamour" drug among the elite in fashion, show business and music.

"What's glamorous," asks Westlake Police Captain Turner, "about someone vomiting into a jail cell toilet? That's the heroin addicts we see."

Young, attractive and chic, Dina and Ross (not their real names) could pass for fashion models. They've been clean for 11 months. Dina, from out West, moved to Cleveland last year to attend college. That's where she met Ross, who grew up in an East Side suburb. Dina never did drugs in high school, but Ross had a long history of serious drug experimentation and dealing.

The two began going to all-night psychedelic dance parties called "raves," smoking pot, doing Ecstasy and snorting cocaine. Soon they were shooting cocaine. Eventually they fell in with a group of heroin-using friends and began experimenting themselves.

"We began using [heroin] only one night on the weekend," Dina says. "And then not too much. But pretty soon it would be both nights of the weekend. I was a waitress and always had cash. I didn't feel like I was spending too much.

"Let me put it this way: The first time was in February [1999]. For the next two months, I could take it our leave it. By May, there was regular use, and by August it was every day. We knew what we were doing was wrong, so we just did more because it made us forget.

"When school started in the fall, we tried to stop, but the physical addiction was there. We began using a $20 bag a day between us, and when we quit, we were doing 10 bags a day and using stolen credit cards to get the money. Every morning we'd drive downtown to 105th and Adams to score.

"My own arrogance was unbelievable. I thought no one like me could be an addict. I was a straight-A student on a full scholarship to a prestigious school. I came from a good home, good parents, I always had good jobs. But every time I tried to quit I'd start right up again three days later.

"I wanted to get better, but I didn't know how. I didn't have the slightest idea how to quit. I felt like I wanted to die *a lot*. Eventually my dad found out that I had used my credit card to charge $4,000 in cash advances. That's how I got caught.

"Looking back, I didn't realize how fast you can get addicted," she says. "Or how available it is."

The road to recovery from heroin addiction is long and arduous. "It's like climbing out of a deep pit," Collins says. "But people do get well. We see miracles every day. People walk in like train wrecks and after a few weeks we see health return, spirits brighten, as they rediscover themselves. To see that person blossom again is astounding. There is no greater joy in a doctor's life."

But the tragic stories far outweigh successful ones.

"We recently had a woman in her early 20s come in for her first time for heroin treatment. She was a single mom, with a 5-year-old kid, from the suburbs," says Roche of Stella Maris.

"She did really well, exceptional. We were so proud of her when she left. We were sure she would turn her life around. But it didn't work out," says Roche fighting tears.

"She went home, bought some heroin, shot up and hung herself."

A DAY IN THE LIFE: BOOSTING, BUYING AND BANGING

Tom (not his real name) is on what he hopes is his final mission.

While most of Cleveland is still in bed on this frigid Saturday morning in January, Tom is up and about. He needs a fix bad.

Tom, 43, wants out of the heroin life. He's lost nine friends over the last two years to drug overdoses, AIDS, complications from hepatitis, and jail.

But this morning, he's "dopesick." The symptoms include chills, fever, sweats, nausea, cramps and aching joints. Heroin withdrawal doesn't kill addicts, but many often wish it did. Tom has decided to "get well" before detoxing a final time.

An addict for seven years, he has become a skilled thief to support his habit.

Tom pulls the battered, filthy van he calls home onto I-90 and heads west to a shopping center he knows well. He pulls into the parking lot and leaves the engine running. He ties shut the string closure at the bottom of his parka to form a pouch around his hips and heads into a supermarket. Three minutes later, he's back in the van, heading out onto the road. He pulls 10 cans of Similac infant formula from his coat and drops them, one at a time, on the floor. Each can retails for $10.39.

Tom heads back to Cleveland. He stops at a convenience store where he has unloaded stolen formula before. The fence gives him $4 a can. With his ill-gotten $40 in hand, Tom heads to his dope house to score.

He parks a block away, in an empty lot off a side street. Five minutes later, back in the running van, Tom has two "bags," or glassine envelopes, each containing a quarter gram of a light-brown powder. He opens the glove compartment and pulls out a spoon. He fills the spoon with snow from the ground and lets it melt on the dashboard. Pouring the powder into the water, he tears a cigarette filter in half and places it over the liquid. He sticks his needle through the filter, and into the mixture, to strain out impurities.

Tom draws back the plunger. He finds a vein in the crook of his reed-thin right arm, slips the needle in and drives the plunger down. His chemical mission complete, Tom's demeanor becomes more relaxed. He's less edgy and driven.

"If I worked this hard at a $5-an-hour job, I'd be a millionaire by now," he says. "Most people have an image of what a heroin addict is, but the drug does not discriminate. I'm not this person you see today. I wasn't raised like this. This is bad shit. Revolting.

"As a kid, I wouldn't steal a piece of candy. I come from a nice family in Gates Mills. I had every opportunity for a decent, successful life. I have a wife and two kids I don't see. I had good jobs, my own company, made a lot of money, built my own house. I lost everything."

March 12, 2000

INSIDE THE MIND
OF A STALKER

She called it quits.
He wouldn't have it.
He told her she'd be sorry.
Now he's going to spend the rest of his life guaranteeing it.

"I got my dad's handgun, then I walked back and forth in front of her house waiting for her. It was pure fate she never came out when I was there. It was God's will. I might have killed her."

This is the voice of a stalker. You'd never know it if you saw him on the street. He's a tall, well-groomed 38-year-old man with boyish good looks. His clothes are neat, if casual, and he smiles easily. He grew up in an upper-middle-class neighborhood in a southwest suburb of Cleveland. He finished high school and married his high school sweetheart, but his addiction to crack cocaine brought the rocky marriage to an end after only three years.

But he never let go of his ex-wife. Even though she obtained restraining orders against him, even though he repeatedly was in rehab for his drug addiction, even though he was arrested and eventually sent to jail, he was compelled to keep her in his control. His obsession with her has been the one constant in two lives wracked with chaos and pain.

The text and tone of his comments about his ex-wife are familiar to Mary. She knows a man just like this. She has her own stalker.

"Eventually, he'll probably kill me," says Mary (not her real name) as she sits calmly in her Northeast Ohio living room. "And I'm OK with that. I know that's a weird thing to say. But it's hard for other people to understand what I've been through."

Mary has been stalked for more than 10 years. She has been raped, physically abused and humiliated by her stalker. She has suffered harassment, from being phoned at home 50 times a day to being followed on foot and by car. She's lost jobs because his inces-

sant phone calls disrupted her workplace. She's received threatening letters in the mail and been accosted in public. She's been in
therapy for six years to deal with the emotional and psychological damage inflicted by her stalker. She moved 70 miles outside of
Cleveland to put some distance between her and her stalker. She
obtained restraining and protection orders against him, and police
enforce them. But the stalker is still very much in her life.

He's her ex-husband. They have a child. He has visitation
rights.

*"I have 13 felony convictions: Two for stalking, one domestic
violence, three drug possessions, assault, conspiracy, aggravated
burglary, receiving stolen property, uttering forgery. People in
court don't believe it when they see my sheet."*

Experts say almost all stalkers have criminal records. They
not only have difficulty with personal boundary issues, they have
problems with laws. Pathologically self-centered people, they care
only about what they want or need that moment, consequences be
damned.

When people hear the word "stalker," they most often think of
headline grabbers like former Cleveland firefighter Thomas Mc-
Carthy, who kept tabs on more than 2,200 women and this year
pleaded guilty to rape. Or they think of West Side rapist Ronnie
Shelton, currently at Trumbull Correctional Institution, serving
3,198 years, the longest sentence in Cleveland legal history for his
attacks on 29 women in the late Eighties.

Richard Adamowski, a 37-year-old Willoughby man, joined the
Greater Cleveland stalker hall of shame last month when he was
sentenced to 18 years in jail for slashing the face of former girlfriend Stephanie Nobilio with a razor. "If I can't have her, nobody
can," he said, reciting what has become a stalker cliché before dis-
figuring her.

All these men are stalkers. But so was Margaret Ray, the woman
who broke into talk show host David Letterman's house throughout the Nineties, before committing suicide at age 46. Or Mark
David Chapman, who murdered John Lennon in 1980 and whose
first request for parole was denied last month. Or John Hinckley,
then 25, who fired on President Reagan in 1981 to impress actress

Jodie Foster. Or Robert Bardo, who in 1989 shot and killed actress Rebecca Schaeffer in the doorway of her Los Angeles home after hiring a private detective to help him find her.

A stalker can be a random killer—or a rapist hiding in the shadows. A stalker can be an ex-spouse or lover unwilling to let go—or a complete stranger who happens to cross your path. A stalker can be a neighbor who takes offense at the arrangement of dogwood trees in your front yard—or a clerk at the corner store who imagines a cosmic, unspoken connection between the two of you.

A stalker could be a co-worker who needs a friend and decides it's you. If you are a doctor, it could be a patient; if you are a minister, it could be a member of your congregation. If you regularly visit Internet chat rooms, it could be anyone.

"Stalking and cocaine go together like eggs and bacon. I had all kinds of scams to get money for cocaine. After I had spent all the money and done all the drugs, I'd start to get mean and thinking about her. Thinking about what a bitch she was. I'd go over and over it in my mind. My behavior would get erratic. It scared her."

It's not surprising that stalkers are prone to abusing drugs and alcohol. Stalking is obsessive-compulsive disorder in its most extreme form. Using drugs and drinking serves several purposes. It can be a form of self-medication. Getting high can put obsessive-compulsive behavior on temporary hold; it can provide an escape or respite from the out-of-control activity. But the urges only come back stronger when the person is sober. On the other hand, depending on the individual, abusing alcohol or drugs can be like pouring fuel on the fire. In either instance, the result is a person who is highly unstable and dangerously unpredictable.

"Stalking is a very old behavior. It has only recently become a new crime," says J. Reid Meloy, Ph.D., an associate clinical professor of psychiatry at the University of California's San Diego School of Medicine.

His book, *Violence Risk and Threat Assessment* (Specialized Training Services, 2000), contains some of the latest findings on stalking. The news isn't good.

"The numbers [of stalkers] are much higher than we ever

thought, and they're also on an increase. Each year, 1 million women and 400,000 men are stalked. That's much larger than earlier estimates," he says.

Meloy has found virtually all stalkers share three characteristics: They have had psychiatric problems, they have abused drugs or alcohol, and they have criminal records.

"You could call them people who have a lot of problems," he says. "*One* of which is stalking."

Stalkers often have two other traits that go hand in hand. They have above-average intelligence and are generally under or unemployed. This gives them the smarts and the time to pursue their victims.

"Stalking is enormously time-consuming," says Meloy.

Locally, Candace B. Risen is the go-to person on the psychiatric side of sex crimes. Risen, a clinical psychiatric social worker, runs the sex-offender program at the Center for Marital & Sexual Health in Beachwood. Many of her clients are referred by the court system. She's often consulted by the FBI and other law enforcement agencies for her experience, expertise and insight regarding high-profile cases involving stalking and sexually deviant behavior.

"Stalking is not one thing. There are many forms of stalking," she explains. "There's your personal stalker, where there's a specific attachment to an ex-spouse or lover. Or a serial stalker, who doesn't know the victims. They are two very distinct groups who are diagnostically different."

Meloy says modern society, a high-tech world where people are more likely to meet anonymously on the Internet than at the local bowling alley, provides an atmosphere that can stunt the development of normal social skills and foster antisocial behavior such as stalking.

"Forming appropriate attachments to others is something people learn from their families," he says. "As we see more single-parent homes, when we have fewer neighbors who know each other as the social fabric becomes less tight-knit, it leaves fewer models. The world gets more impersonal. It leads to a lack of social skills, fragmentation, alienation, loneliness and anger. That mix is potentially ominous."

Risen says serial stalking is most often an obsessive-compulsive sexual desire or fantasy that begins as a response to a real life dilemma.

"What happens is, the dream life takes over," Risen says. "The script or the ritualized behavior is the answer to a problem. It's a misguided way of coping. Perhaps the real life problem is being consumed by feelings of inadequacy. When these adolescent longings meet puberty and are coupled with erotic feeling, they can turn into aggression.

"These feelings aren't random. They come from somewhere. And they're kept alive by extensive fantasizing. Thinking about these rituals becomes intoxicating, like an altered state."

"Once I called up a towing service and had her car towed from work . . . I pissed in her gas tank and ruined the engine. I wore out the redial button on my phone calling her at work. She used to get reprimanded because of my calls. I know she changed jobs a few times because of me."

Stalking victims are extremely vulnerable in the workplace. It's an ideal environment for harassment and humiliation. The stalker can use a person's place of employment like a stage to play out attention-getting stunts. The cars of stalking victims—unprotected in large parking lots—are frequent targets.

Popular culture plays a role through television, movies and music. Stalking behavior is a recurring theme. Think of the persistently amorous cartoon skunk Pepe Le Pew or the relentless girl chaser that Harpo Marx played in movies. And it is characterized in ambiguous ways.

"There's a dual message in the media," Meloy says. "Stalkers are often the subjects of comedies or romance movies. Look at *[There's] Something About Mary*, four guys obsessed with the same woman. True love perseveres. Look at the lyrics to the Police song "Every Breath You Take." We have a Calvin Klein perfume called Obsession. There's a general acceptance of the phenomenon. And in many cases it's highly romanticized."

But Meloy emphasizes that the social and cultural elements take a back seat to the one think he believes all stalkers share: A profound psychiatric disorder.

"I tried to keep her hostage. . . I broke into her house, took scissors and sliced up all the clothes in her closet . . . I removed the starter coil from her car so many times it looked like I had a collection of

*them . . . I slashed three sets of her tires . . . I smashed her wind-
shield with a brick."*

Stalking, even if it seems utterly free of reason, still has its own
rhythm. Stalkers honor different anniversaries than most people.
They remember the time they first saw someone or the date they
were divorced. They may orchestrate menacing in ritualistic ways
that make sense only to themselves. The activity tends to build and
escalate, often ending in a showy, and usually violent, crescendo.
Then it can unexpectedly cease. Sometimes it is the stalker's way
of keeping the victim off-guard. Other times, the stalker is afraid
of crossing the line and getting caught. Being arrested and hauled
into court is an example of stalking backfiring on the stalker.

One Cleveland man's actions caught up with him recently in
Rocky River City Hall. The man, who was in the courtroom with
his attorney, was being sentenced for menacing by stalking. His ex-
wife was there, as was his probation officer. The man had violated
a protection order by talking with his ex-wife in public. She tried
to ignore him. He persisted in conversation and even asked her out
to dinner.

The ex-wife also wanted to address her concerns about her son's
attitude when he returned from weekend visits with his father. She
said her son came back angry, rebellious and made pointed, critical
remarks that sounded like his dad.

The man's attorney told Judge Congeni-Fitzsimmons that the
man had successfully completed a nine-month stay in a drug-and-
alcohol rehabilitation facility, held a steady job and was preparing
to find a place to live on his own.

Congeni-Fitzsimmons could have jailed the man for six months
for violating the protection order. But both the ex-wife and the
judge wanted him to build on his newfound sobriety. The judge
gave him a break, putting him on probation for three years and
stipulating that the man and his son attend anger-management
counseling once a month.

The man, wearing jeans, a T-shirt and rubber flip-flops, became
agitated.

"I don't want to be the bad guy in this," he said, his face turning
red. "He [my son] has been through *enough*."

The attorney, alarmed by his client's belligerence, thanked the
judge *for* him. But the man kept insisting that anger-management

counseling was a bad idea. Breathing hard, he looked out of the courtroom window to avoid eye contact with anyone. He was not aware of how he was coming across to the judge or observers in the courtroom.

Congeni-Fitzsimmons says later, "These people have a hard time seeing they've committed a crime. It's all about power and control. It's like a personality trait so strong it becomes a psychosis."

Timothy Boehnlein, a psychology assistant at the Center for Domestic Violence, a private, non-profit agency in Beachwood, counsels stalkers the center treats.

"The stalker is using power to control another human being. What they don't see is that they are out of control when they're doing it. The stalker isn't controlling himself. We have lots of relapse when it comes to stalkers," Boehnlein says. "We *expect* relapse. The key is thorough assessment and using it to figure out a treatment."

Congeni-Fitzsimmons first began seeing stalking victims and their frustration with the legal system while a county prosecutor from 1978 to 1980, and then as a federal prosecutor through 1985.

"The problem with the law back then was that the majority of stalking offenses were not felonies. They were punishable by up to a $1,000 fine and six months in jail. That's not much of a deterrent. I've seen examples of men stalking women *from jail*. Then the law changed in 1994 so that anyone with a prior stalking offense against the same person could have it bumped up to a felony. That law was changed [again] last March and now states that anyone with a prior stalking charge against anyone will have their charge raised to a felony."

"She got a temporary restraining order. I had to stay 500 feet away, no calls, no mail, no contact. I broke that by sending her flowers from rehab and got one year in jail. While I was in jail, I hired a hit man to break her legs so she wouldn't be able to go anywhere. I was caught for that before it happened and got aggravated conspiracy."

To say a stalker won't take no for an answer is a grave understatement. Stalkers are impervious to warnings, admonishments and punishment. They not only do what they want, they only *hear* what they want. They appear to be hard-wired toward practicing stalking. As if it's in their DNA. This makes therapy an iffy proposition.

When Timothy Boehnlein has a caseload of 30 clients, five of them will be stalkers. The majority are domestic stalkers (ex-husbands and ex-boyfriends) whose behavior escalates and almost always culminates in a violent or explosive incident.

"Typically these guys are operating out of emotional reasoning," he says. "There's an irrational thought pattern in place, a kind of skewed thinking, and they tend to be emotionally delayed. They use denial and minimization to justify themselves."

After talking about their childhoods, clients in therapy are asked by Boehnlein to slow down the thought process that leads to stalking.

"We show them they don't have to act on every emotion or impulse they feel," says Boehnlein. "We try to give them other choices and alternative ways of reacting to situations. We offer tools they can use to challenge the irrational thoughts."

Boehnlein also contacts the stalkers' victims to corroborate their stories.

"Stalkers are masters of manipulation," Boehnlein says. "We stress accountability and responsibility. No excuses."

Boehnlein's work with stalkers has led him to two important conclusions: Stalkers can't stop stalking without professional help, and women being stalked need to be the primary providers of their own safety, collecting evidence against those who stalk them. Police departments lack the budgets, manpower and time to protect stalking victims 24 hours a day.

> *"I mailed her a package of dog crap. I would park my car in front of her parents' house at night burning and screeching my tires on the street to get attention. Once, we were in the car fighting and I ripped all her clothes off. Another time, we were on a busy freeway and I got out of the car and took the keys and left her there. Another car almost rear-ended her. I was sorry it didn't."*

A domestic stalker in a fit of pique can be completely devoid of rational thought. That person can go from dead calm to rage in seconds. The delusional stalker who targets celebrities can turn violent, too. It just takes a little longer. Imagined intimacy is more difficult to act upon.

WOIO Channel 19 co-anchor Denise Dufala has been an on-air television personality for more than 14 years. Last February, a

Parma Heights man was charged with menacing by stalking for sending 18 letters to Dufala and her relatives. He was placed on three years' probation and ordered to undergo three months of in-patient psychiatric care after he pleaded guilty to two counts of the charge. The man's attorney said he had a history of mental illness and needed treatment. The judge told the man that if he violated his probation he would receive a year in prison.

Dufala is matter-of-fact about the incident.

"That's just one of the stalkers you found out about," Dufala says. "For every one you hear about, there are two others you don't. For a woman on television, dealing with stalkers is a constant way of life. It's part of the business. You wish it wasn't that way. It's unfortunate but true. Any anchorwoman can tell you the same stories."

WKYC Channel 3 anchorwoman Romona Robinson tells a similar tale.

"I have a stalker file at home," she says. "These are people with mental problems who don't take their medicine. I've had both man and women [stalkers]. They think they love you, they think you love them. People ask me why I'm so private. You have to be. There are precautions you take, but to some extent there's nothing you can do. I still have to go out and talk to people. I can't be a prisoner in my own home. I don't want to overemphasize it, but I don't want to diminish how frightening it can be either."

Dufala's and Robinson's stalkers, like most people who prey on high-profile media figures and celebrities, are delusional stalkers. They read into what television personalities say and find personal messages. They develop connections and relationships that don't exist. Dufala says most of these people can be stopped from stalking before they begin.

"I'd say that 99 percent of the people who stalked me were surrounded with family who knew that person had a problem or knew he was going overboard with some inappropriate behavior but failed to do anything about it," she says. "Too often people feel embarrassed to bring it up because of the stigma that mental illness carries. But getting someone the help or medication needed is a lot less embarrassing than having that person appear in the newspaper or on television for having stalked someone."

"When I got out of jail, I went and saw her on the second day. I was preoccupied with her day and night. I called her all the time,

telling her I was going to kill her, kill myself. I asked why she was
doing this to me. I told her I would make her sorry."

Consequences mean nothing to stalkers. Punishment is an abstract concept. They are totally focused on the subject of their obsession.

"Early on it was hard to get your arms around the law on stalking," says Cleveland Municipal Court Judge Judge Ronald Adrine, who has been a municipal judge for 19 years. "Stalkers seem to know how to come right up to the line of the law without crossing it. That's where it gets tricky.

"The worst case I saw involved a man who was obsessed with his deceased brother's fiancée. When he first came before me, it wasn't clear that his dough was not completely baked. He was very convincing. He really believed she was playing hard to get. This woman's life was completely destroyed. She was terrified. You had to listen hard over a long time to decipher this man's mental state.

"It's a dicey issue," Adrine adds. "A lot depends on your level of experience. You need to be sensitized to things that might sound otherwise overblown. Each case is so different, you're never 100 percent sure."

"Right now I'm all about staying sober, working the program, going to meetings. I'm trying to learn from my mistakes. I even have a relapse prevention plan. If I feel like I'm tempted, I talk to people, I don't isolate. I get to a meeting, call a sponsor. But I've even had problems calling my sponsor too much. He told me to cut that out."

Good news on the stalking front comes in small packages. Stalking is finding its way into the arena of public discussion. Meloy, of the San Diego Medical School, says education and understanding will ensue.

Popular anti-depressants, such as Prozac, have helped curb some obsessive-compulsive cravings, says Risen, the Beachwood psychiatric social worker. She also notes that over the course of a 30-year career, she has seen behaviors such as domestic violence and the sexual abuse of children, once thought too horrible for public consideration, receive the attention of medical, social and legal authorities. Now that awareness is being raised about the devastating effects of stalking, there is hope more can be done to deter offenders.

"I know my ex-wife is scared of men now. How does she know when one will turn out like me? She takes a lot of precautions."

It's impossible to underestimate the extent to which a stalker, even one who never acts violently, can destroy a victim's life. Over time, through relentless menacing and on-again, off-again harassment, the stalker throws the victim into a state of near-constant fear that is profoundly debilitating. Victims describe the feeling as a slow but steady descent into a deep, dark madness.

Mary, the stalking victim, has remarried and has a child with her new husband. She's learned to manage the fear that once controlled her. Though she has found a way to cope, there is still a feeling of resignation.

"I always compare it to having a chronic or terminal illness," she says. "You have good days and bad days. But it's always there. You learn to live with it.

"Hopefully it's not terminal."

October 22, 2000

HUNTING THE MAN
BEHIND THE MASK

On television, police solve almost every crime in an hour.
This real life case took 24 hours.

As Detective Jim Butler typed in the Web page address of a suspected pedophile, a devil's mask popped up on his computer screen.

He was responding to a call from the 3rd District police station. Officers had a report from the parents of three girls, one 13, the other two 12 years old. The girls said they had been sexually assaulted by a man they had met in an Internet chat room.

Butler glanced over at the photograph of his own kids on the desk in the Sex Crimes Unit on the sixth floor of the Justice Center downtown. It was just after 9:30 a.m. Thursday. He would be seeing them this weekend. That always lifted his spirits after a week of this grim business.

Butler looked again at the screen. The top image featured the suspect in the vivid red, hideously gleeful devil's mask complete with horns and bloody fangs.

Next to it were the words, "this is me . . . if u don't like it then get the fuck out! im not here to impress anyone cause i got it going on for myself. im a tattoo artist, and also a freak."

The other pictures showed a young, beefy, Hispanic man, mugging for the camera. The three girls had developed an online relationship with him. They knew him only as "Joey."

He was the man behind the mask.

10 A.M. – GOING ALL OUT

At the 3rd District on the East Side, there was already a sense of urgency about this case.

Only two days before, the body of a young girl, found one mile from the site of the rapes, was identified as 11-year-old-Shakira

Johnson. Shakira had been missing for five weeks. The girl's killer was still at large.

Third District Cmdr. Andy Gonzalez, 44, read the report about the three girls early Thursday morning.

Normally the rape case would have bounced directly to Sex Crimes. But because of its heinous nature, and the involvement of children from the 3rd, Gonzalez wanted it. Butler was on his way to the station house on Payne Avenue to help out,

He had been with Sex Crimes only two years but loved the work. He is well-suited to the singular focus of the investigations. He uses the psychology degree he earned from Wittenberg University. Butler didn't join the force until age 34. Before that, he had been a reporter for several Cleveland radio stations. But he had always been drawn to police work.

At the 3rd, Butler told Gonzalez, Capt. Luis Cumba and Lt. Michael Baumiller he was going to call the girls' parents and have them bring the kids in. As other detectives began to arrive for their shifts, Baumiller told them to hang loose.

One of the detectives, 41-year-old Bruce Garner, was supposed to work his second job, as a security guard, at the end of his shift. He needs the extra money to support his wife and three children, the oldest about to go off to college. But Baumiller made it clear this could be a long day. They were going all out for this one. If Butler's interviews yielded good information, everybody would be involved in the pursuit and capture of "Joey."

Butler is gifted at interviewing kids. At 6 feet 6 and 280 pounds, he is imposing. But also protective. He speaks with a smooth baritone that's both authoritative and comforting. It was made for radio. Now he employed it helping scared kids relay painful experiences.

The three girls arrived at 10:30 a.m. with their mothers. The group huddled together self-consciously. The detectives, sitting in their cubicles, talked quietly about what children the kids were. Baumiller, 52, with more than 20 years on the job, noted the Strawberry Shortcake attire on one. There was nothing even slightly sexual about these girls.

Butler introduced himself, telling the moms and girls what to expect. He escorted the first girl to a back office, asking her questions and typing the answers on an old electric typewriter. As he spoke, Butler looked for eye contact and other physical cues that might indicate fear or deception. It didn't take long to determine that there really was a bad guy out there. More importantly, he learned that "Joey" had a standing offer to meet with the girls again.

11 A.M. – A STORY EMERGES

The girls' stories were plausible and unrehearsed—and familiar. They met "Joey" in an Internet chat room in September 2003. The conversation quickly turned to sex. He was full of questions. Did they have boyfriends? Did they ever do stuff? He sent them the link to his Web page. The one with the devil mask. The exchanges continued for several weeks. He gave them his cell phone number. For the girls, this was a strange, exciting adventure. "Joey" was cool. He told them he was a repo man, a guy who reclaims cars from deadbeat customers.

He asked them questions, always flirting. Had they ever done "it?" They giggled in embarrassment writing back "no!" The "Joey" behind the mask was driving obsessively toward one goal. To meet them in person.

He used teasing and flattery to entice them to come to the RTA bus station on War Avenue off East 71st Street near Slavic Village on Oct. 7. The girls knew they would all be there together. There was safety in numbers. What could happen?

They met "Joey" around 5 p.m. at the bus stop. He didn't waste time. He suggested playing what Butler called every pedophile's favorite game: Truth or Dare.

He told them to pick a category. If they chose Truth, he asked an embarrassing sexual question. For Dare, he challenged them to join him behind the bushes.

Manipulated by the game, one by one, each consented, and each was raped, police say.

The oldest girl finally broke it up, saying they had to go. They left feeling confused and coerced.

Would they tell their parents? No way.

Three weeks later, an older sister overheard a phone conversation between two of the girls. She convinced her sibling to talk. Parents got involved. The 3rd District detectives got the report Oct. 23.

In the interview room, the girls told Butler they were hurting and confused. He said he couldn't tell them how to feel. But the police could make sure "Joey" never did this again.

2:30 P.M. – A PLAN

The interviews done, Lt. Baumiller suggested to Cmdr. Gonzalez that one of the girls could call "Joey" on the pretext of wanting another meeting. Gonzalez and Butler liked the idea. Butler approached the families in the detective bureau. The 13-year-old and her mother agreed to help.

Butler, Capt. Cumba, the girl and her mom went to a Vice Unit office where there was a phone. Butler coached her. She made the call around 2:45. He marveled at her calm efficiency. "Joey" quickly directed the conversation toward sex. Would she and the other girl come to his house? Would the other girl agree to sex with him?

She played him masterfully, telling him what he wanted to hear. And it was all on tape.

Finally, he said he had to take a shower. Could she call back in 30 minutes?

The tension in the room swelled silently as the minutes ticked by. At 3:15 p.m., the girl called "Joey" again. He was ready to pick the girls up, he said. Same place. On War Avenue. She told him she had to get her friend. She said she would call back when they were near the bus stop. He said he would be waiting for the call.

3:30 P.M. – SETTING THE TRAP

Butler gave a quick briefing to Bruce Garner, Ron James Jr., and the dozen or so other detectives assembled in the community room. He shared his expertise from working in Sex Crimes. If "Joey" fit the pedophile profile, there were things they should know.

One, he would show up on time. His attraction to sex with kids was all-consuming.

Two, if confronted by police, he would run. Not only run, he will run over you to get away, Butler said.

Three, if he is a repo man, as he told the girls, there is a good chance he is armed. Repo men often carry guns.

Four, pedophiles don't fare well in jail. He will do anything to avoid jail, including putting a policeman in a position where he would be forced to shoot "Joey."

Capt. Cumba, 52, passed out maps of the area. Undercover cars would be waiting at key corners in the neighborhood. Cumba, the girl and her mother would be sitting where they could see "Joey" come off Interstate 77. Once the girl identified "Joey," they would wait for him to turn left on War Avenue and head down to the bus stop. Police hoped to apprehend him there. The trap was set. The adrenaline was pumping.

Cumba drove an unmarked car with the 13-year-old girl and her mother. He wasn't optimistic. In more than 20 years on the job, he had never seen these setups work. Not once. But his experience was with dopers. They were always too high to make appointments on time or at all.

But Cumba had a personal desire to see "Joey" locked up. When Cumba was a patrol rookie in the 6th District, he got a call about a female in distress on Fulton Court. He happened to be on Fulton Court at the moment of the call. He interrupted two men raping a female. It was a gruesome scene. He called for backup and arrested the men.

But the charges were later dismissed. The girl was mentally disabled, unable to testify on her own behalf. The experience still haunts Cumba.

3:48 P.M. – 'JOEY' SHOWS

The 13-year-old girl said "Joey" drove a green Taurus. She called him on her cell phone saying she and her friend were there; seven minutes later, a green car rolled by.

"That's 'Joey,'" she said.

Cumba was floored. He got on his radio and alerted the other officers. "Joey" was in the area, driving a green Mercury Mystique, a Taurus look-alike.

The chase was on.

"Joey" didn't turn left on War Avenue as expected. Three blocks past War, he took a left and headed toward the UPS terminal. When he reached the end, he turned left again. The police tried to box him in. As soon as he saw a car in his rearview mirror, "Joey" gunned his engine and turned left again, now heading east toward East 71st.

Just before the intersection, an unmarked car blocked "Joey's" path. Detective Scott Zenkewicz, 33, opened the passenger side door. He reached for his weapon when "Joey" punched the accelerator and zoomed toward the undercover car. Zenkewicz jumped back in and his partner, Detective Mike Alexander, 37, punched the gas just in time.

"Joey" skirted the rear of the car, missing it by inches, going up on the sidewalk and turned north once again on 71st. As cops converged from sidestreets, he jumped from the moving vehicle, hit the ground and took off down Claasen Avenue behind the Victory Tavern. His car kept going on 71st, eventually crossing the yellow line and smashing into a parked truck.

An undercover police car pulled up to "Joey," now on foot, blocking his access to the street. He looked to hop a fence behind a house only to find Tank, a massive Rottweiler, snarling on the other side. There was nowhere to run.

"Joey" had a decision to make.

4:15 P.M. – TIME TO DECIDE

"Joey" turned and faced three police officers who had weapons drawn. They all shouted at him repeatedly.

PUT YOUR HANDS UP!

GET ON THE GROUND!

He stood there with his hands up. He kept asking, with a torrent of profanity, what they wanted. He said he hadn't done anything. Detective. Bruce Garner, only six feet away, pointed his Smith & Wesson at "Joey" over the roof of a parked car. Garner shouted again and again for him to keep his hands up.

Suddenly "Joey" cursed Garner, officers said, and reached with both hands for his waistband.

Garner fired one shot from his 9mm weapon, hitting "Joey" on the lower right side of his chest.

"Joey" put his hands back up.

"I can't believe you shot me," he said.

He remained standing while the three officers pointing guns continued to yell at him.

GET DOWN ON THE GROUND!

He lifted his shirt, showing the officers his bullet wound.

PUT YOUR HANDS UP!

GET DOWN ON THE GROUND!

Finally Detective Ron James Jr., a 37-year-old son of a cop, approached "Joey" and with two other officers forcibly put him on the ground.

An officer called for an ambulance. Lt. Baumiller Butler arrived on the scene. Baumiller had served two years on the Use of Deadly Force Team. He knew what to do. He escorted Garner back to the lieutenant's car, an arm around his shoulder, and sat him down.

He took Garner's gun.

4:23 P.M. – SAVING "JOEY"

James handcuffed and frisked "Joey," who was lying on the ground. There was nothing in his waistband. He was unarmed. He began crying, asking James not to let him die. He was not a bad guy, he insisted. He had a kid. Please don't let me die, he kept asking James.

James knew "Joey" was going into shock. He was losing blood. The detective took off his jacket, bunched it up and put it under "Joey's" head. Then he ran across the street to the Victory Tavern to get some bar towels to stop the bleeding.

Just a few feet away, Baumiller talked to Garner while they waited for Homicide and Internal Affairs to arrive.

Baumiller tried to prepare him for the rest of his day. He would tell his story about the shooting repeatedly to various officers and officials. Baumiller assured him it was a clean shooting. Garner kept looking outside the car in "Joey's" direction. Is he OK?

Is he going to make it?

Is the ambulance here yet? Where's the ambulance?

Baumiller said he would check on "Joey." He told Garner three witnesses had seen "Joey" go for his pocket. But he had no gun.

James returned from the Victory with bar towels. "Joey" pleaded with James not to leave him.

"Don't let me die," "Joey" said.

Five minutes later, the ambulance arrived and James accompanied "Joey" to MetroHealth Medical Center on West 25th Street.

Police had "Joey" in custody, but a nagging question remained. Was he the man behind the mask?

5 P.M. – GETTING AN ID

Butler called in the license plate number on "Joey's" Mercury Mystique. The plate came back with the date of birth and Social Security number of Edwin Diaz. Butler drove back to the Justice Center to see if Diaz had a criminal history, and to write warrants allowing him to search Diaz's home. He wanted to make certain that Diaz was in fact "Joey."

Butler got a Lorain Avenue address on the near West Side for Diaz, then sent an officer over to guard Diaz's residence, making sure no one removed anything before detectives got there.

Diaz had several felony convictions. He had been arrested and done a couple of years in prison for drug trafficking, drug abuse, possession of criminal tools, carrying a weapon while on probation, receiving stolen property, and grand theft auto. No sex crimes.

Butler got a call from the 3rd District. The word at the hospital was that Diaz came close to death twice but was resuscitated both times. He was expected to survive.

At 7:30, Butler and Detective Andy Williams drove to Judge Timothy McGinty's house in West Park. The judge read the search warrant and signed it.

Butler and Williams drove to Diaz's place. They met Greg King from the Internet Crimes Against Children Task Force and went inside.

The house was neat and sparsely furnished. It seemed Diaz lived there alone. Butler went upstairs and found Diaz's bedroom. There was a Dell computer and a video editing machine. Diaz had a video camera and lights set up for making home movies. Butler said he couldn't help wondering if that was planned for the girls. There was porn on Diaz's hard drive, but nothing indicating there had been other contact with minors.

Then Butler saw it. Right next to the computer. The red rubber devil mask from the Web pages was there in plain sight.

Butler was relieved. Diaz was "Joey."

1:30 A.M. – HOME ALONE

Butler sat on the couch in his one-bedroom apartment on Lake Shore Boulevard—a pile of shoes by the door, a cardboard box of neckties on the table with a month's worth of newspapers. The television was off.

He looked at the picture of his kids on the wall as he smoked his last cigarette of the day. His 13-year-old boy, his 11-year-old daughter. They would rent some movies this weekend. His ex-wife was good about visitation.

Butler stayed up a little longer thinking about the day. There was all that paperwork waiting for him back at the office.

Police work was usually as messy as his apartment. But not today. They had Diaz off the street. Got him in less than 24 hours. That had never happened to Butler before. They still needed to prosecute the man behind the mask. There would be a lot more reports to file before this one would be over. But first, maybe some . . . sleep.

•   •   •

EPILOGUE

Detective Bruce Garner was assigned to a non stress-related position for 2½ months and during that time was prohibited from working his second job. He is now back at work. He has not been cleared in the Diaz shooting.

On Nov. 7, Edwin Diaz, 35, was arraigned in Cuyahoga County Common Pleas Court. He was released on $50,000 bond. Police also learned that he did work towing cars.

On June 1, Diaz pleaded guilty to three counts of rape, one count of felonious assault on a police officer and one count of failure to comply. He agreed to serve 10 years in prison and to be labeled a sexual predator.

Formal sentencing is scheduled for Aug. 11.

The three girls remain in therapy but "are getting on with their lives," one of their parents said.

ABOUT THIS STORY

To put together this story, *Plain Dealer* reporter Michael Heaton used various police documents and interviewed Detective Jim Butler, Cmdr. Andy Gonzalez, Lt. Michael Baumiller, Capt. Luis Cumba, Sgt. Terrence Shoulders, Detective Bruce Garner, Detective Ronald James Jr., Detective Scott Zenkewicz and Detective Chris Bush of the Cleveland Police Department.

Also interviewed were a bartender and several patrons from the Victory Tavern. The owner of Tank the Rottweiler and the parents of one of the victims, all of whom requested anonymity.

Requests to interview Edwin Diaz and his attorney Gerald Smith were declined as was a request to interview Assistant Cuyahoga County Prosecutor Michael Horn.

July 11, 2004

FUGITIVE TRACKERS

*Tracking down elusive suspects on the run
is the mission of this relentless task force*

LAW & ORDER

Retiree Lindsay Smith was in his easy chair chatting with a neighbor when he was slammed in the face from behind with a pistol. His nose and eye socket shattered.

Blood soaked his shirt, pants, the chair and carpet. His assailant, a blue bandana over his face, pulled the 78-year-old to the floor. He kicked him repeatedly and demanded money.

Out behind the house on West 130th Street in Cleveland, two other attackers beat Smith's son, Dale, 47, who was checking on his elderly father while his mother was out of the country.

The thugs bound the younger Smith's hands behind his back, dragged him into the house and dumped him under a table. His father, curled up on the floor with broken ribs, was still fending off a hellish flurry of kicks and blows.

The neighbor, Zartrina Williams, screamed as the old man's attacker fished some bills from his wallet; the other two intruders ransacked the house.

When the thieves finally ran, Williams called the police. Lindsay Smith was robbed of $210 and change. Dale Smith lost $18, two credit cards and his keys. The father was in the hospital for a week. His son was released that day after treatment.

Zartrina Williams soon confessed to planning the Aug. 15 crime with her brother, Jason Williams, Alphonso Basemore and Orlando Jones. Her brother and Basemore were jailed within the week. Only Jones, Zartrina's boyfriend, the one with the most extensive felony record of the three, ran before police could find him.

Jones, 20, was charged with aggravated robbery, felonious assault, kidnapping and aggravated burglary. He was on the loose in Cleveland for three months when he came into the sights of FBI

Special Agent Phil Torsney and the Cuyahoga/Cleveland Fugitive/ Gang Task Force.

On most mornings, Torsney rises at 4 a.m. to run five miles. Chasing bad guys requires that he stay in shape. At 50, the 5-foot, 11-inch Torsney still weighs 150 pounds, the same as when he was played soccer for the University of Maine Black Bears.

Fifteen years of tracking suspected murderers and rapists and armed felons have made dressing routine. After his run, he puts on jeans and running shoes. A hoodie over a long-sleeve T-shirt. Over that, an olive-green, Kevlar bulletproof vest.

He holsters a .40-caliber Glock semiautomatic with 15 rounds in the clip. He snaps a Motorola two-way radio on to his belt. He fills the vest pockets with a flashlight, cell phone and notebook and pen for the names, addresses and license plates he scribbles down.

He clips handcuffs to his vest and another pair to his belt, in case it's a big day.

Before leaving the house, he grabs one of the half-dozen peanut butter-and-jelly sandwiches he makes each Sunday night. He says they always taste better when his wife makes them.

He drives a government-issue Ford Crown Victoria. In the trunk is the "Key to the City," a 35-pound battering ram.

Today's FBI is more likely to use spreadsheets and wiretaps than breaching tools to fight crime. Like the Key to the City, Torsney and the task force are throwbacks to a simpler form of law enforcement. They don't investigate crimes; they wait until the bad guys are identified and run them to ground.

It's not glamorous and it can be dangerous, but Torsney would not do anything else.

He's taught police school in Afghanistan for the FBI and, as a park ranger, drove airboats in the Everglades. But he loves the run-and-gun pace of the streets. "I never wanted to sit behind a desk," he said. "I'm not an administrative kind of guy. I don't like meetings. All our meetings take place over the hood of a car."

Since Sept. 11, 2001, street crime has dropped on the FBI's list of priorities. Terrorism, counterintelligence and computer crime now top the list. Meanwhile, violent crime is on the rise locally and across the country.

Officers from the Cuyahoga County Sheriff's Office, Cleveland police, the Ohio Adult Parole Authority and the Cuyahoga Metropolitan Housing Authority police make up the task force. Since its formation in 1991, the squad has made 2,798 arrests. The violent felonies break down to 333 for murder, 414 for armed robbery, 313 for rape, 54 for attempted murder. The rest are miscellaneous drug, theft, parole and escape offenses.

Torsney is the leader of an ever-changing team. Members serve at the discretion of their departments. It's a sought-after assignment that provides invaluable experience for new officers.

Sometimes, when fugitives learn the task force is hunting them, they turn themselves in or leave town. By late November, Orlando Jones had done neither.

THE CHASE IS ON

On Nov. 27, Jones learned that he was the *Plain Dealer* Fugitive of the Week—a designation made by Torsney and the task force. The same morning his picture ran in the paper, informants began calling the FBI with tips regarding his whereabouts.

At 7 a.m. the next day, Torsney huddled with task force members in a parking lot at East 93rd Street and St. Clair Avenue. He had an address for Jones and passed around his picture.

Torsney, Sheriff's Detective Mike Domonkos and first-year FBI agent Randy Garber knocked on the door. A woman wearing only a towel let them inside.

Torsney told the woman to feel free to get dressed. Several times. It didn't seem to bother her. Her preschool-age son was excited to meet the police. The woman sat on her bed and said Jones had been there but had left the day before. She kicked him out after seeing his picture in the paper but had no idea where he went.

Torsney was polite and deferential, which is his way. The younger guys on the team—and they are all younger—look to him to set the mood. When Torsney gets agitated, which is rarely, they know it's time to crank it up.

"Does he have a girlfriend?" Domonkos asked the woman.

"I have a girlfriend," said the little boy. Everyone laughed.

Torsney explained the seriousness of the crime. Said there was reward money available. If Jones wasn't guilty, he needed to come in and get it straightened out.

They left a business card and headed for another address. Half a mile away, Torsney pulled over. An anonymous caller to headquarters had a Collinwood address for Jones. Half a dozen officers regrouped at a convenience store parking lot. Torsney assigned positions, and the team moved out.

Two officers guarded the back of the two-story single-family house while four went up on the front porch with guns drawn. They knocked. A woman let them in. One officer thought he saw a figure run toward the back of the house as he entered.

The team outside in back shouted. Someone had opened the back door and closed it. Inside the house, some stairs led to the basement, while others led to a second floor. Jones could have gone either way. If it was Jones.

Torsney and Domonkos went down to the basement. Garber and Sheriff's Detective Eugene Sharpe started up the dark stairs.

Garber approached the first landing and popped his head around the corner. At the end of the unlit hall stood a figure wearing a black T-shirt and black pants. Garber swung back to Sharpe. "Someone's up there."

He couldn't tell if there was a weapon. Garber and Sharpe trained their guns on the top of the stairs.

"Come on down," Garber shouted. "The first thing I want to see come around that corner are your hands."

Several seconds ticked by. A pair of empty hands appeared from the shadows followed by the man in black.

"Face the wall and put your hands behind your back," Garber ordered.

Garber and Sharpe each grabbed an arm.

"Why'd you run up there?" Sharpe demanded.

"I was scared, man. I was scared," said Orlando Jones.

Garber, Sharpe and Torsney put Jones on the floor face down and handcuffed him. The man accused of beating Lindsay Smith was finally under arrest. The hunt was over.

A NEW DAY, A NEW HUNT

At 7 a.m. eight days later, Torsney gathered the troops in yet another empty parking lot, this time on East 105th Street. This morning, they were looking for a man who last August put a woman in the hospital. She needed 15 stitches after he hit her.

A half hour later, James Boles awoke in his bedroom on East 106th Street to see three members of the task force surrounding his bed. They arrested him for felonious assault. Boles complained as they brought him downstairs.

"Man, I could have cleared this up with one phone call," he said.

"Should have made that call," an officer said.

Orlando Jones is in jail awaiting a Wednesday, Jan. 17, pretrial hearing. Zartrina Williams pleaded guilty to planning the home invasion and was sentenced to six years in prison. Jason Williams pleaded guilty and awaits sentencing, and Alphonso Basemore awaits trial. Boles is free on bond and has a pretrial hearing Monday.

January 4, 2007

ART WORLD FIND YIELDS FORTUNE AND FORGERY

Lakewood native discovers treasure

While there are undoubtedly a million stories in the Naked City, Tom Warren's is a work of art.

His tale unfolded amid the money-drenched 1980s New York City art scene, where ego, greed and ambition collided daily. It involved the late, great art superstar of the decade, Jean Michel Basquiat, and a darkly eccentric street artist named Alfredo Martinez. Not to mention charges of forgery, missing money and an FBI sting.

But that's getting ahead of the story.

Tom Warren, a 28-year-old photographer from Northeast Ohio, joined the Big Apple's art scene in 1982. For him, it was bohemian heaven. A freelance photographer, he also was working as a carpenter and living the artist's life from a Soho loft. Warren's roommate, Anton Fier, was a drummer for the Lounge Lizards, the coolest band on the local underground scene.

Warren had access to all the best, hip parties in downtown Manhattan. For a young man from Lakewood with a degree in photojournalism from Kent State University and a genuine love of art, life couldn't get any better.

Then, outside a party one night, he stumbled upon some discarded works of an artworld superstar—and into a harsher segment of the art community.

On a warm evening in June, Warren left a wild gathering at the downtown loft of rising art star Jean Michel Basquiat (pronounced Bas-kee-ot). The 22-year-old former graffiti artist had emerged on the scene and was soon to be one of Andy Warhol's proteges. And very rich. Dealers and collectors were circling the young painter like crows around road kill.

Artist Julian Schnabel, journalist Rene Ricard, rock star David

Byrne and actor Vincent Gallo were among the celebrities partying with Basquiat that night. It was a celebration of Basquiat's part in a group show at the blue-chip Marlborough Gallery curated by Diego Cortez.

Warren had been to Basquiat's first one-man show some months earlier and was knocked out by the artist's powerful, neo-primitive style. He was Warren's favorite young talent.

Warren stood in front of the Crosby Street loft as the party raged on inside, he recently recalled, when he saw a bunch of drawings he recognized as Basquiat's work scattered on the sidewalk and amid a pile of garbage on the curb. It looked as if someone had gone through Basquiat's trash, examined the drawings and discarded them.

Warren couldn't believe his good fortune. He quickly scooped them up and took them home. There were more than two dozen drawings in all.

In the following weeks, Warren showed the treasure to some artist friends and even gave a couple of drawings away as gifts. Warren was hanging out at the Mudd Club, the Red Bar and Danceteria with up-and-coming artists, musicians and every kind of netherworld poseur and celeb. Word of his find made its way through the art world circuit and back to Basquiat.

A month later, Warren was having a drink with friends in a Times Square art hangout called Tin Pan Alley. Basquiat happened to be there shooting pool and recognized Warren. He told Warren he had heard the photographer was giving his work away. Basquiat was concerned that Warren, by giving his drawings to dealers or collectors, was reducing the value of the rest of his paintings.

Warren assured the artist that he had only given two pieces away and they were both in the hands of artists who were fans of Basquiat.

Basquiat nodded. "That's cool," he said. "I guess you found thousands of dollars."

Six years later, Jean Michel Basquiat was the hottest young artist on the international scene. His paintings routinely fetched seven figures. But fame and his own appetite for drugs consumed him. That same year, 1988, he was dead of a heroin overdose at 27.

Although New York's art scene has many fine, upstanding and reputable people, the industry is not regulated.

"The art market has always lent itself to making a fast buck—a kind of classy, class-conscious, socially climbing, visual three-card monte. Call it sleight of eye," said Phoebe Hoban, a New York-based journalist who is the author of *Basquiat: A Quick Killing in Art.*

"Particularly in the 1980s . . . art collecting and consumption reached a giddy high, creating a seller's market that could be readily manipulated by those with questionable scruples."

FATEFUL MEETING

In 1992, Warren met an artist and sometime curator named Alfredo Martinez at the studio of a painter where Martinez worked as an assistant. Martinez, who stood 6 feet 5 and weighed 300 pounds, was an eccentric character known for his work with guns. He once curated a show in which an installation featured artists behind a Plexiglas wall firing a machine gun at a target.

Martinez also had a questionable reputation. Another artist, Josh Harris, told *Art and Auction* magazine that Martinez was adept at copying artists' painting style. "They're damn good," Harris said of Martinez's imitations.

Others in the art world were less generous in their descriptions of Martinez. Artist and collector Simon Cerigo, who introduced Warren and Martinez, called the Brooklyn, N.Y., native a "self-involved nut."

Warren, now a photographer for Sotheby's Auction House, had no professional dealings with Martinez until two years ago, when Martinez asked him to exhibit some of his photographs in a show Martinez was curating. "He was very complimentary talking to me," Warren said of the experience. "He said that my photographs were so good that [renowned art dealer] Larry Gagosian should be courting me. . . . He kept saying he loves my work. But then as a kind of afterthought he asked if he could exhibit a couple of my Basquiats as well. I said sure."

The show went off without problems, and Martinez promptly returned Warren's Basquiats. That is why Warren had no misgivings last year when Martinez invited him to show some photographs at a group exhibition in a warehouse in the Williamsburg section of Brooklyn.

As before, Martinez asked Warren if he could borrow and show a couple more Basquiats, to which Warren agreed. This time, Martinez asked to see the authentication receipt for one of them. Warren had had several of the drawings approved by a Basquiat authentication committee, headed up by the artist's father, Gerard Basquiat.

Cerigo told Warren he would be crazy to lend his Basquiats or anything else to Martinez.

"But I said to myself then, this is the last time I'll do this," Warren remembered. Though he got his originals back, he was one time too late.

According to a press release issued by the FBI on June 13 of this year, after that second show, Martinez sold New York art dealer Leo Malca two Basquiats for $38,500. Martinez said he obtained them from an old girlfriend of the artist.

Buying two Basquiats for $38,500 is an incredible bargain. Last May, a Basquiat painting from 1982, *Prophet I*, sold for $5.5 million, the most ever for one of his works. The market for Basquiat's work has never been hotter.

Malca told authorities he became suspicious and began comparing the drawings he purchased with digital images of Warren's originals he obtained from another dealer. Once he determined that he had purchased forgeries, he confronted Martinez.

Around 9 p.m. last Feb. 16, Warren said, someone buzzed his Queens apartment. He looked at the monitor and saw Alfredo Martinez and two other people he didn't recognize. It was Malca and his assistant. Warren buzzed the three of them up.

According to Warren, Martinez came through the apartment door like a freight train, bellowing: "Tom, sit down! Tom, where's the money?"

The photographer said Martinez continued his harangue. "Tom, give Leo his money!"

The more he carried on, the more it became clear to Warren that this bit of bad theater was all for the benefit of Malca. Malca was sort of standing back, trying to get a read on Martinez's performance, Warren said. After an hour, Malca had seen enough. He and his assistant were out the door, leaving Martinez with one statement.

"I want my money," Malca said over his shoulder.

With Malca gone, Warren said, Martinez broke down crying. He went from hostility to humility in 10 seconds. Warren said Martinez admitted forging the drawings. He talked about being homeless and how life on the streets had driven him to criminal measures. He begged Warren to give him the original Basquiats. He said he was going to kill himself. Warren finally got him to leave early the next morning.

Warren said he called Malca a few days later to explain his unwitting role in what seemed to be a forgery scheme. He said Malca seemed convinced that he was in cahoots with Martinez and remained suspicious and aloof. Warren did nothing for several months and waited to see what would happen.

Martinez, on the other hand, apparently went on a Basquiat selling spree. Dealers in Manhattan got word in April that three more Basquiats had surfaced on the market. Once again, according to an FBI report, Martinez was brokering the deal. His story again was that he had obtained the drawings from an ex-girlfriend of Basquiat. One of the dealers called Malca, who told her not to trust Martinez, and the FBI began its investigation. It set up a sting in late May, and Martinez offered an undercover FBI agent posing as a socialite five Basquiats for $145,000.

The agency arrested Martinez June 11. Shortly thereafter, Warren, now 48, was questioned about his part in the alleged scheme. Warren and his lawyer explained what happened. According to agents investigating the case, Warren was completely cleared.

Martinez is still in jail awaiting a Nov. 18 court date. According to his attorney Ronald Garnett, he will plead not guilty.

Malca's $38,500 has not been recovered. Tom Warren is having the balance of his collection of drawings authenticated by the Basquiat estate.

October 14, 2002

WHEEL OF MISFORTUNE

The secret, hard life of a Gypsy

Legend has it that Gypsies were blessed by God when one of them stole the nail that was intended for Christ's heart during the crucifixion. As a reward, they and their descendants were forever exempt from the commandment "Thou shalt not steal."

Zelda* tells another story. In 1966, at age 15, she left Ohio to escape an unhappy family situation and moved to Boston with her 20-year-old Gypsy boyfriend. She spent the next 20 years with his family, telling fortunes, defrauding her customers out of tens of thousands of dollars, bearing six children and moving around the country at least 15 times. Two of her daughters were sold into Gypsy marriages, and both have recently left that life.

When Zelda left California and her Gypsy past in 1986, she returned to Ohio, remarried, had a child, started her own business and became a Christian. Shortly after her return, she vowed that if she could ever get her daughters out of the Gypsy life, she would do whatever she could to expose the dishonesty of Gypsy fortunetelling.

"The most money I ever made in one session was $10,000," she says. "I had a woman client that I had been advising for a long time. She told me there was a man who wanted to marry her. She wasn't sure if she loved him, or if he was the one for her. She told me he had money. I found out his phone number and got in contact with him. I knew she would do anything I told her. So I went to him and told him I could, through the spirits, get her to marry him. We met in a hotel room and he brought the money. Then I just went back to her and told her she had to marry this man if she was ever to be happy."

The ability to gain someone's trust as a fortuneteller is not a talent most people are born with. When Zelda first joined her husband in Boston, his family had reservations about her because she was gadje, or not of Gypsy blood. But they felt she was young enough to learn and dark-complected enough to look the part.

Zelda fought the pressure to tell fortunes at first, but after a year she was making money for the family as a reader and adviser. Her education was sitting and watching her mother-in-law tell fortunes. "They told me I would have an exciting life of complete freedom from hard or dirty work. And that I would make lots and lots of money. I was taught not to deal or associate with anyone outside of the Gypsy world. They taught me to speak their language, to dress like them, to follow their customs. They were Serbian Gypsies, and they considered themselves of the highest class because they weren't involved in pickpocketing or break-ins."

In 20 years of fortunetelling, Zelda was arrested once, during her first year with her new in-laws. "It was for a $10 reading in Lansing, Mich. The police told me they were really after my mother-in-law. I got off with a fine and suspended sentence. I was too scared to tell fortunes for a while after that. But before long I was back at it again."

Zelda's story is about one of the oldest con games known to man. It's about a life of crime and a secret society shrouded in mystery and history. Rom, as Gypsies call themselves, left Northern India 1,000 years ago. Around the 14th century, they migrated to Europe where they were driven from one country to the next because it was believed they were liars, sorcerers, thieves and whores. They were persecuted during the Spanish Inquisition, taken into slavery in Eastern Europe, and, during World War II, a million were put to death in Nazi concentration camps. Even today they are one of the main victims of harassment and oppression by the Neo-Nazi movement in East Germany.

There are more than a million Gypsies in the United States, and while they remain one of the nation's most insular ethnic groups, new generations of men are beginning to assimilate, tearing at the once tight-knit fabric of this community. (It is important to note that not all Gypsies live the life of criminals. Zelda distinguishes between the Rom Gypsies and Americanized Gypsies. "Americanized Gypsies have given up that way of life," she says. "They have jobs, pay taxes and send their kids to school. They are hard-working, good American citizens. They have chosen to live in what Rom Gypsies call 'the world.'

Zelda's story illustrates the similarities between Rom Gypsy and mafia life. Both are romanticized and vilified by Hollywood and the public. Both have histories that involve crime, blood oaths and codes of honor. But the reality of both sects has been shredded by the same thing: greed.

"Gypsies taught me to look at other people, gadje, as nothing more than money," says Zelda. "They have their own laws, their own court. The only way they will use the American court is if they can take advantage of it."

One example she cites is that of a fortuneteller moving in on another's territory. The family that was there first won't hesitate to turn the newcomer into the police, she says. And contrary to the book by Peter Maas, later made into a movie, there is no "King of the Gypsies."

"Every Gypsy man is the king of his own family," Zelda says. "The women are treated like slaves. Gypsy girls are given no education beyond reading and writing. Around age 15 they are sold in arranged marriages for anywhere from $1,500 to $5,000. Then they belong to the in-laws. If there's a divorce, you get your money back. Children are raised being taught to marry for money—not love. A daughter-in-law, if she's a good fortuneteller, can make a lot of money."

Gypsy life is full of unusual rites and customs. The concept of marime, or something that is unclean or defiled, holds great sway over everything Gypsies do—from the clothes they wear to the behavior of women and the preparation of food.

A woman's skirt is unclean and must never be touched by a man. They must be washed separately from other clothes. A woman must never pass in front of a Gypsy face to face unless she has a baby in her arms. A woman cannot step over a man's clothing, or an electrical wire. She must pick it up and pass under it to avoid being polluted.

Utensils used for preparing food cannot be washed or kept with items that touch the body. The body is separated into three sections. From the waist down is considered marime, from the waist to the shoulders is neutral and the head is sacred. Even the house is divided into clean and unclean areas. The front of the house is for gadje and is often where fortunes are told. A woman may not go into a bathroom if it is within the sight of a Gyspy man.

There are many ways of fortunetelling: tea leaf reading, palmistry, handwriting analysis, tarot cards, astrology and character readings. Gypsy women who make a lot of money are called "gifted agents." But the real gift, Zelda says, is finding desperate and gullible people. A Gypsy fortuneteller uses manipulation and intimidation to separate these people from the money in their bank accounts.

The clients, she says, come from all walks of life; from the very educated to the ignorant. More often than not, people come to fortunetellers with problems in romance and marriage. At first the fortuneteller is feeling the client out, looking for believers with money. A person who is a smart aleck or is uncooperative will be given a quick, superficial reading and sent on his or her way. Someone who shows an emotional weakness will be developed slowly.

"For example," says Zelda, "a woman comes in and says her husband is seeing another woman and she's obviously very troubled. You begin by easing her pain by saying that the husband really does love her, but this other woman has put a spell on him. You tell them what they want to hear, and imply that you—through God—can fix it. They must prove their faith in God.

"You don't charge the woman the first time. You tell her to come back again, and this time bring a pound of coffee and a pound of sugar. You say something about the bitter and sweetness of love and how this is an offering to God. All Gypsies do all day is drink coffee, and this is one way they get it free. Then the next time you tell the woman that you need special things to do the work to change her situation. It might be beeswax candles or incense. Then you charge her $50 or $100 for them. You might even give that back to her to gain her trust.

"The next time she returns you've told her to bring an egg or a tomato that she put under her pillow the night before. You tell her to bring it in a white handkerchief that has never been used. You put it on the table, light the candles and begin doing your prayers or whatever. Then you smash the egg or tomato. But what you've done is slip some Spanish moss, which enlarges when dampened, or a leech, or a big moth, or some ugly-looking chicken bone in the handkerchief. When you open it up, it looks horrible and you say that is the evil that has been causing the person problems; in order to get rid of it, you say you have to take $200 to the church, or to the graveyard to bury it. If they hesitate about the money, you can say, 'Does that money mean more to you than your husband? Than your soul? Than me? You've brought this evil into my house, into my presence?'

"Once they give the money, you keep asking, 'Are you giving this money freely to God? You're not going to have bad feelings about it later? Do you believe God can solve your problems?' You want to make sure they're not going to have a change of heart and run to the police later. Once that's cleared up and you have that money, you say, 'We've gotten rid of the evil in you, now we can start working on your husband.'

According to Zelda, the process can take up to a month. But the fortuneteller is steadily gaining the person's trust and doggedly working to determine how much money she has in the bank. The fortuneteller will say she's thinking of three numbers—$3,000, $10,000 and $15,000—and will ask the client which figure is closest to her savings. Then she knows what she's working with.

Another ploy used is the "switch." The frightened client will be told to bring $1,000 in a specified currency—twenties, fifties or hundreds. Again, it must be wrapped in the white handkerchief and worn on the person's body the night before. All details must be strictly adhered to for "the work" to be completed. Since the fortuneteller knows exactly how high the stack of currency will be, she'll have her own bundle made of plain paper. The client brings the money, and during the prayers and candles, the switch will be made. The client believes the bundle before her is the money she brought. The fortuneteller will then put it in a tall receptacle, spray lighter fluid on it and ignite the stack of plain paper, telling the client the money is being burned as an offering to God.

Again the client will be asked if she feels good about her offering to God. Any bad feelings, she'll be warned, could ruin "the work." The fortuneteller is always monitoring the client's mood and emotions, looking for ambivalence.

There are many gimmicks—and even more ways to get the money. A dark-haired client will be told to bring hair from a brush. The fortuneteller will rub it with the "black snakes" that kids light with matches on July 4. The client's sample of hair is ignited and she sees black snakes crawling from the ashes. The evil must be removed.

Clients who aren't wealthy or who don't have large bank accounts will be told that the fortuneteller, because she likes the client, will put up the money needed for "the work," and that the client can pay it back in weekly installments. Most clients are too scared to miss a payment.

Since becoming a Christian, Zelda has experienced a lot of pain and anguish about her past. She regrets having exposed her children to that way of life, especially the two daughters who have recently left Gypsy marriages.

"I see the pain that they're going through to readjust. Gypsy life is a crazy cult. I left my husband five times during the 20 years I was in Gypsy life. But I kept going back. He was torn himself between the Gypsy life and American life. He got involved with drugs and seeing American women on the side. I eventually had this identity crisis and told him I had to leave the life, and he gave me his blessing. Two months later, he and the woman he was seeing fell off a 50-foot bridge in Los Angeles and died. Once I left, it took me a year to get rid of the feeling of oppression. And I see that in my two oldest girls now. I know what they're going through. It's hard."

Sitting in her shop with two of her daughters, Zelda acts out how she would manipulate and intimidate a client. She's convincing in the role and has to stop herself. "I get goose bumps from doing that," she says.

Dredging all this up has given her bad dreams, she says, and she prays for God's protection. She recalls one client who wanted to accompany her to the graveyard to bury $350. She tried to discourage him by saying that she'd be seeing spirits and dead people. Still, he insisted. She said she'd have to be naked. He said he'd go naked. Finally she said he'd have to learn to speak six languages to say the prayers. He said he'd learn. She asked him why he wanted to come. "If my wife finds out I spent this money, I have to find out where to dig it back up," he said. "I gave him back his money and told him I'd put it up myself," says Zelda. "That only made him trust me more."

Her oldest daughter, Maria (not her real name), now in her early 20s, was much more successful at fortunetelling than her mother. She has made as much as $80,000 in one session. When asked what she might say to a prospective client, she answers, "I would say, 'There is someone in your past. Someone you once cared for very much and who you still think about now.' That's true of almost anyone," she adds. "Most people tell you more about themselves than you end up telling them. It can get to be an addiction with people."

When asked if there isn't a certain thrill involved in swindling people out of large amounts of money, all three women shake their heads. "It's not a thrill, there's always fear," says Zelda. "I know a woman doing time for taking $130,000 from a girl who shared a bank account with her father.

"You're always afraid it's going to come back on you and you'll get caught," says Maria. "Most people are too embarrassed to tell anyone, but you never know."

"When I first started to tell this story," says Zelda, "I wanted to warn people about fortunetellers. But I also hoped that Gypsies would read this and realize that this is not the way to live life. They use the name of God and Jesus, but they don't believe Jesus was the son of God. They like Jesus because they think he was the greatest con artist of all time."

From time to time, the three lapse into Romany, the Gypsy tongue. When asked where it comes from, Maria says, "It's a combination of a bunch of other languages. It's not like any other." And then pausing, as if this just occurred to her, she says, "Even their language is stolen."

*Not her real name. "Americanized Gypsies have given up that way of life. They have jobs, pay taxes and send their kids to school. They are hard-working, good American citizens."

November 8, 1992

CROSSING THE LINE

Cocaine brought down lawyer James Columbro.
Now he wants a second chance.

James Columbro sat in his Justice Center office, obsessed with a single thought. It was the spring of 1989, and the assistant Cuyahoga County prosecutor had to write three briefs and prepare for a murder trial. He was teaching a course in business law at Cuyahoga Community College, doing pro bono work for a battered women's shelter and nurturing a small private practice.

But he wasn't worried about his workload. When it came to work, he had always been an animal: the more the better. And the courtroom? Colleagues boasted that next to Columbro's name in the dictionary it read: "Excellent trial lawyer." It wasn't money. He made $55,000 that year.

Columbro was craving cocaine, an addiction he had been feeding for four years. But today, like so many days before, he had promised himself he would quit.

Instead, he got up, locked the door of his office, poured a foot-long line of uncut, Peruvian blue-flake cocaine across his desk, rolled up a dollar bill and snorted half of the cocaine into his right nostril. The drug did what it was supposed to do. And then some. His heart began pounding like a jackhammer. Sweat poured down his face, and the top of his head felt like it was about to explode. His body was internally combusting.

He was scared, very scared. He started saying "911 prayers": "Oh God. Sweet Jesus. Please don't let me die. I swear I'll never do this shit again. Please let me live." He gripped the desk with knuckles now alabaster from the effort.

And the rush passed. He survived the chemical tsunami. He put his head on his arms and gulped air as the drug permeated his body. It was then he noticed the six inches of cocaine still on the desk. He tightened up the dollar bill and finished the rest of it without a thought to his promise.

That's when Columbro, 37, began to suspect he had a problem.

But drugs were only half his problem. Columbro didn't even flinch over the source of his drugs, the Scientific Investigation Unit of the Cleveland Police Department. SIU held all drugs confiscated by the narcotic units. And Columbro had been stealing cocaine from the evidence locker for four years.

He had a "foolproof system." He called the unit and requested the evidence on a particular case that involved drugs. Once the drugs were delivered in their Ziploc bags, he snorted what he found and replaced the cocaine with baking soda.

The SIU officers had no reason to suspect Columbro. After all, he had helped draft the Law Enforcement Trust Fund that allowed money confiscated from crime scenes to be used for law-enforcement needs. Columbro was one of the good guys.

What they didn't know was that Columbro had crossed the line. He had the equivalent of a $1,000-a-day drug habit, once snorting 500 grams of cocaine in two months.

After four years of abuse, he had lost 30 pounds and looked emaciated. He couldn't sleep when he wanted and couldn't wake up when he tried. He stayed up for four straight days, then slept all weekend with the help of a bottle of scotch. He couldn't stand or sit still for more than a few minutes. He began to lose his memory and concentration. He was isolated from his colleagues, his wife, Linda, and their two children, Michael, 7, and Jackie, 3. His marriage was near collapse.

Then, in the summer of 1989, the Cleveland Police Department tightened its procedures relating to confiscated drugs. Instead of using Ziploc bags, the drugs were stored in heat-sealed plastic bags.

The next time Columbro called for evidence from SIU, he saw the new bags. He didn't care. He ripped open a bag containing crack cocaine and began crushing the rock with his fingers. He snorted the dust, but it had little impact. Crack is meant to be smoked.

He sent the bag—torn and with the cocaine missing—back to the evidence room. This time he made no effort to replace the drug with baking soda. He was too far gone to care.

Two days later, Columbro answered the phone call from County Prosecutor John T. Corrigan's secretary requesting his presence. Once in Corrigan's office, he was confronted with the overwhelming evidence of his theft and drug abuse by Corrigan and two staff members.

Columbro barely denied the accusation. He eventually confessed, and agreed to waive his rights and plead guilty to 36 counts of drug abuse and theft in office. In an hour, Columbro's career was over.

Five years later, he wants it back. Today, Columbro is clean. He hasn't had a drink or touched drugs since that day when he lost it all. He was banned from holding public office and his license to practice law was indefinitely suspended after he was released from the Hocking Correctional Institution in southern Ohio. He served 11 months of an 18-month term.

This month, he will petition the Board of Commissioners on Grievances and Discipline of the Supreme Court of Ohio for his license back. The board is under no time requirement to answer his request, although he can re-apply every two years.

Last year, the disciplinary council received 3,449 complaints. Of those, 16 percent to 20 percent were drug- and alcohol-related.

"Drugs and alcohol are a significant mitigating factor. If—and it's a big if—the attorney is successfully pursuing recovery," says Geoffrey Stern, head of the disciplinary council of the Supreme Court of Ohio, the license is likely to be granted.

Columbro is hopeful.

"As a former prosecuting attorney, I know this better than any-one: A man has to be held responsible for his actions," says Colum-bro. "You punish behavior. It's not an indictment of your birthright. It doesn't mean you shouldn't live. Enough is enough. The state of Ohio has gotten its pound of flesh, its retribution. The sentence was levied out. The sentence was completed."

But Columbro's application is controversial, legal professionals say, not only because of his addiction but because he stole cocaine while in office.

"I'm glad to hear that Jim is five years sober and doing well," says Edward Kovacic, who was Cleveland's police chief at the time of Columbro's guilty plea. "I congratulate him, I really do. But all is not forgiven. I believe there has to be permanent, lasting con-sequences for people who break the law. Especially those who are sworn to uphold it. There has to be a higher standard. What's to stop everyone from going out and trying cocaine if they feel there's a second chance for them?"

Not surprisingly, Columbro disagrees.

"Now why can't I be permitted to go back to work? Athletes go back to sports, businessmen go back to business. Actors go back to movies. Some people will say I deserve what I got. Well, it's been gotten. Those in my profession who say I don't deserve my ticket back have a very unenlightened view of crime and punishment."

Bill Haase is the director and administrator of the Ohio Lawyer's Assistance Program, which helps lawyers with drug and alcohol problems. The group assisted Columbro during his hearing in which his license was suspended. And it is helping him in his appeal.

"We're tough. If a lawyer doesn't show genuine remorse and appreciation, if he doesn't follow the requirements in terms of sincerity about his sobriety, we throw them out," says Haase.

After Columbro was released from prison in 1991, he returned to his wife and children. The family was desperate for money, so Columbro sold magazine subscriptions over the phone. He also did snow plowing and landscaping.

"Thirty-six felonies puts a hell of a crimp in your resume," Columbro says.

He also began a drug-monitoring program, including urine screening and visits to a psychologist. He attended a 12-step program. Then, in May 1993, he began volunteering with Haase at the Ohio Lawyer's Assistance Program.

"Jim has been the most effective asset we have as a speaker on the issue of substance abuse," says Haase. "He tells his own story and brings the charisma he had in the courtroom to fellow attorneys who need to hear it. He has been effective in interventions. He is a good example of what a person who has been felled by this disease can do to turn his life around."

Columbro also volunteered at Cleveland Alcoholism Services, a treatment center for alcoholics, and at Freedom House, a nonprofit rehabilitation center for substance abusers located on Cleveland's near West Side. He applied for and won federal assistance ($3,600 in tuition), to pay for the Project for Addiction Counselor Training (PACT) to become a chemical dependency counselor.

"Jim was willing to learn and I figured he needed a chance," says Jack Mulhall, Freedom House's founder and director of rehabilitation who gave Columbro a job as a counselor at $250 a week. Freedom House treats men and women recently released from prison with substance-abuse problems, as well as court-ordered evaluations and other cases.

"If these kids don't trust you, you don't stand a chance of helping them. And we get two or three new ones coming in every day.

Jim's a bright guy and he's been there, on both sides of the line. He's streetwise and gets respect. Respect is everything here. I consider Jim and Phyllis Eisele-Curran, who trained Jim, the two best counselors in town."

Columbro may be an effective counselor, but he wants to prove that he is trustworthy enough to practice law again.

"Being a lawyer is what I am, how I think, and the biggest part of me," explains Columbro. "I don't have any idea what area I would practice in, although criminal defense, assisting the chemically dependent, seems most likely. I could also be helpful as a lawyer to facilities which work with alcoholics and the chemically dependent."

One thing is certain. If Columbro wins back the right to practice law, he will not return to the prosecutor's office. And, lawyers say, it is unlikely he would be offered a job with a large law firm.

"For now, I'm leaving that up to God to decide," says Columbro.

"There was nothing in my past that would indicate that I was an alcoholic or would grow up to be a drug addict," says Columbro, now 43, in the kitchen of his Westlake home. Columbro grew up in Shaker Heights, the product of a loving family.

"Because I didn't have a problem. Even though I got caught drinking homemade wine on the bus in grade school at St. Dominic's, I didn't have a problem. Or in high school at Cathedral Latin, when I would leave at lunch to go to Lum's and drink. I was class president and played varsity football. So you know I didn't have a problem. Or going to frat parties at Villanova [University] and drinking until I got physically ill. See, still no problem. Blacking out on my first weekend of leave during basic training for the Marine Reserve in Quantico. I attended study groups at bars in law school where we'd drink pitchers of beer. I not only didn't have a problem, I knew everything," he says in the cadence of a recovering addict who has told his story many times.

But what Columbro didn't know, his fellow recovering addicts later told him, was that he suffered from "terminal uniqueness."

"That feeling that there's no one in the world quite like you," explains Columbro. "Well, let me tell you: This is an equal opportunity disease."

Columbro graduated from the Delaware Law School in Pennsylvania in 1977 and became a Cuyahoga County prosecutor one year later. He began in Juvenile Court, working on child custody cases, then was rotated to the Justice Center courtrooms, where he prosecuted every indictable felony, appearing before all 33 Common Pleas judges.

By 1982, he was in charge of a courtroom, supervising other prosecutors. That year he married Linda, who worked at Juvenile Court, routing cases to attorneys. Four years later, at age 34, he ran for Juvenile Court judge against incumbent Betty Willis Ruben and lost by some 20,000 votes. After the election, he was assigned to the major trial division, which handles homicide, rape and all drug violations.

After he failed to win a judgeship, Columbro applied at several Cleveland law firms and was turned down by all of them. His frustration over his career mounted. He began to drink heavily. The V.O. Manhattan straight up with a twist was his poison. Two or three at lunch, and then after work one at John Q's, one at the Harbor Inn, one at the Flat Iron and then maybe a pitcher of beer at Mitchell's Tavern near his Westlake house before going home.

"I had typical alcoholic thinking," he says. "Everything was wrong. None of it was my fault. I had a handle on the prosecutor's job. I was comfortable in terms of doing the work. I thought I had arrived but was still unhappy. That feeling of, 'This is it?' I was drinking to reward myself, drinking when things were bad. It was a constant pattern. And the pattern took off on me.'

It was only after he burned a hole in his stomach with the alcohol that he turned to drugs.

"Even during the worst times I never gave up hope," says Linda Columbro, Jim's wife of 13 years. "Everyone told me to leave him. He told me to leave him, that I was crazy not to. But you don't leave somebody with a disease. You don't throw people in the trash. Ultimately, I didn't want my kids to be without a father, so I ruled it out."

"How my family suffered," Columbro says ruefully today. "There is no difference between the man who abandons his family and the addict who lives in the home. Because the addict really isn't there. He is not there emotionally or spiritually."

In August 1988, Linda gathered her family around Columbro and confronted him about his behavior. Columbro denied any drinking or substance-abuse problems and promised to behave more sanely. Nothing changed.

A year later, Linda found a packet of cocaine in his suit pocket. Again, she assembled the family and tried to confront Columbro about his abuse. Again, he lied his way out of the confrontation with promises.

But he could barely hold his act together at work. A narcotics officer recalls Columbro dictating a search warrant while standing on his desk.

"I thought he was having a nervous breakdown," the officer recalls.

These days, Columbro chats with neighbors, gardens, attends karate lessons with his son, and begins his day at 6 a.m., making lunches for his children. The healing process at home took a long time. He had to earn back the trust of his wife and family. His son had to repeat second grade and required counseling while Columbro was in prison.

"The guilt and shame is debilitating," says Columbro. "Addicts and alcoholics don't realize the harm we do our loved ones and depths to which they are affected. There is no way I'll ever be able to make amends to my kids, except to be there for them from now until the time they're ready to leave me."

Linda, who now works full time for a small industrial-manufacturing company, is "100 percent confident" Columbro will not relapse. He still continues a documented urine-screening program twice a month.

"After being in prison, after losing almost everything, after seeing what's been taken away, he would never . . ." says Linda.

Columbro concedes he might not practice law again.

"I thought I could get away with it. I practiced drug use. I became an addict. Being an addict has consequences. And when you are in a position of public trust, those consequences are severe," says Columbro.

He recalls that when he was sentenced to 18 months in prison by Judge Patricia Gaughan, a woman he had worked with in the prosecutor's office, he told the court, "I'm coming back a better man, a better husband, a better father, a better lawyer."

"Three out of four ain't bad," he says now.

September 17, 1995

PASSPORT REQUIRED

CHILDREN OF HOPE

*A Catholic priest from Cleveland fights to
save children in El Salvador's civil war*

Finally the villagers decided they had to flee. For weeks the fighting between the guerrillas and government soldiers had been drawing closer to their homes in El Salvador's northern Chalatenango Province. It was too dangerous to work any longer in the surrounding coffee and sugar plantations. They packed up their few possessions and headed for the Sumpul River 30 miles away, intending to cross into neighboring Honduras and safety

Among them was a dark-haired, dark-eyed boy of 12 named José Careoza. José had never known his father. He clung closely to his mother during the trek and again when the group paused on the bank of the Sumpul. On the other shore they would be safe. The group waded into the river. Suddenly the foliage of the far bank erupted in small-arms fire. Honduran soldiers had been waiting in ambush. The villagers panicked. Bodies fell. José's mother was shot and slipped below the surface. The boy scrambled to shore. The survivors fled the way they'd come. The Salvadoran Army held them for a while, then church workers trucked them to the capital, San Salvador, where they were taken to a squalid refugee camp. A few days later a tall, chain-smoking gringo ambled into the camp. He was Ken Myers, a Catholic priest from Cleveland who had been working in the country for six years. As he chatted with a group of women, they told him about the boy whose mother had been killed on the border. Myers asked José whether he wanted to live in his parish in Zaragoza. The boy said yes. There would be hundreds to follow him, but on that day in 1980 Jose became the first member of the Communidad Oscar A. Romero (COAR) ...

"Have you brought a bottle of booze and the *New York Times*?" Father Myers asks. The visitor has not. Myers points into the distance toward the airport and says with mock sternness, "Go back!" But three years after he took in José, it's hard to imagine Ken Myers, 42, turning anyone away. The priest, a cigarette dangling from his lips, is now standing in the same refugee camp where he found José. He visits the camp and others like it weekly, though it's less a camp than a shantytown of surpassing misery.

Some 500 refugees from the countryside live here in the teeming downtown of San Salvador in tin shacks slapped together, jammed against each other around the perimeter of what once was a soccer field. There is no sanitation, and the smell of human feces is overpowering. Small children, some of them naked and all of them filthy, scamper around, oblivious to their surroundings. Old men and women sit dejectedly in front of their shacks, staring across the ruined field. The whole compound crouches in the shadow of an abandoned seminary, whose bullet-pocked walls speak of the violence that brought the people to the camp.

Myers, towering over the gaggle of refugees who follow him everywhere, learns there are no orphans for him today. After a few more cigarettes and conversation with the kids in Spanish, he climbs into his yellow Toyota pickup truck, fumbling on the dashboard for his cigarette lighter while backing slowly into the heavy traffic on the road to Zaragoza. When Myers first arrived in the country, his soft-spoken manner and air of unhurried calm earned him the nickname Padre Lento—Father Slow—and it fits.

"Most of these people are from up north where the fighting is going on," he says. "Their homes have been burned. They've lost their husbands and their land. Without papers, if they walk the streets, they'll be put in jail. The church provides food. I find a lot of my kids in camps like that."

He accelerates into the flow of jammed buses and empty cabs for the 30-minute drive to the orphanage. The city falls quickly behind, replaced by lush jungle and an occasional cornfield hacked into the side of a mountain. Some 10 minutes into the trip he slows for a crowd gathered in the roadway. The people are staring dumbly at a young girl of 7 or 8 years lying on her side at the edge of the road. Blood has run from her mouth and dried. "She's dead," Myers says flatly. "Hit by a car. I stopped for her on the way up to the camp, but is was too late." Then he adds, "Ambulance service around here is not the greatest."

Indeed, the death of one more child goes unnoticed in a country now in its fourth year of savage civil war. Since October 1979 an estimated 36,000 Salvadoran civilians have been killed in the fighting between leftist guerrillas and the shaky, U.S.-backed government. About the time the girl in the road had died, in fact, the leftists were claiming that more than 100 of their noncombatant sympathizers, including women and children, had been massacred by government troops in three small towns in northern El Salvador. A long list of such atrocities has marked the fighting, which intensified after the murder of the man for whom Myers' orphanage is named. Oscar A. Romero was the Catholic Archbishop of El Salvador, an outspoken man who sympathized with the nation's desperate poor. As he raised the chalice of Communion wine during a memorial Mass in March 1980, Romero was shot to death by a gunman in a small chapel in San Salvador.

"After that, things got pretty tense in terms of people traveling and going out at night," says Myers. "I had a meeting with the Sisters and we decided our work was changing. In the mid-1970s we tried to recruit and instruct lay people to know the Bible and religious doctrine," Myers continues. "They were to pick up the slack where we didn't have enough clergy to go around."

At that time Myers was working out of a rectory in Zaragoza that was about the size of a two-car garage. He had just gotten permission from the church to build a three-room school, which he intended to use for night adult-education classes. But, Myers says, "The refugee centers were growing. I came up with the idea of using the school to house kids, since a lot of them weren't being cared for." As the number of orphans grew, COAR needed more space. In 1982 Myers bought 15 acres from a Belgian couple who belonged to his parish. On the land, a 10-minute walk into the hills outside Zaragoza, he started building.

As Myers' pickup truck bumps into the driveway leading to the orphanage, he stubs out another Delta Suave filter cigarette. The lane is lines with coffee plants and plantain trees. To one side is a long, low chicken coop housing 500 hens. The chickens provide an egg a day for each of COAR's 180 children, and the rest are sold. At the end of the driveway, nestled between steep hills, is the community clinic, a wooden building with a large cement porch. On one hill perches the Casa Grande, an old mansion that now contains a small store, the community's kitchen and the living quarters of the three nuns who help Myers run the orphanage. On the other hill behind the clinic rise the 15 cement buildings where the kids bunk, up to 20 in each house, according to age and gender. Siblings are kept together. Each house has a supervisor—an older child or a widow. There is no insulation or carpeting on the cement floors— just rows of bunk beds, a large communal table for meals and the kids' nightly homework, and a bathroom. The electricity works most of the time, and there is running water. Fourteen of the spartan buildings are occupied now, while another serves as an office.

Just beyond the houses a larger building is going up: Myers wants to use it as a high school. Nearby, a former chicken coop has been turned into a wood-working shop where the boys are taught carpentry.

Under the tropical sun, Myers parks the truck and walks into the clinic, the domain of Sister Stanislaus Mackey, 67, a wiry nun of boundless energy. Like her colleagues-Sister Audrey Walsh, 62, who is quiet and commanding, and Sister Mary Pat O'Driscoll, 34, who is gentle—she is a registered nurse. All come from Ireland, where they joined the Congregation of the Sisters of Charity of the Incarnate Word, and all have been at COAR since last January. Sister Mary Pat takes care of the babies and the house for toddlers under 4. Sister Audrey supervises the whole community.

Father Myers finds Sister Stan treating an ailing old man from Zaragoza. "When we first got here so many of the little children were malnourished, and they all had lice and worms," she says. "Once they begin to eat a balanced diet, their minds become sharper. They get a sense of importance when people stop commenting on their illnesses." The children bear little resemblance to those in the refugee camps. They are clean, healthy and full of life, but Sister Stan says it's a big job teaching them good habits. Most had never seen an eating utensil, much less a toothbrush, and must be repeatedly dissuaded from eating dirt.

Their mental health also gets care. "It's the saddest thing in the world to see someone so young whose nerves are shot," says Sister Stan. "Little Nelson had awful fear when he got here. He got very emotional whenever anyone would say anything about his parents' murder. But as time goes on he has begun to see that he's part of a community that loves him here at COAR. We can never replace his parents, but he begins to feel that the loss is at least bearable.

"What moves me most," Sister Stan continues, "is their longing for love. They miss their parents so much that they cling to you. The other thing that strikes me is their gentleness. I think when God took their parents, He gave them something very special."

At noon the kids run back to their houses for a meal. Myers explains that in the afternoon the older children will replace the younger ones at the school's desks. All the kids have chores. The older boys learn masonry on the construction projects and teach the younger ones. The girls work in the laundry and kitchen—no small task in a community that consumes 400 tortillas a day, not to mention beans, rice, cheese and milk. The daily schedule is structured but not rigid, and there's always time for soccer or guitar lessons given by Sister Mary Pat. "COAR is based on the theory that the kids are bound together by the service that they give to each other, not by the institution," says Myers.

The priest seems bound by both. Born in Norwalk, Ohio, the eldest of three children of a gas-company employee and a housewife, he entered Borromeo College in Cleveland in 1960. Four years later he went on to St. Mary Seminary, where he was drawn to missionary work.

After his ordination Myers was required to get experience in Cleveland parishes for five years before beginning his mission. "I can see the wisdom of that now," he says. "My biggest supporters have always been the people of St. Pat's in West Park and St. Mary's in Olmsted Falls." Myers finds the dollar-per-child-per-day budget of the orphanage in various ways. Some of the money comes from the Cleveland Diocese, some from the Catholic Relief Services, some from other churches and charities. A Catholic parish in Florida sends $100 each week. "You just have to have faith the support will come," says Myers. The money so far has helped some 1,000 children who have passed through COAR. Whenever possible, the staff places children with surviving relatives, keeping at COAR only those who have no one else.

That evening the community grows even more. Four young brothers, all wearing oversize baseball caps, show up at the door. Their parents had been arrested the night before. Myers introduces the boys to the community and assigns them a house. Shaken, the boys, ranging in age from 5 to 10, reappear, afraid to stay in the strange house. Myers reassures the youngsters, and Sister Audrey walks them back to their new home. "That's common," says Father Myers. "They're still not sure about who we are and what we're doing."

Father Myers and the nuns have no such doubts. As night falls the priest puts on his robes and says Mass for the community. Afterward the children head to their houses. Myers helps serve the evening meal to the kids whose house he supervises. Then he joins the sisters in the Casa Grande for dinner and the usual discussion of the day's events. Lupita isn't urinating, one says, could she be ill? Jaime didn't go to school today. What's for Sunday dinner; should we kill some chickens?

Later they discuss an American Jesuit who had just been found dead in the hills of Honduras. All of the nuns had volunteered for the hazardous work, and Sister Stan and Sister Audrey had previously seen dangers in Guatemala. "There," Sister Audrey says, "the government began by introducing one restriction after another. Pretty soon there's a curfew and certain places you can't go. You're not constantly thinking about your life being in danger. You do what you can."

Four of COAR's houses are named for the three American nuns and one lay worker who were raped, murdered and thrown in shallow graves in El Salvador nine months after Archbishop Romero's assassination. Members of El Salvador's National Guard have been accused of the crime. Father Myers knew and worked with two of the slain women, and all the COAR staffers know that they could be the targets of such madness as well.

Sister Stan, however, says that her fear has lessened since coming to El Salvador. "I feel that God is always with me," she says. "I feel that I should put my life at stake for something as important as the lives of these children. If they shoot my head off tomorrow, I don't mind. I feel I've done my best," she continues. "I love these children. We sow our destiny here. We don't walk this way again, and very few are walking it now. I'm sure all the Sisters feel privileged that the Lord has called us here."

After dinner Father Myers strolls onto the porch. He's working on the day's 10th cup of coffee and umpteenth Delta Suave. "The whole operation may seem haphazard," he says, looking over the village, "but the key is to adapt to changing situations. We're not just building houses. We're taking care of children. You can't lose sight of that." He glances at his watch. "We don't despair here," he says, rubbing his eyes. "I wouldn't even say we get discouraged. We just get very, very tired." Then he heads up the path to the simple house he shares with the children. And, if anyone should, he sleeps the sleep of the just.

December 5, 1983

PATH OF THE WARRIOR

*Barry Toll went from the circus to special forces
in Vietnam. There was another circus waiting
for him in the Nixon White House.*

1968. Barry Toll hunkers down on the jungle floor in the tri-
border area where Laos, Cambodia and Vietnam meet at the Ho
Chi Minh Trail. The heat, humidity, vegetation and variety of animal life make for a kaleidoscopic sensory experience. The dense
mountain rain forest is one of the world's most beautiful—and
harshest—environments. Toll, code-named

"Circus" for his years performing on the high wire with the Great
Wallendas, is a sergeant, 4th Infantry Division LRRP/K Co. 75th
Army Rangers. He wears a black bandanna in place of a helmet,
and his fatigues bear no patches, markings or other identification.
His pack, supplies and weaponry are foreign issue and untraceable.
Only the whites of his eyes show through the olive green-and-black
waterproof camouflage grease that covers his face.

Toll is a team leader. The Special Op directives in Cambodia
and Laos include collecting intelligence on enemy numbers and
location, destroying munitions, snatching North Vietnamese Army
(NVA) officers, planting sensory devices and "neutralizing" as many
of the enemy as possible. Its mission is "to gather strategic intelligence for the president."

Beginning with John Kennedy in 1962, border intrusions are
under direct authority of the president of the United States. The
top-secret activities are unknown to all but the highest government, military and intelligence officials. The soldiers have signed a
written agreement: If killed or captured, the U.S. government will
deny knowledge of their existence. Toll and his comrades are on the
front lines of a secret and illegal war.

The NVA is, however, well-aware of the guerrilla force. They call
them *hoac si vê mát,* "men with painted faces." While the North
Vietnamese both fear and respect them, they also are eager to cap-

ture or kill them. Each dead member has a $10,000 piaster price on his head. Caught *alive* each brings $100,000 piasters. The average annual income in Vietnam is $300 piasters. LRRP operatives are walking winning lottery tickets.

The dangers of war aside, the jungles of Southeast Asia offer myriad forms of disease and death. The ecosystem is like a churning organ, a relentless, grinding and insatiable tropical maw. Life feeds on death. Toll has four days of enemy surveillance just 3 kilometers from the Ho Chi Minh trail in Cambodia to inventory the possible forms of his demise.

He is here with two other LRRPs, Frenchie and Adair, as well as two Montagnards, Rhoi and Jac, members of a separatist mountain tribe that has fought the Vietnamese for generations. The CIA employs them for special operations. The team's very presence violates international law.

Toll's dedication to the Eastern philosophy of Taoism serves him well on the long nights in the jungle. He meditates, practicing kundalini and hatha yoga hours each day when off watch, mentally and rhythmically repeating his mantra until his mind empties of all superfluous thoughts while maintaining hyper-mental alertness.

Movement could draw the attention of the North Vietnamese, and a battalion could be as close as 20 feet away. Swatting bugs is not a good idea. Yet the mosquitoes carry the threat of malaria, strains of which defy Western medicine. Then there's amebic dysentery, which can easily kill a man inside of 10 days. There's dengue fever, bubonic plague and gangrenous jungle rot, a danger with every boil, blister and scrape. The leeches in the jungle are attracted to the smell of salt and ammonia in human urine. To keep them at bay, the team wears condoms at all times. They can't apply insect repellent: The chemical smell could alert the NVA to their whereabouts.

In fact, 48 hours before every mission all LRRPs (Lurps), the acronym for men on Long Range Reconnaissance Patrol, cease eating anything other than indigenous foods, mostly rice and dried fish. They quit drinking alcohol or bathing with soap or using toiletries, lest the smells give them away. Conversely, when the wind is right, a Lurp can smell the Vietnamese, who spend much of their time in tunnels where cooking fires smolder. A whiff of stale smoke will cause the hairs on the back of a Lurp's neck to stand up.

The scene is nightmarish.

Eastern philosophy teaches that the most direct path to enlightenment is through prolonged exposure to imminent death. But first, says Toll, you must survive. Then, you have to emerge from the experience sane. Toll likens these missions to dangling his legs over the edge of the abyss and gazing in.

In the course of 24 hours, Toll might encounter an ark's worth of wild animals. Snakes are everywhere. An 18-foot python slithers by. Cobras and banded kraits, two of the world's deadliest snakes, are common in the jungle. Cobras mate for life and travel in pairs; when Toll sees one, he makes a mental note to keep an eye out for the other. Later in the day, a full-grown 400 pound tiger prowls by. The tiger, upwind, doesn't smell him. Toll wonders if he's hunkered down in the tiger's hunting grounds and if the cat will be back later that night looking for a snack. He can hear the monkeys chatter in the trees as a monitor lizard the size of a small dog lumbers by.

The teaching of Lao Tzu, the father of Taoism, are close to Toll's heart here in the jungle. He thinks of the saying from the *Tao Te Ching*, Taoism's most sacred book: *"Those who know how to live can walk abroad without fear of the rhinoceros or the tiger. They can enter battle without being wounded. Why is this? Because they are beyond death."*

There is no talking on the four-day range patrol mission. All communication is by hand signals. Sleep is at a minimum. Government-issued amphetamines fuel them on five-mile-long hikes over hilly terrain toward the interior and throughout the mission. Each team member is an expert, trained in at least two military disciplines and cross-trained in each other's specialties. Adair is a radio tech and medic. Frenchie is an expert in explosives and languages. Rhoi knows geography and maps. On this mission, Toll's team is trying to locate NVA headquarters by monitoring troop movements. The information will be used later to launch massive B-52 air raids.

It takes great self-control to sit in the same location for days at a time without being detected. During the long nights in the black jungle, Toll, wired on Dexedrine, takes his mind off snakes, leeches and mortar fire by thinking of home, his wife Mary, infant daughter Loretta, and strawberry banana splits.

He recalls growing up in Cleveland: His buddies back in the

old Collinwood neighborhood, playing baseball, going to Indians games at Municipal Stadium, collecting baseball cards and player autographs.

He remembers his family's move to St. Petersburg, Florida, after his dad, a union official at Addressograph Multigraph in Cleveland, died. There were hours spent in the St. Petersburg library reading everything they had, especially books on Eastern thought and religion. Toll was the only 14-year-old Taoist in St. Pete who had read the entire *Bhagavad Gita* and *Upanishads*, both sacred books in Taoism. There were afternoons boating and fishing with friends, most of whom were transplants from other Northern cities, and a bit on the wild side for the likes of the then-sleepy Florida town. Toll literally learned the ropes and the trapeze at the St. Petersburg Youth Circus. It was a taste of show business, and he liked it. He was very good on the high wire, and when the Wallendas found themselves short a performer, they called Toll. He ran away to join the traveling troupe. He was 16.

Toll remembers being drafted just when everything was going so well. He was 19, leaving the Wallendas and heading to New York to pursue an acting career when FBI agents came knocking at the door of his mother's house in St. Petersburg, wanting to know why he hadn't registered for the draft. He thought about going to Canada, but his mother talked him out of it. "You will be a witness to history," she told him. She couldn't have known how prescient those words would be.

1967. The Army puts Toll through a battery of intelligence testing, and the high school dropout scores high enough to qualify as a third-year college student. An instructor tells him his I.Q. is 182. He's classified "rare and unusual" and is recommended for training as an intelligence analyst.

Instead, the Army decides it needs fodder. He is shipped off to Fort Polk, Louisiana, for training at a place called Tigerland. It means only one thing: The jungle. He is headed for Vietnam.

In March 1968, with the Tet Offensive raging, Toll takes his place on the field of battle at Dak To: 105 Americans are trying to take a hill in the Central Highlands against 365 NVA. It is a protracted, vicious, bloody firefight that lasts five days. Chaos reigns. When it's over, American soldiers—the 23 still alive—own the hill. Toll is the first American to reach the top.

Back at home, Lyndon B. Johnson announces he will not seek re-election. He halts the bombing of North Vietnam and publicly calls for peace talks. Martin Luther King Jr. is assassinated in Memphis. His death brings about rioting in 130 American cities.

After three battles, Toll realizes if enemy fire doesn't kill him, the lack of U.S. Army coordination on the battlefield will. He wants more control over his future, whatever it takes. He volunteers for Lurp training, an intense month of physical and mental conditioning: A seven-mile run wearing a 30-pound pack in the morning, 18 hours of classroom instruction, then another seven-mile run before turning in. The course has a 65 percent washout rate.

As the sun rises over the triple-canopied jungle ceiling, Toll is mentally recounting his past Lurp missions. This will be his ninth, he thinks, but quickly snaps out of his reverie. Less than 50 feet away he sees enemy troops patrolling. He alerts his team with a low wave as he prepares them for possible escape, evasion and extraction. The sounds of birds and bugs become deafening.

A plan is in place should the team be compromised. They have planted a variety of explosive devices in an arc 30 feet out on the perimeter of their encampment. There are tripwires, toe-poppers and Claymore mines. The tripwires set off grenades, the toe-poppers will blow the toes off a foot, and the Claymores will spray 750 large ball bearings straight ahead for 150 feet like a shotgun blast. The explosion is capable of cutting a dozen men in half.

Minutes later, an unlucky North Vietnamese soldier moves too close to the Lurp team and a trip-wired grenade takes him out with a concussive blast.

It's time to move. Fast. Toll quickly radios the location of a landing zone a mile away where the team will meet a chopper. The escape drill has the team leaving in single file. The men peel back. The point man, the Montagnard Rhoi, unloads two clips of bullets from his AK-47. Then Frenchie stops, tosses a grenade and puts down some short fuse mines to discourage pursuers. Adair and the other Montagnard do the same. The team leaves an array of explosive hard-ware in its wake.

At the landing zone, a helicopter swoops in under fire. In minutes, the team boards, and the chopper begins to lift when Toll notices Frenchie is missing. He looks down and sees him waving in the clearing. He was pinned down during the retreat. NVA troops are arriving at the tree line and laying down heavy fire.

Toll tells the pilot to land again. The pilot shakes his head "no" as the chopper takes some heavy dings from the groundfire. Toll pulls his side arm, a Browning high-powered 9mm, and points it at the pilot's head. *"Take it down."* After some quick and heated negotiations, the pilot agrees to take a low pass at Frenchie. Toll has two men hold him by his ankles as he hangs from the helicopter. Frenchie sees him coming and leaps off a tree stump up into the two-handed grip. Toll swings him into the bird while bullets fly.

Mission accomplished. No one dead. No one left behind. Enemy regiment located. Frenchie turns to the pilot, grinning like a madman.

Tonight, there will be a party back at the base. Dope and booze and prostitutes. Lurps are not subject to Army regulations. They even carry get-out-of-jail-free cards signed by General William Westmoreland. The cards instruct military police not to detain them.

Two weeks later, on the night before his next mission, Toll awakens with a 106-degree fever. After going in and out of consciousness, he is put in a metal container and packed with ice. He begins convulsing and, since his dog tags ID him as Catholic, he is given last rites as his men and the field commander file in the hospital ward to bid him a warrior's farewell: Adair, Frenchie, Rhoi, Futrelle, Bartholomew, Hess, Wood, Loftus. They say prayers. There are no Taoist monks available. Not in the U.S. Army anyway.

Toll's team is told he will not live. Their mission is cancelled and they are replaced by another Lurp team. A comatose Toll is medivaced to Zama Army Hospital in Tokyo, where he is treated for malaria and tropical jungle fevers of unknown origin.

To the hospital staff's surprise, Toll emerges from the coma after nine days. At 6 feet tall, he has wasted away from 180 to a mere 109 pounds. He soon learns the Lurp team that replaced his—made up of some of his closest friends—was wiped out in a firefight two days after being "inserted" in Cambodia. After a month, Toll leaves the hospital. But even if Toll wanted to return to the jungle, he can't. The malaria could return. His days of active combat are over.

Barry Toll is going home.

1973. Toll is a staff sergeant in an elite unit assigned to the World Wide Military Command and Control Systems at Langley Air Force Base, Virginia. During the past four years, Toll has been formally recognized as one of the Army's top-rated operations and intelligence specialists serving in a series of Joint Service staff posi-tions dealing with highly classified information. His assignments have taken him to Hawaii, Europe and Asia. His team is one of five charged with around-the-clock duty to administer "doomsday" orders in the event of nuclear war. Toll jokingly describes the job as "practicing blowing up the world."

The team, led by a four-star admiral, is on three days, off seven. They monitor world events, often from a 707, poring over sensi-tive, high-level intelligence bulletins, maintaining a posture that prepares them to brief the president for a worst-case scenario.

The early Seventies are troubled for American national security. Toll is behind the scenes at every juncture: The anti-war demon-strations at Kent State and Jackson State in Mississippi. The tur-moil over the *New York Times* publication of the Pentagon Papers, the massive top-secret history of the illegal U.S. role in Indochina. The accusations of dirty tricks and sabotaging of political enemies at the Nixon White House that culminates in a "third-rate bur-glary" at the Watergate Hotel.

Internally, the Joint Chiefs of Staff are convinced that Richard Nixon and Henry Kissinger are operating their own secret agenda in Vietnam. Toll knows the "peace with honor" agreement Nixon signed in 1973 isn't worth the paper it's written on. Nixon's state-ment to the American people—"All our POW's are on their way home now"—is a lie. Toll and others in the loop know an estimated 350 Americans are still being held secretly in Laos.

The missing men are something Nixon and Kissinger desper-ately needed to conceal. The first Article of Impeachment pending before the House of Representatives alleged "Conduct of an illegal and unconstitutional war in Cambodia and Laos." Large numbers of American soldiers captured in Cambodia and Laos would be *proof* of an illegal war.

With the Watergate indictments of Bob Haldeman and John Ehrlichman, former Attorney General John Mitchell and many Nixon Cabinet officers, the government is in disarray, and the Joint Chiefs are near mutinous. One of Toll's duties is to keep track of who is in line to succeed the president. The almost constant round of musical chairs makes his job a nightmare. Nixon nominates the German-born Kissinger for secretary of state after William Rogers is forced to resign. In this poisoned climate, the Senate confirms

Kissinger's nomination. Toll believes that Kissinger is being rewarded for sticking by Nixon while others fled, were fired, or went to jail.

Toll has come on duty after a two-week hiatus. It's October 6, 1973. His Doomsday Team is put on Presidential Alert. Sixteen hours after arriving at work, an alarm goes off in the Communications Center, and the team is notified that the Egyptian Army has crossed the Suez Canal. Only the United States and the Soviets know that Israel has nuclear capability. Toll sees top-secret exchanges between Nixon and Israeli Prime Minister Golda Meir wherein she vows to use nukes against Egypt rather than surrender one inch of territory. The Soviets are threatening to supply Egypt with nukes as well. This is nuclear saber-rattling at its most alarming. It is the closest the United States has come to a nuclear war.

Nixon orders that Kissinger be added to the National Command Authority (NCA) succession list. The secretary of state is normally fourth in line for the presidency, preceded by the vice president, speaker of the House and president pro tem of the Senate. But Toll knows the Constitution provides that no American citizen can succeed to the presidency unless that person is a natural-born citizen of the United States. Toll alerts his supervisor, the battle staff commander, Colonel Wallace Crompton, a man he respects immensely.

Crompton, then the senior colonel in the U.S. Marine Corps, is a legend, having risen to colonel from a Marine private. Toll knows Crompton was as disgusted as he was by the intelligence they were privy to. He told everyone within earshot that he would soon be resigning.

Vice President Agnew is preparing to resign over tax charges. Toll sees the message from the president ordering them to add Kissinger to the NCA. "Colonel, I cannot lawfully obey any National Command Authority order from Henry Kissinger, because he cannot constitutionally succeed to the presidency. I need to know what you are going to do about this, because I may not be able to perform my duties," Toll says.

Crompton, his face crimson in anger, tells Toll to assemble the battle staff team and get the NCA's 707 aircraft aloft.

After solemnly gathering the team 40,000 feet over the Atlantic, Crompton asks Toll to speak his mind before the staff. He does so in no uncertain terms. After murmurs of outrage from the other seven team members, Crompton instructs Toll to immediately query the National Military Command Center at the Pentagon as to the validity of the order and to copy the White House. The plane becomes library quiet. This is a national security showdown.

Toll sends the query. Landing at Langley some hours later, he's called into the Communications Center and told there is a phone call from a general officer in the National Military Command Center. To take the call, Toll steps into a top-secret "phone booth."

Crompton and the others stand by, unable to hear Toll's words in the soundproof booth but able to see his intense, agitated responses.

As Toll emerges from the booth, an alarm sounds. For all they know, Israel has just nuked Cairo. The team is airborne in less than 90 seconds, heading out over the Atlantic, getting lost in the cover of a phantom flight profile of a commercial aircraft vectoring overseas to Europe.

In the air, after confirming that the nuclear crisis has passed for the moment, Toll reports that the general officer at the Pentagon had forwarded the challenge of Kissinger's authority to the White House. Chief of Staff Alexander Haig had responded: "I just talked to the Old Man [Nixon]," he said. "The list stands as issued."

The eight team members are silent. It occurs to Toll that he is standing where Lyndon Johnson was administered the presidential oath of office with Kennedy's blood-spattered widow at his side. A dozen feet behind Toll is the rear door from which Kennedy's casket emerged after that fateful day in Dallas. The plane's tail number is 26000. Back then it was known as Air Force One.

He thinks of these events, the long, drawn-out war in Vietnam and the effect it's had on American lives. How decisions each president made have dominoed down through the years to bizarre moments such as this.

Toll turns to Crompton. "Colonel, I need to know what you are going to do if we receive an order from Henry Kissinger because I cannot lawfully obey one from him regardless of what the president says."

The colonel does not hesitate. Looking at each member of the president's nuclear control team, he says, "Barry, I'll tell the son-ofabitch to go to hell."

Toll can't disguise his relief. "That's good enough for me, sir."

Toll heads back to the bunks in the rear compartment. A thousand images race through his mind. He is shaken, but resolved. He sits in a leather command chair and thinks about the ghost of Kennedy that hovers somewhere in this plane, the secret war Kennedy started and the men, his brothers-in-arms, who Nixon left behind in Laos.

Then he cries.

July 4, 1975. Toll has put in two years as a member of the Doomsday Team working for the White House. He shows up for his shift out of uniform. He's had enough. He shocks everyone with the words, "I can no longer perform my duties or wear the uniform in good conscience. I am going home and requesting immediate discharge."

Within minutes, the White House sends a Flash Override message around the world ordering the revision of the current secret codes and replacing them with new ones. The FBI, the CIA and the Defense Intelligence Agency convene for an emergency security damage assessment meeting to decide what to do. They must have a plan in case Toll considers defecting. They also must have a plan should Toll go to the media to talk about the U.S. government's foreign policy.

Toll has no intentions of defecting, although he is outraged and angry at presidents and a government he sees hiding behind the guise of national security for its own political ends and, in the process, abandoning more than 350 American soldiers in Southeast Asia.

Toll the patriot has become Toll the outlaw. Nobody quits the military. He doesn't care if he is put in the stockade. But if he is, he tells them, his first call won't be to a lawyer. It will be to a syndicated columnist, Jack Anderson or Sydney Schanberg of the *New York Times*.

After a 45-day debriefing session, he heads home. He just wants to disappear. He is unaware that St. Petersburg is well on its way to becoming the marijuana smuggling capital of the United States. It's a great place to get lost.

In St. Pete, Toll hooks up with several high school buddies who are running a marijuana smuggling operation. He turns his back on a life of service in the highest echelons of national security.

Still bitter and disillusioned, he blames the treachery of Nixon and Kissinger for his abandonment of an otherwise exemplary military career and his current life of crime. He sees his turn to crime as payback for a morally bankrupt government. During the last horrific year of the Nixon presidency, everything was out of control. On at least three occasions, Toll's Doomsday Team received memos from Secretary of State Kissinger and other Cabinet officers to ignore all orders from the Oval Office until further notice. The implication was that Nixon was incapacitated. Toll assumed he was drunk. It was another indication of the profound instability of Nixon and his administration.

Toward the end of his time working for the government, Toll could no longer keep quiet about his feelings regarding the POWs and MIAs. He began illegally leaking information about SOG operations and consequent cover-ups regarding POWs and MIAs to Republican Representative Pete McCloskey of California. The congressman used the information during the McCloskey Hearings to determine what U.S. policy was in Southeast Asia. The hearings led to the first article of impeachment regarding the "illegal and unconstitutional war in Cambodia and Laos."

Toll's expertise in covert operations makes him popular with the South Florida smugglers. They are millionaires many times over from importing marijuana, but their hit-and-miss methods have more in common with Cheech and Chong movies than they do with anybody's idea of organized crime. Shipments are intercepted and smugglers are arrested.

Toll brings military discipline and a world of technical know-how to his friends' drug dealings. He teaches them how to sweep their homes and offices for listening devices. He instructs them on government methods of surveillance. He tells them how marijuana bales in South America are tracked by satellite until they arrive in the United States. He buys radio scanners that allow the smugglers to monitor the air waves, listening for federal frequencies that tell them which law enforcement agencies are active and where.

Toll uses mountains of illegal drug money to outfit a van with the latest communications intercept radio equipment. He helps the smugglers bug the feds. The vehicle becomes a mobile anti-arrest unit. He buys a Bell Ranger helicopter to spot Coast Guard cutters up and down the waterways on both the Atlantic and Gulf sides. He teaches smugglers how to ferret out and manipulate informants, detect wiretaps and spread misinformation. He shows them how to employ diversionary tactics, including "accidentally" sinking an old boat on the Atlantic coast when a big drug shipment is coming in on the Gulf.

Toll is paid with a percentage of profits from the increasingly successful operation. In less than four months he is a millionaire. Now able to finance his own operation, Toll recruits the best men from each group he was hired to help and forms his own organization. He is the embodiment of the 'high life.' He and some other smugglers form a rock 'n' roll production company to hide their assets and launder their cash. When the IRS comes snooping, they fold the old company and start another under a new name. They book the Eagles, Loggins & Messina, Fleetwood Mac and other touring bands, including a local favorite, a guy named Jimmy Buffett.

Toll has a permanent all-access pass to money, drugs, Lear jets and limos. There isn't a party in the United States or Rio de Janeiro he can't get to in four hours or less. Since he can't report his cash, he spends it. His accountant estimates Toll spends $3,800 a day on sundry items, the best restaurants, most expensive clothes, gifts for friends and family, not to mention cars, boats and other big-ticket toys. He and his partners like to brag, describing themselves as people who "don't count money."

Toll quickly learns that crime, however profitable, does not pay. Maybe *because* it is so profitable.

Toll and his pals in St. Pete, now also into cocaine in a big way, are caught by the Drug Enforcement Agency when dealers roll over on distributors and distributors roll over on the smugglers. Toll is asleep in a Detroit Metro Airport motel room in Romulus, Michigan, where he'd gone to meet up with his drug partners. When the phone rings, no one is on the line. Toll knows it's the police calling to make sure he's there. He quickly flushes his coke down the toilet and drops his Smith & Wesson .357-caliber Magnum down a heating duct just before police kick in his door. They drag Toll out of the room and cuff him, naked in the winter chill, to the second floor railing.

They don't find anything in the room, but it doesn't matter. An arrested associate cuts a deal and implicates Toll in a conspiracy to distribute drugs. There's no avoiding jail time, even though Toll hires the best lawyers money can buy. He's sentenced to seven years but serves only two. He's on strict parole for the remaining five.

On March 31, the night before he enters the world's largest walled prison, in Jackson, Michigan, Toll flies to Cleveland for the final night of the Eagles' *Hotel California* tour at the Richfield Coliseum. He goes backstage to say hello to the opening act, his old friend Jimmy Buffett. He celebrates his last night of freedom with the Eagles and Buffett. As the sun rises on April Fools' Day 1977, Toll drives to Jackson to surrender to prison authorities. Four months later, sitting in his prison cell, Toll hears a new, oddly catchy Caribbean-flavored song that seems to be playing on every radio station on the dial.

Some people claim that there's a woman to blame,
But, I know, it's my own damn fault.

The song is Jimmy Buffett's "Margaritaville."

1992. Toll can't believe what he's about to do this morning in Washington, D.C. He's in a suit and tie and has a fresh haircut. He's heading off to appear before the Senate Select Committee on POW and MIA Affairs. Reviewing the testimony he's about to give, he wonders what it will be like to have all five living presidents angry at him.

After his release from prison, he'd bounced around for a year, avoiding the feds who wanted him to testify against his former associates. By the fall of 1985, his marriage now history, he'd heard through the grapevine that it was safe to come home. Toll was completely free of the legal system for the first time since his arrest at that motel in Michigan in 1976.

Toll, still a follower of Taoism, begins his *Sadhu* period. Like one of India's hundreds of wandering yogis who live off alms as they seek to become one with God, Toll settles back in St. Petersburg and divests himself of all earthly belongings, seeking simplicity and spirituality. He gives up all drugs and alcohol, and refrains from sex. Living off his military pension, he resides in Florida and helps his mother and grandmother care for an invalid aunt.

Toll spends his free time studying American history, specifically military history and issues related to national security. He concentrates on how war changes men and the differences between the soldiers of World War II and Vietnam. He wants to understand why the war in Southeast Asia was so devastating for so many American soldiers. Toll believes Harry Truman was right when he said the two worst things he had ever done as president were signing the National Security Act and creating the CIA in 1947. His research confirms his belief that every president since Truman has systematically abused the Constitution under the guise of "national security." Toll believes that a license to lie to Congress and the American people represents the gravest threat to democracy.

After several years of extensive research, scholarship and personal exposure to presidential decision-making, Toll envisions himself a self-made academic. He acquaints himself with the Freedom of Information laws and masters the use of the Internet to find information.

He finds an esoteric Military Forum chat room on CompuServe's network that intrigues him. Up to this point he's been avoiding the POW/MIA issue. While he knows most of the people involved are sincerely seeking the truth about relatives, he's also aware that mixed into the movement are kooks, wannabees and phony fundraisers exploiting people's misery for profit.

It's increasingly difficult to ignore the families seeking closure regarding their loved ones. He knows if a credible investigation is begun, he will testify.

1990. Toll's phone begins ringing, and reams of unsolicited material begins arriving in the mail. His fax machine burns out, and his computer is flooded with e-mail. The messages are all requests from families trying to find out what happened to their sons, their husbands, their dads. Realizing he cannot address the thousands of requests piecemeal, he agrees to speak at a national convention in Washington, D.C. At the Willard Hotel, a stone's throw from the White House, he addresses a POW/MIA convention for the first time. He promises three years of time to the cause and talks about how and why the White House misrepresented and underreported soldiers lost in Cambodia and Laos.

In June 1992, Toll appears before the Senate Select Committee on POW/MIA Affairs headed by Senator John Kerry of Massachusetts and Senator Robert Smith of New Hampshire. Toll gives his testimony in a sworn deposition about much of what he had witnessed while working as an intelligence specialist and Doomsday Team member for the Nixon White House.

He tells the committee it was the opinion of the Joint Chiefs of Staff and the U.S. intelligence community that an estimated 350 U.S. POWs and MIAs were alive and were held captive in Laos in 1973 after the Peace Accords were signed and that President Richard Nixon had that information. Toll says that Nixon was given that analysis in intelligence briefings on several occasions. Toll also tells the committee that he was privy to information indicating POWs were transported from Laos and Cambodia to the Soviet Union and to the People's Republic of China.

"The truth must come out now," declares Toll.

The POW/MIA movement has discovered Barry Toll. One month later, in a series of precise and carefully measured disclosures, he begins revealing what he knows on the CompuServe Military Forum. CompuServe Magazine publishes a feature story on Toll's experiences in Vietnam and as an intelligence specialist with access to sensitive secrets from the Nixon White House. In 90 days, the CompuServe Military Forum chat room membership grows from 4,000 to 38,000.

Toll is interviewed for print, radio and television, demanding the U.S. government come clean on the issue. His testimony generates more than 100 articles and columns written by writers with viewpoints as varied as the liberal Sydney Schanberg, formerly of the *New York Times*, and the conservative Robert Caldwell of the *San Diego Union-Tribune*.

The POW/MIA Affairs Committee disbands in January 1993. The Senate Committee issues a report concluding that men were left behind. But the findings are obscured in the otherwise long and fuzzy document. The national press lets the story fade.

Toll stresses all along to the families that the POW/MIA issue is not going to be won quickly or easily. Too many politicians and military and intelligence personnel have too much to lose by releasing documentation that would reveal the truth. Toll borrows a popular aphorism claiming there is little accurate history until 50 years after an event. Toll tells the families they have 30 years in Vietnam and the truth will surface completely in the next 20.

Toll's commitment to the POW/MIA families is almost up. The effort lands him back in the White House. After years of presidents, Congress and executive agencies avoiding the truth by keeping the secret war in Southeast Asia classified, the POW/MIA buck has landed on President Clinton's doorstep. It's a thorny issue. Even though none of it is Clinton's fault, the secret of men left behind carries with it a "kill the messenger" stigma should he decide to open the archives.

Clinton asks Toll to consult with National Security Adviser Anthony Lake on the continuing Vietnam conundrum. The POW/

MIA issue still threatens the normalization of relations between the United States and Vietnam. In 1994, Toll, with the help of former CIA Director George Carver and General Eugene Tighe, chief head of intelligence for the Defense Intelligence Agency, present their findings on the POW/MIA issue for Lake. Toll's team reports the same facts of the war's hidden history. They are impossible to discredit.

Toll's persistence pays off. Clinton, in an effort to appease the POW/MIA movement after lifting the trade embargo against Vietnam, issues an executive order for massive declassification of 3 million documents relating to Vietnam. It is as decisive a victory as Toll has ever seen for his work.

Toll retreats to Hawaii, knowing his service to his country is finally complete.

The warrior is finally at rest.

May 27, 2001

IN THE LINE OF FIRE— AND JOURNALISM

From covering a story to taking cover

Michael Laughlin looks down at the dirty cement floor. He winces in the heat. So thirsty. A round from an AK-47 burns the flesh deep in his right shoulder. Sweat stings the oozing lacerations where two other bullets grazed his face and neck. He wonders how much blood he can lose before it becomes life-threatening.

Laughlin and three other photographers are hiding in this small, concrete-block home in Port-au-Prince, Haiti, just blocks from where a political march just ended. The sound of the gunfire intensifies.

The "chimere," former president Jean-Bertrand Aristide's armed thugs, close in on the house. Even back in the dark kitchen, Laughlin hears three different types of automatic weapons firing just outside in the courtyard. It's open season on journalists.

"Get under the table," shouts Peter Bosch, a photographer from the *Miami Herald*. "Two more are shot."

Laughlin looks at the table in the back room off the kitchen. It's against the wall. There's discarded pieces of wood and other household junk underneath it. Maybe even a rat or two. It's 84 degrees and sticky. He's woozy, dehydrated and bleeding. He's not sure he wants to get under that table. If the chimere overrun the house, it's not where he wants to face the end.

The police have abandoned the area, the marines aren't responding to phone calls, and three people have been shot. Fearing the worst, Daniel Morel, a Haitian photographer with Reuters news agency, runs out the front door and jumps a fence to get help. Laughlin fantasizes about a drink of cold water and concentrates on staying calm. Breathe deeply, he tells himself.

"We have to run," Bosch tells Laughlin. "If you're not up to it, get under the table and we'll come back for you."

Laughlin struggles to move his 5-foot-11 and 220-pound frame just a few feet to the floor under the small table. The pain in his right shoulder and arm is killing him. Ten minutes later, Bosch, his silver ponytail swinging behind him, bursts into the kitchen. Morel is back with an ambulance. But the gunfire keeps the vehicle 100 yards from the house. They have to go. Now. Laughlin tells Bosch he'll try. He'll do anything for a drink of water.

"If we get out of this, we're going to a strip joint tonight," Bosch tells Laughlin, helping him to the front door.

In the fear, pain and confusion, one thought occurs to Laughlin: There are no strip joints in Haiti.

He and Bosch open the flimsy front door and run like hell.

TWO DAYS EARLIER

Michael Laughlin and reporter Sandra Hernandez arrive Friday, March 5, in Petionville, Haiti, to cover the turmoil following the ouster of Aristide for the *South Florida Sun-Sentinel*.

Laughlin's wife, Kathy, isn't thrilled about this three-week assignment, but he considers the story important and is glad to be covering it.

To appease his wife, he put in for vacation the day before he left. This year marks their 10th wedding anniversary, and they plan to travel to Europe for two weeks in May to celebrate.

On Sunday, March 7, Laughlin rises at 7:30 a.m. in room 220 at the clean and modern Hotel Montana in downtown Port-au-Prince. Breakfast is a dozen Fig Newtons brought from home in South Florida.

He leaves his valuables in the hotel safe, taking with him only 10 $1 bills and a large bottle of Evian water for the march. Rule No. 1 for foreign journalists in Haiti is: Don't drink the water.

Downstairs in the lobby, Laughlin and Hernandez meet their driver, Raymond, sending him ahead to the presidential palace where the 12-mile march will end.

The sun climbs in the sky, and the temperature rises with it. As does the humidity.

It's quiet with little traffic. People are walking to church. Several hundred Haitians gather for the march.

By mile three, thousands of people are joining the parade. Laughlin buys his first bottle of water, drinking half and pouring the other half over his head. He lights a cigarette and looks for more photo opportunities.

Three miles later, a marcher picks Laughlin's pocket in the sardine-like crush of the crowd. His money gone, he'll have to wait until he meets Hernandez and Raymond at the end of the rally before he can buy any more water. At mile 10, foreign volunteers give him some water and offer Haitian currency. He smiles and says no thanks. He'll be with his driver and back at the hotel soon.

At noon, the marchers reach the presidential palace, where Haitian firemen hose them down to cool them off. The crowd is jubilant. But there's trouble, too.

Laughlin sees *Miami Herald* photographer Peter Andrew Bosch, who tells him one man already has been shot by snipers and they ought to call it a day. It's not worth risking injury, or worse, he says. A team of Haitian SWAT police arrive to investigate.

Laughlin, Bosch and other photographers follow them up a side street off the plaza where more shootings have been reported.

Laughlin runs ahead, finding a safe, corner enclave on the Champs de Mars. The police like the spot, too, and follow Laughlin. Photographers across the street want pictures of the police without Laughlin in it. They yell for him to move. He takes a picture and then joins his colleagues across the street.

Automatic-weapons fire rings out from the rooftops. Everyone finds cover. Laughlin steps back around the corner of a building. There is a lull in the shooting.

Peering out from around the building, Laughlin looks for the source of the gunfire. In an instant, he is hit as debris and dust fly off the stucco wall behind him. He feels like he's been pounded in the shoulder with a sledge hammer. A flood of thoughts races through his head. Then he sees the blood soaking through the right shoulder of his navy blue T-shirt. He's been shot.

A Haitian man runs up, grabs Laughlin and says, "Let's go." They run 50 feet down Champs de Mars to where the other photographers are huddled. Bosch is irritated. "Damn it, Mike, I told you to be careful," he says to Laughlin.

Five minutes later, there's more gunfire in the streets. Bosch and the other journalists take Laughlin into a courtyard. They look at his wounds. They ask can he move his arms and fingers. He can. Bosch tells Laughlin he'll be OK—if he doesn't bleed to death.

The front doors to half a dozen homes line the courtyard. When bullets rain down from above, the photographers see an open door and Haitians beckoning. They all pile in out of harm's way. Bosch walks Laughlin into the back of the house, sits him down at the kitchen table, then returns to the front door to check the street.

A woman who lives in the house puts rubbing alcohol and a towel on Laughlin's wound and applies ice to his head and shoulder. Her kindness for a stranger overwhelms him. Though she can't speak English and he knows no Haitian, he tells her he loves her and thanks her. It's a brief moment of quiet tenderness amid the constant barrage of rounds outside.

Some folks are at the front door; a Haitian photographer is working his cell phone in hopes of summoning help. New York Spanish television correspondent Ricardo Ortega and another Haitian man get hit by rifle fire as they re-enter the courtyard. Ortega takes two rounds in the stomach; the Haitian is hit in the hip. Bosch returns to the kitchen to tell Laughlin to hide under the table. Daniel Morel escapes and goes for help.

OUT OF THE WAR ZONE, A SENSE OF RELIEF

After the ambulance arrives, Bosch and Laughlin are the last of the group to reach it. The vehicle is so full they can't close the double doors in the back. Laughlin is no longer worried about dying from his wounds. He's worried about dying from new wounds. They all holler for the ambulance to move.

Two blocks away, the driver misses a turn. The car stalls as the driver puts it in reverse. In the excitement of the moment, he floods the engine. The staccato whine of the starter makes every second last an eternity. After three tries, the engine ignites, and the vehicle rolls on. Ortega is moaning in pain. The wounded Haitian man is eerily silent and still. Laughlin feels a sense of relief as the ambulance passes civilian Haitians going about their Sunday routines. They're out of the war zone and headed for Canape Vert Hospital not far away.

Laughlin enters the hospital under his own power. A U.S. Marine stationed at the door looks at his wounds with a mix of revulsion and horror. The hospital floor is covered with fresh blood. Four people have died and 30 were wounded by the suspected chimere snipers. Doctors begin working on Ortega. The wounded Haitian man never made it out of the ambulance. Laughlin is given a Dixie cup of water and a large square bandage and told to wait.

From where Laughlin sits, he can see Ortega's feet while doctors try to save his life. An hour later, loss of blood and dehydration begin to overwhelm Laughlin. One of the last things he remembers is the doctors pulling the sheet over Ortega's head.

Laughlin feels himself drifting toward unconsciousness. A doctor finally notices, gets him a gurney and starts an IV drip with a bag of saline solution. Another doctor uses a large syringe to put pain medication in the IV. Sandra Hernandez visits Laughlin, and he asks her to get his pants. In a pocket is the digital card that contains his photos. Laughlin, feeling the drugs, imagines a kaleidoscopic light show on the ceiling.

A captain in the French military tells Laughlin he's being transferred to a U.S. MASH hospital out by the Port-au-Prince airport. Morel agrees to transmit Laughlin's photos to the Sun-Sentinel and call his wife, Kathy, before she hears about him on CNN. Twenty minutes later, Laughlin is loaded onto a military helicopter in front of a huge crowd of fascinated Haitian onlookers.

At the MASH unit, Laughlin's wounds are cleaned and redressed. The shot of morphine they give him isn't anywhere as good as the painkiller at Canape Vert. But he's not complaining. Four hours later, at 10 Sunday night, he is awakened and put on a C-130 and flown to Guantanamo Bay, Cuba. There, he is the only person in the hospital and receives X-rays and more examination of his wounds. He can have all the water he wants.

Just after midnight, he gets to call Kathy. It's the first time they've talked since Saturday night.

"Hi bunny," he says.

"It's so good to hear your voice," Kathy says, near tears. His flight to Miami's Jackson Memorial Hospital leaves the next day. He wishes he had some Fig Newtons.

April 4, 2004

TINKERBELLE AND
THE COST OF A DREAM

*Robert Manry's solo voyage across the Atlantic
proved to be a difficult journey for his family*

A skinny girl in a lime-green, two-piece bathing suit parks her bike in the stand at Manry Park in Willowick. She whips out a cell phone from her shoulder bag and hits a button with her thumb.

"Mom, I'm at Manry," she says loudly into the phone.

Just behind her, sitting at a picnic table, Douglas Manry shudders.

"That freaks me out," he says, listening to this stranger use his family name so casually. "I still can't get used to that."

The girl is 10, maybe 11, a time when life is fun and carefree. She's about the same age as Douglas Manry was 40 years ago when his father's famous voyage eclipsed his childhood and that of his older sister, Robin.

The park was named for their father, Robert Manry, after he sailed a 13½-foot boat 3,200 miles alone across the Atlantic in 78 days. At the time, it was the smallest sailboat to cross the ocean. Wednesday marks the anniversary of that historic landing in Falmouth, England.

In 1965, Bob Manry, a *Plain Dealer* copy editor and modern-day Magellan, mesmerized two continents with his navigational prowess, courage and endurance. His feat was celebrated for months on both sides of the Atlantic with press conferences, parties and parades. There were television appearances, magazine spreads and two book contracts from Harper & Row. There hadn't been an adventurer of his stature since Charles Lindbergh.

Bob Manry's naive nautical achievement captured the imagination of a nation mired in political strife and social unrest. For almost three months, the tiny *Tinkerbelle* competed with the war in

Vietnam, inner-city race riots and an emerging culture war called the Generation Gap for front-page headlines across the country.

While Manry helped people recall a simpler time and celebrate old-fashioned values, he could not shield his own children, who were swept away by the turbulent times. The skills that aided him in his triumph over the perilous North Atlantic were little help when human nature and fate combined to rain hell into his once-idyllic home life.

Douglas Manry and his 14-year-old sister rode the media tidal wave that came behind *Tinkerbelle's* odyssey. The memories of those experiences and the way they played out are bittersweet for the siblings even today.

For the Manrys, the park in Willowick is doubly symbolic. The carved wood sign, with the image of *Tinkerbelle* and the words "Manry Park," represents a period in their lives when the world seemed a place of endless possibility and promise, an experience that marked their lives and relationship forever. In retrospect, the park is also the place where few today even know who their father is or what he accomplished. It's also where Douglas once spent the night while homeless.

When Bob Manry set his course June 1, 1965, he knew there would be trouble on the horizon. He just had no idea how much. Or how deep it would run for those he loved most.

> Earlier . . . Robin and Douglas had broadcast the news to their
> friends that we were going to get a boat, so nearly all the children
> of the neighborhood were waiting for us on our return home.
>   – From the book *Tinkerbelle*, by Bob Manry

An ad for a 30-year-old, 13½-foot Whitecap class sailboat, selling for $160, catches Bob Manry's eye. In 1958 dollars, it isn't inexpensive. It becomes the *Plain Dealer* copy editor's obsession, like a third child in the family, after daughter Robin and son Douglas.

Manry first caught sailboat fever when a speaker from Germany, visiting his high school class, gave a talk about his adventures on the high seas. After that day, he read many of the great seafaring accounts, and especially enjoyed Joshua Slocum's *Sailing Alone Around the World*.

At home in Willowick, he returns the boat to its former seaworthy state. The vessel becomes a center of family activity. The Manrys takes no vacation without hauling the little craft behind their station wagon. They enjoy camping and sailing *Tinkerbelle* on small lakes in and around Ohio and Pennsylvania, and in Canada. It's their golden time together, away from the bustle of suburban life.

Their summer vacations have all the warmth and humor of a 1950s family sitcom. Dad does know best when it comes to fixing anything. Mom lovingly cares for the kids. Robin and Douglas delight in the simple pleasures of popular culture. It's the dawn of rock 'n' roll, but their vacation photographs from the era look like a high school Home Economics film reel.

Although neighbors doubt *Tinkerbelle*'s aquatic reliability, Manry confounds them in the summer of 1964 when he and Douglas sail the boat 200 miles across Lake Erie in heavy weather. The newspaperman—described by colleagues as quiet and socially awkward—dreams of greater glory for his little craft.

In the winter of 1964, Manry first mentions to others a plan to make a trans-Atlantic voyage with an attorney friend in a 26-foot boat. No one seems impressed. When the lawyer—who was never identified—backs out at the last minute, Manry decides to go it alone. In *Tinkerbelle*. He tells only his family.

He plans extensively for potential disaster. He stuffs the boat with buoyant foam. He prepares for lightning, for navigating by the stars, for loss of food and water, for hull damage, for torn sails, even for a bout of appendicitis. He packs antibiotics for illness, and Dexedrine to stay awake.

On May 23, 1965, Manry, his wife, Virginia, and brother-in-law, John Place, tow the boat to Falmouth, Massachusetts. Douglas and Robin stay home with their grandmother, Blanche Place. Manry spends three days alone putting the final touches on *Tinkerbelle*.

Harbormaster Bill Litzkow is kidding when he asks Manry if he's off to England.

Manry has never been more serious in his life.

On June 1, he sets sail for Falmouth, England. As he shoves off, Manry hands the harbormaster a letter for *The Plain Dealer* informing his employers that he is sailing the Atlantic alone in *Tinkerbelle*. A few days later, after reading the note, a *Plain Dealer* editor realizes that Manry is news.

Sailing also helps to keep a man aware of his lowly place in the
universe, especially if that sailing involves celestial navigation
and its concern with the sun and the stars.
— From *Tinkerbelle*

Manry's first night at sea, luminescent microorganisms wash
over his bow, providing an electric vision that leaves him in ecstasy.
The next night he finds his boat dead in the water, in a dense fog,
in the middle of busy Atlantic shipping lanes. Manry sits, terrified,
as potentially deadly cargo ships pass on either side.

Manry has good days and bad. He battles storms and enjoys the
sun. *Tinkerbelle* sits still for hours at a time, "becalmed." On his
best day, he sails 87 miles at his top speed of about 7 knots, or 8
miles an hour.

The *Plain Dealer* stories begin appearing just days after his de-
parture. Reporters write about Virginia, the kids, neighbors and
the family pets. The paper even publishes one of Manry's letters
handed off to a passing ship. The Manry family articles are a hit
with readers. It doesn't hurt that Manry is a newspaper copy editor.
His colleagues at other papers around the country take an exceptional interest in his progress.

As Manry continues to sail east, he dips into his medicine bag to
stay awake during storms or favorable winds. One Dexedrine tab
keeps him alert for 20 hours. But then come full-blown hallucinations, both visual and auditory, that last for hours until he passes
out from exhaustion.

During two of his three major hallucinations, Manry's mind
conjures up peril for his family.

In the first, his daughter is kidnapped. In the second, assassins
target his son.

By the time he is three-quarters across the ocean he has been
swept overboard six times, saved only by a lifeline. He almost col-
lides with a sleeping shark, he breaks two rudders and, during the
first storm, he loses radar equipment. For a short time on the last
leg of the journey, he is reported lost. Royal Air Force planes begin
a search. After 24 hours there is still no word on Manry's location.
His relatives in New England are angered when reports on their
brother are cut short for news about Frank Sinatra and Mia Far-
row's wedding.

Manry has no idea his trip is causing a stir on both sides of the Atlantic. He left U.S. shores with no fanfare. He expects nothing more when he arrives. He has $700 to transport himself and his boat back to the States.

The international media swarms when it becomes clear that Manry will eventually reach British shores. The *Plain Dealer* is not about to miss out on a unique promotional opportunity. The paper offers to fly the Manry family to England to meet *Tinkerbelle.*

Robin protests. She says the kids in the neighborhood will consider that "stuck-up." Besides, she will miss seeing her new boy-friend at the Willowick Community Day fair at Dudley Park.

On August 9, with Manry some 300 miles out, *The Plain Dealer* is scooped. Channel 5 reporter Bill Jorgensen hires a boat to take him out to *Tinkerbelle* for a three-hour interview with Manry while the family and Team PD waits in England for his arrival. The tran-scripts of the television interview run in the rival *Cleveland Press.*

The *Plain Dealer* counters a week later by rushing Virginia Manry out to *Tinkerbelle* for pictures of the couple smooching joy-ously. Manry reaches Falmouth Harbor on Tuesday, August 17, at 7:30 p.m. He agrees to be towed in because of the danger of sailing with 300-plus vessels in the water, along with 50,000 people wait-ing on shore to greet him.

Manry is 40 pounds underweight but in good spirits. His cal-culations were impressively accurate. He arrives two days after his August 15 prediction and with plenty of food and water to spare. The pandemonium that greets him is almost more of a challenge for the shy, self-deprecating Manry than 78 days alone at sea.

> All I wanted to do basically was to achieve the dream of an ocean voyage I'd been harboring for nearly 30 years by crossing the Atlantic to England, and I wanted to do it with as little fuss as possible.
>
> – From *Tinkerbelle*

When Bob Manry lands at Falmouth Harbor, he goes down on all fours to kiss the ground. Falmouth Mayor Samuel A. Hooper is there to greet him with the throng. Everybody wants a piece of Bob Manry and his storybook adventure.

The crowd surges forward, cheering on Manry and his family. As Bob, Virginia, Robin and Douglas are swept down the dock by the crowd, Manry takes a last, sad glance back at his faithful *Tinkerbelle*. She kept him and his family's dreams alive on the water. Who will look after them now?

Every major news organization on both sides of the pond is represented in Falmouth. The *Plain Dealer* has a team of three. The British papers *Daily Mirror* and *Daily Express*, among others, are all over the *Tinkerbelle* landing. The BBC, AP and UPI are well represented. A young reporter named Dan Rather is there for CBS. Syndicated columnist William F. Buckley Jr. weighs in, calling Manry a hero. The *New Yorker* publishes a "Talk of the Town" item, saying Manry is a champion to copy editors everywhere.

It's a good time to be Bob Manry's kid. Your wish, their command. *Plain Dealer* publicist Russ Kane takes Douglas shopping for some cool Carnaby Street clothes. He buys hip-hugger pants, a leather wristband and pointy-toed Beatle boots known as "winklepeckers."

Daily Mirror photographer Eric Piper regales Robin with tales of his photograph sessions with the Beatles. She asks for a jar of mud from the Mersey River. "Beatle Mud." She gets it.

The Manrys are given the entire top floor of the Green Bank Hotel, the fanciest digs in Falmouth. Douglas tells reporters he has a thing for Shirley Eaton, the "golden girl" from the James Bond movie *Goldfinger*. She shows up, gives the boy a peck on the cheek and wrings the occasion for all the publicity it's worth.

The Manry circus rolls into London, where more press festivities await. The family stays at a much more upscale hotel than the Green Bank in Falmouth, eats at fancier restaurants and receives even more media attention. The *Plain Dealer* arranges for the family to take the *Queen Mary* ocean liner home, with *Tinkerbelle* on board.

To Douglas and Robin, it seems the dream will never end. Robin finds romance on the return trip. When the ship stops in France, another Bond girl, Claudine Auger from *Thunderball*, comes aboard to meet Bob Manry. The vaunted sailor is somewhere else on the ship. Douglas happens to be in the cabin and takes the introduction.

The *Queen Mary* docks in New York at Pier 90 after a five-day crossing. It's another flashbulb-popping, reporter-shouting media orgy.

Manry appears on three television shows while in New York: the

Today Show with Hugh Downs, *What's My Line?* with John Daly
and the *Steve Allen Show*. Allen asks Manry how he kept the little
boat afloat. Manry tells his host he filled the ship with polyethyl-
ene. "I thought you sailed alone," Allen quips to great laughs. Polly
Ethylene, get it?

While in New York, Manry also visits the office of *Life* magazine,
where he negotiates to sell his story and photographs.

When the Manrys land at Cleveland Hopkins Airport, there is
yet another crowd waiting. They are cheering and holding "Welcome Home" signs. Only the Beatles earned a more exuberant reception there. Manry is a celebrity at the dawn of celebrity culture.
And he's not even home yet.

> Did I have the right to endanger my life, even slightly, and
> consequently jeopardize the future of my family? . . . With much
> soul-searching I answered these questions in the affirmative,
> although I am willing to concede I may have been wrong in
> doing so.
>
> – From *Tinkerbelle*

More than 10,000 people turn out for a parade and party in
Manry's hometown of Willowick, followed by a luncheon at The
Willo restaurant for more than 400 select admirers. Bob Manry
is given a new Honda motorcycle, two portraits of himself, an en-
graved plaque, an honorary membership in the Kiwanis Club and
an award from Governor Jim Rhodes for the advancement of the
prestige of the state of Ohio.

The rock band The Twilighters plays its hit "Be Faithful," Bob
Manry gives a speech that day and his legend is secure.

All the while, Robin and Douglas keep each other's confidence.
They are beginning to wither under the *Tinkerbelle* spotlight. The
attention was fun, but now it's becoming frightening. The loss of
personal control is unnerving. They feel like public property. Emotionally, they cling to each other. Although they never feared for
their father's safety at sea, they now fear for their own at home.

Almost immediately after the family returns from England, people start to harass them.

It begins with prank phone calls. Hang-ups at first. Then people
come on the line saying Bob Manry is nuts. Some neighbors said he
was crazy before *Tinkerbelle* ever touched water. Now that Manry

has accomplished the impossible, it's like a slap in the face to some in the blue-collar suburb.

Douglas first realizes it's going on while shopping with his mother in downtown Cleveland. He hears her, distraught, confiding to a salesperson that people are questioning her husband's sanity.

What's this about, he recalls wondering.

On almost every garbage collection day someone kicks over the trash cans on their tree lawn. Things are ugly for Douglas, now 12, at school. He's wearing his hair longer than other boys in the seventh grade. He has cool clothes from England. He's an artist, not an athlete. The greasers, the "tough" guys, target him. They trip him in the hall. They spill his books. When the teacher isn't looking, they bounce basketballs off the back of his head in gym.

Robin, 15, isn't having much fun, either. She is accused of bragging about having met the Beatles. She never met them, nor said she did. But the gossip flies. Former friends turn on her. She often comes home from school in tears.

In the summer of 1966, the local outdoor recreation center in Willowick is renamed Manry Park. Bob Manry is still enjoying fame and popularity. But things become worse for his kids. Socially, Douglas and Robin are under siege.

Douglas peers out his front door every morning to make sure all the other kids have already walked to school. It's his way of avoiding his tormentors. But every time Manry Park is mentioned over the school public-address system, which is often, the teasing, the shoves, the catcalls begin anew. Douglas comes to despise his last name.

Bob Manry busies himself with his book, *Tinkerbelle*, and giving speeches about the adventure. He can't really relate to his kids' problems. Tension in the home builds. Virginia Manry is concerned enough to arrange for both children to see a therapist. Robin finds comfort in the sessions. The doctor offers Douglas "primal scream" therapy. But Douglas isn't interested in subconscious motivations.

In 1967, Bob Manry signs a book deal and uses the advance to buy a 27-foot sailboat, which he names the *Curlew* after a British waterfowl. He's sold the idea of sailing around the Eastern Seaboard of the United States with his family for a different kind of nautical narrative. This one involves attempting to communicate with two increasingly disaffected teenagers who want nothing to do with their square parents, much less spend a year with them on a small sailboat.

But the Manrys, including their dog, Chris, and their cat, Fred, set sail. They are gone a full year. Douglas keeps up with his schoolwork through a correspondence course. Robin opts to repeat her junior year in high school.

The kids and their parents argue frequently aboard the Curlew. Bob doesn't care for the kids' music, clothes or hairstyles. Or the surly, noncommunicative attitudes that accompany them. During port stops, police in the South harass Douglas because of his long hair. Several times they pick him up for vagrancy, then release him into his parents' custody. This only adds to the generational bickering on the boat.

But in other ports, the Manry kids, now 13 and 16, encounter sailors, free spirits and nonconformists who are pursuing an alternative lifestyle. They are hippies, and some of them have read Bob Manry's book. They want to meet him. Manry will have no part of them. He sees them as a bad influence on his children. The kids think their dad is being at best uptight, and at worst, a hypocrite.

The *Curlew* trip ends in late 1968, and Bob Manry prepares to write his book. The *Tinkerbelle* story is three years old and the demand for his speeches is waning. Robin and Douglas return to school. The *Curlew* voyage is one more reason for other kids to feel they are oddballs and outsiders. But local hippies, and there are some in Willowick, befriend the kids.

On May 3, 1969, Robin and Douglas skip school, cruise around in a friend's car and smoke a little grass. Their dad is in New York giving one of his *Tinkerbelle* talks and their mother is in Pennsylvania visiting their ailing grandmother. Later in the afternoon the kids drive by their house to find a police car in the driveway. They wonder if they were reported missing from school.

Police are there because their mother was killed that afternoon in a freak one-car accident on the Ohio Turnpike near Youngstown. Virginia Manry's mother, Blanche Place, had died at home the same day. Neither knew of the other's death.

The family is stunned. The Manry kids dread the future without their mom. She was always the more understanding parent and the go-between during the ongoing arguments with their dad. Virginia's death also gives them one more reason to despise their *Tinkerbelle* fame. Thanks to the attendant publicity, the obituary in *The*

Plain Dealer and the photo of the "Manry Death Car," the kids must now grieve publicly.

Some days later, Douglas is standing on a Willowick street corner when another kid drives by, slowing down only to shout, "Hey, Manry, your old lady died." Douglas simply shakes his head.

By 1970, Bob Manry is beset with woes he never imagined. The former sailing hero, best-selling adventure writer and famous family man is now a widower with two teenagers he hardly understands. He also is facing a book he cannot write because he is overcome with grief. His finances are shaky. He is lonely and in great personal pain. He begins to date, bringing more scorn from his kids.

The following year, Manry marries Jean Flaherty, a friend of his deceased wife. The enmity between the kids and their stepmother hangs in the air like poison. Two months after the marriage, Manry and his new wife are out with another couple. Manry suffers a massive heart attack.

The man who braved the Atlantic in a tiny wooden boat dies in the back seat of a car. He is 52.

> "Only 12 miles to go," I told *Tinkerbelle*.
>
> The thought brought on a faint stabbing of pain. The voyage was almost over. It was in its hoary old age, moving swiftly toward its end, its death.
>
> – From *Tinkerbelle*

Manry's will determines that insurance and savings, $42,000, as well as proceeds from the later sale of the family's house, will be divided among his widow and his two children. Robin and Douglas' aunt, Louise Manry, a copy editor from New York City, comes to live with them. She stays for a year until Douglas is 18 and graduates from high school. Louise Manry's heart breaks for her niece and nephew. All three are uncomfortably numb. There isn't much talk about their father's death, but Aunt Louise remembers feeling that his spirit is with them. She regards them as normal teens in abnormal circumstances.

After Louise Manry moves back East, Robin Manry takes her money and enrolls at Kent State University. Douglas takes a trip to an artist colony in St. Ives, England, where he is still remembered as the son of Bob Manry. He makes a small splash as a celebrity painter there, garnering some favorable reviews, but he feels lost and moves back to Ohio after about eight months.

Douglas can't access the rest of his inheritance money until he turns 19 in a few months. He doesn't drive and has no home or job. He's been living off $25 a week disbursed by his father's estate. For a time, he stays with Robin and her volatile, unstable boyfriend in Kent. When that doesn't work out, he stays with friends and neighbors in Willowick until the weather warms.

Without money, or real plans for the future, alone in the world, Douglas Manry finds himself homeless, sleeping in Manry Park or at Cresthaven Beach. On his first night huddled on the Manry Park aluminum pool bleachers he can't help but notice that at least this park has provided him with something. All he thinks about is returning to England to study painting once he has his inheritance.

In 1973, with less than $14,000 to his name, Douglas Manry returns to England, where he stays for eight months. He travels around, trying to start a new life for himself in a place where he had once felt so welcome, so special.

He finally realizes the glory is gone when he enters the Green Bank Hotel in Falmouth. There is nothing in the lobby or anywhere else that marks that once-happy, historic occasion of his father's landing.

The world has moved on, and now Douglas Manry must, too. He finds work on the iron ore boats of Lake Erie for a short time, and then takes a job as a banquet chef at the Cleveland Athletic Club in downtown Cleveland.

Today, Douglas still works at the CAC. He continues to paint and show his work whenever possible. He has been with his partner, Justine, for 18 years. They live in West Park with their dog, Juliet, and several cats.

Robin is single and lives in New York, where she moved in 1978. She works as a waitress and shares an apartment with her cat, Chavo.

Both Robin and Douglas have made peace with their past. And they wish their parents could have lived to know them beyond their rebellious teen period. The passage of time has given them a deepened appreciation for all their parents sought to provide.

Each year it's financially feasible, the two siblings travel back to the U.K. for a vacation. The last trip was in 2004 to the Isle of Skye in Scotland. They sometimes fantasize about buying an island in Scotland when one of them hits the lottery. Robin recently described their Skye vacation:

> A perfect place for Douglas and me. Mountains, moors, fog, sea. heather, ruins. Haunting beauty. We've been traveling together for over 10 years now and each [trip] is always the best. But Skye was something special. A wild, bleak countryside. It's great to explore a place together and reminisce, too. We understand each other very well, I think. We've always been close. What can I say? There is no one like a good brother.
>
> We don't know when our next trip will be. But we know there will be one—someday—and we have lots of great memories.

August 14, 2005

Information for this story came from:

Tinkerbelle (Harper & Row), Bob Manry's first-person account of his trans-Atlantic voyage.

Newspaper clippings from *The Plain Dealer* News Research Center.

Special Collections Librarians William Barrow and Cecilia Hartman of the Cleveland State University Library and Cleveland Memory Project.

Bob Manry's son, Douglas; daughter, Robin; and sister Louise Manry; current and former *Plain Dealer* employees including Alex Machaskee, Al Andrews, Russ Kane and Mike Roberts; and former *Life* magazine proofreader David Greisen.

Fred Landsman and Lynn Ischay, who confirmed the Willowick school experiences of Douglas Manry.

Steve Popovich, who reconstructed the Willowick celebration for Bob Manry.

Steve Peplin, who provided sailing and solo sailing records.

John Logue, who offered access to the boat *Tinkerbelle*, which the Western Reserve Historical Society owns.

CITY STREETS

J.J. CUISINE AND THE CASE OF THE THEATRICAL

I was sitting in my office on Thurman Street, savoring the successful completion of a job and considering cracking a cool bottle of Chardonnay in the refrigerated compartment of my desk.

It was a day like any other, only more so. I was feeling pretty pleased with myself, having just broken a goat-cheese counterfeiting ring. A couple of mugs were doctoring some damp dairy products and pawning them off on unsuspecting owners of nouvelle hash houses. I'd grabbed hustlers in the past pushing skim-milk mozzarella as the real thing and gave them some rhythm. But phony goat cheese? That's where I drew the line. You'd be surprised at the number of queer birds in the food racket. I've probably met every one of them.

The name, by the way, is Cuisine, J.J. Cuisine, just like it says on the door to my office. J.J. Cuisine, R.I.—Restaurant Investigator. I'm a professional food snoop, a privateer of the palate, a gourmet gumshoe, a slophouse dick. When a guy in the food business gets in a jam he can't handle, he comes to me. Like French champagne, I'm expensive but worth it.

I was in a good mood that day. Business had been booming. I was busier than a flea on a fat broad and needed some rest. I'd given my secretary, Bunny—a full-figured, rattle-brained doll—the day off. I was on the blower giving one of the boys over at the D.A. (that's Department of Agriculture in my line) the raspberries about the feds getting caught with their pants down on the goat-cheese caper when I noticed a skinny silhouette against the frosted glass of my door.

I got off the phone and hollered for whoever it was to come in. There stood some old guy in glad rags. He was well under 5 feet with a pencil mustache, pin-stripe suite and matching fedora. "What can I do for you, Pops?" I asked.

"My name is Vincent," he stammered, wringing his hat like a piece of pastry. "Short Vincent."

I'd heard the name. The guy was a legend. Emphasis on the word "was." Short Vincent had once been host to no less than eight restaurants and lounges on a street off East 9th that was only 485 feet long. We're talking one-eleventh of a mile. That was some years ago though, late 1940s and '50s. Things began falling off in the late '60s and now the only place left was the Theatrical, the restaurant that had originally anchored all the action.

Vincent told me a tale of woe that had my heart bleeding like a wet beef burrito. In the good old days, it seems, the street was like something out of a Damon Runyon novel. The nights were alive with guys and dolls, bookies and bustouts, show girls and be-bop boys. Gangsters, judges, entertainers and complainers all lent their threads to the warp and woof of a boom-town time that this city hasn't seen the likes of since. Besides the Theatrical there was Kornman's, the Frolics Café, Hollenden House's Crystal Room, the French Quarter, the 730 Lounge Bar, the Elbow Room and Les Gals.

Vincent regaled me with stories of yore. One about famed bar owner Hymie Mintz deciding to run for the state legislature and when asked about the Taft-Hartley bill replying, "I already paid it!" A story about inveterate gamblers Honest Yockim and Shoes Rosen flying back from a prizefight in Pittsburgh during a lightning and rainstorm of biblical proportions, wagering furiously on whether the plane would go down. Of a guy named Race-Horse Richard who actually ran against, and beat by 70 yards, a 3-year-old thoroughbred aptly named Hard Luck Joe out at Cranwood Park. This same guy had earlier offered to do some flagpole sitting for a charity bazaar held on that busy little street. He was the first one to see the tornado coming and hit the deck before the twister touched down in one place and one place only—Short Vincent's charity street fair, reducing it to rubble in seconds.

Vincent was an animated little dingus while he told these long-forgotten tales. He kept looking at me, trying to gauge my interest. I tried to appear indifferent because I knew exactly what he was getting at. I knew what he had come down for. This was just the comedy routine before the main event. He wanted me to help restore the Theatrical, the only jewel left on his tarnished crown. What could I tell the guy?

"Vince," I began as calmly as I could. "I just don't think I'm your man. We're talking about an institution of the past. This is a sucker's bet for me, a no-win proposition. I've got a very tough reputation in this town. I'm the golden boy of the bordeaux-and-brie business. The Theatrical is strictly a beef-and-booze joint. The place's popularity peaked before I was born. You're playing me for a sap, Shorty."

Vincent pleaded. The Theatrical was Cleveland history. Business was slow. It should be government-subsidized. It needed the attention of a new breed of eaters. It was like knocking down the Terminal Tower because the architecture had gone out of style. Something could be done, he insisted. Something *had* to be done.

"Look, Vince," I said, as sorry as I could be. "You don't understand my clientele. I do action painting with sauces, I admire aged balsamic vinegar, eccentric risottos, dangerous veal medallions, Provencal grand aoli, translucent sheet pasta embedded with whole herb leaves. I'm into dramatic texture contrast, dolphin-safe tuna, pecorino-encrusted salmon with green apple mint sauce and golden pepper vinaigrette. I'm talking tricolored mostaccioli and baby artichokes! Vince, pal," I said in a loud final sentence. "Am I getting through to you?"

He was a pitiful sight. His shoulders were hanging low and his eyes were on the ground. He was a broken man. He mumbled something about "Thanks anyway, sorry to disturb you." He turned and slowly shuffled out the door.

I felt as if I had just kicked the family dog. I kept telling myself I didn't have the time, I didn't need the money. Right in front of me I had a contract to help a guy with a specialty lettuce organization that would turn the produce industry upside down. I was busy. What could I do?

I jumped up from my desk and ran down to the street. I caught him waiting for the bus. "Vince, tell you what," I said. "I'm not promising nothing. I'll go down to the Theatrical, take a look around, talk to a few people. That's all I'm saying. I'm just saying here, I'm not talking. Capische?"

Old Vince lit up like Christmas tree and, with tears in his eyes, shook my hand. "J.J.," he said. "I know you can do it. If anybody can turn the Theatrical around, it's you. Go down there and talk to a guy by the name of Buddy Spitz. He's the owner. And hey, thanks a million."

I met Buddy Spitz for lunch the following Monday. Short Vincent offered to wait outside and watch my car. Parking had been tough. There was construction going on next door and that wasn't helping much. This is a swell bag of nails, I thought, making a mental note.

Spitz greeted me as I walked through the door. He was the kind of guy who knew a good-looking tie when he saw one, and wasn't afraid to wear it. I liked that. He wore his glasses halfway down his nose like someone who's always doing two things at once. Behind him, the restaurant opened up in a shimmering expanse of mauve and copper. The bar in the center of the room was enormous. There must have been 50 stools. Just behind the bar was an elevated bandstand with a big black grand piano looming above the action. The lunch traffic was brisk. The midtown suits were convening for their midday repast.

The room was lined with big, circular beige-leather booths where large men could eat huge meals and discuss monumental deals. On the walls hung tall spunglass and copper reproductions of Renaissance harlequins. A wall of multicolored glass squares that looked like stained glass from a chapel in Reno separated the bar and dining room from the kitchen. I'd been thrown out of better joints than this. But not many.

This was Vegas décor, circa 1950. The ambience was of opulence and largess. This was a restaurant for a man's man. A customer at the bar described the place to me as "the last bastion of male supremacy." Quaint in a way today. It has always been said of Sinatra, one of the few entertainers of that era who has not been to the Theatrical, that "Frank loves a big room."

This *was* that room.

Spitz took me to a booth in the corner known as Mushy's Table. The sightlines were superior. In his lifetime, Morris (Mushy) Wexler was the Theatrical. He opened the place in 1937 and ran it along with his Empire News Service—a race wire that offered bookies last-minute information on various sporting engagements. The shadow of illegality that eventually culminated in Wexler's investigation by a Senate committee for alleged mob ties only enhanced the Theatrical's reputation as a place to see and be seen.

"I married Mushy's daughter," Spitz told me. "When he called me up and told me I was working for him, I wasn't going to say no," he said, laughing. Spitz gave some background on the place. We talked about the highs and lows. I wanted to hear about the lows. It's my job. The place burned to the ground in 1960. Dire predictions for the end were rampant, but Wexler rebuilt the restaurant, gaining it even greater acclaim and popularity then before. I needed to know more about Spitz's current problems.

He told me times had changed. The eating and drinking habits of Americans had turned 180 degrees. A drink at lunch today is almost unheard-of, and those who do drink after work drive to taverns closer to home because of strictly enforced drunken-driving laws. Though more Clevelanders are coming downtown these days, they're going to Playhouse Square and the Flats. More hotels are supposed to go up downtown but that's going to take four or five years. Fortunately, Spitz owns not only the building but the land it stands on. He's got no landlord to support. Just 65 loyal employees.

Right now the construction of the Bank One building next door is gumming up the works with parking and traffic headaches. It's scheduled to be completed in August '91. Until then, Spitz has scaled back the Theatrical's usual 2 a.m. closing to 8 p.m. Monday through Thursday, and 9 on Fridays.

It wasn't much to go on, but I told Spitz I'd do what I could. I told him I'd need to speak freely with his customers and employees—past and present. He said he'd give me the straight dope. I told him I'd get back to him in a few days. I knew one thing for sure. This wasn't going to be duck soup.

I pulled some files from the morgue, I did some asking around. Two names kept reappearing: Shondor Birns and Danny Greene. Wise-guy racketeers who share the dubious distinction of being shredded by car bombs. Everyone I talked to at the restaurant said the same thing about the two. After awhile it got to be like a comedy routine.

About Shondor Birns: "Sure, he had a few legal problems, he did his business, *but* when he was in the Theatrical he was a perfect gentleman. Said hello, kept to himself, big tipper, nicely dressed, not a big eater, 1,000% a gentleman."

And on Danny Greene: "A quiet man, back booth, never drew attention to himself, a nice guy. No problems. Treated everyone great. Never a problem. A nice man."

I was expecting to hear the same thing from a query about Attila the Hun. "Had a temper, sure. Who wouldn't in his business? But when he was in here? Nothing but manners and style. We loved the guy."

The problem with the Theatrical was that crime, misdemeanor or felony, real or imagined, was its biggest draw and its biggest flaw. Finally I felt I was on to something. I made appointments to talk to some longtime employees.

Erma Fowler and Fannie Stein, the hat-check girls, have a combined total of 27 years racking and stacking lids for the Theatrical. I had to make an ungracious inquiry about their ages, which they graciously answered. Although they made me swear on my mother's grave I'd never reveal them. "I'll refer to you dolls as 'women of a certain age,'" I said.

"Make that 'uncertain age' young man," cracked Fannie. What a pip.

They talked fondly about the Theatrical. They said they'd seen everything there from the sublime to the ridiculous and ran down a list of almost-forgotten entertainers and celebrities. George Raft, Yul Brynner, Milton Berle, Arlene Francis, Liberace, Mitzi Gaynor, Jack Teagarden, Dean Martin, Henny Youngman, Edward G. Robinson, Perry Como. It went on. The two work only the fall and winter season, when the coats are heaviest and hats are more than a fashion statement. Erma talked about her dancing days when she worked the burlesque circuit. I had heard on the street that she played a mean trombone.

"I wasn't a nudie," she told me. "But back then they had policemen around the stage to keep the satyrs in line."

I asked how a couple of gorgeous broads like them had kept the wolves at bay all these years.

"We dealt with all of them," Erma told me. "I remember some of these guys telling me they were looking for a nice girl to go out with. I always told them 'If I went out with you pal, I wouldn't *be* a nice girl.'"

I cornered Randy Moroz who tickles the 88's evenings at the place and asked if the high rollers still come around. Moroz, who heads up the Randy Moroz Quartet, has been there only three years but still has a tale or two to tell.

"One night there was a guy at the bar who was tipping us $50 a song," he said. "The drummer had to go to the bathroom, but I told him to keep playing."

The late, great Glen Covington's band figures heavily into Theatrical legend. One night many years ago a prominent local attorney was sitting at the bar with his date when he felt someone poking him in the head. He turned around to see some big palooka point-ing a .45 up his nose.

"It looked as big as a cannon," recalled the barrister. "The guy was stiff as a board and kept saying, 'I don't like you.' I did some quick thinking and said, 'I don't think Tony Milano would appre-ciate this.' Tony Milano was a big guy in the mob back then. The guy's hand dropped like a rock. 'You know Tony Milano?' Then he wouldn't quit bugging me. He was apologizing and trying to buy me a drink. I just wanted him to leave me alone. Finally he asked me what my favorite song was, Just to get rid of him I said, 'It's Impossible.' Next thing I know he's pointing the gun at Glen Cov-ington up on the piano and saying, 'Play It's Impossible'!" Glen, who was black, turned white, and played the fastest version of 'It's Impossible' you ever heard. Finally somebody got the nut out of there."

Then there's the generic Theatrical Sports Anecdote. It involves a major-league ballplayer of your choice. He was in the Theatrical drunker than a banshee. Couldn't even walk. With the help of a hooker, or two, depending on who's telling it, and two bottles of bubbly, the major-league ballplayer heads loudly back to the hotel in a car provided by the restaurant. The bar patrons, witnessing all this, bet heavily against the guy's team the following day and he a) pitches a no-hitter, b) hits three home runs, c) all of the above.

But for every bout of bad behavior, there's a tale of generosity or human kindness that doesn't leave a dry orb in the house. Bill Veeck, whose 1948 Indians won not only the league pennant and World Series but the hearts of all Clevelanders, was at the bar one night when an admiring fan sent him a glass of beer. In typical Veeck fashion, he found out what kind of beer the guy drank and sent him a keg.

A local newspaperman put it this way, "The bookies were like greeters out of Caesars Palace in Vegas. They'd shake your hand, inquire about your health and family, ask you how you thought the Indians or Browns were going to do that season and buy you a drink. They were like PR men. Then the bartenders were like co-medians. They didn't just pour you a drink. They did a routine for you. And they were some of the funniest guys in the city."

Many Theatrical anecdotes had two acts. The first one took place on the street, the second usually in a municipal court room. Like the one about aforementioned bookmakers Honest Yockim and

Hymie Mintz. The two were booking $2 bets and the beat police-
man kept popping them and dragging them into court. The judge,
who some claim was a horseplayer himself, was irritated that the
cops kept taking his time with these harmless nickel-and-dime violations and kept throwing the case out of court for lack of evidence.
The cops came back with a newspaper, which carried the race results. The judge threw it out. They came back with the racing form
itself. Judge threw it out. Finally the judge said, "I wouldn't charge
these guys if you brought the damn horse up here!"

"If I wrote a book about this place, I'd call it 'I Changed the
Names to Protect the Guilty,'" said Morrie Fisher, who was the Theatrical's night manager and maitre d' for 28 years. "My wife used
to yell at me, saying, 'You son of a bitch, I know you got a broad in
town!' I'd say, 'What are you talking about?' She'd say, 'Nobody can
be as happy as you are to go to work!' She was right. I loved coming in here. Every night was an adventure. You never knew who
was going to come through the door or what was going to happen.
The night Shondor Birns got killed the woman who ran the bar he
had just come out of called me. I said, 'Gee I'm sorry to hear that, I
liked Shondor a lot, but why are you calling me?' 'I couldn't think
of anyone else to call,' she says."

"In the early '60s," continued Fisher, a tan, handsome version
of Danny DeVito, "the Theatrical was the largest dispenser of li-
quor in the state of Ohio. Back then there were three newspapers
in town and every day we were in one of them. It was like a giant
neighborhood tavern. I spent more years with Mushy Wexler than
I did with my own father who died when I was 25. What a guy he
was. We had our nights, we had our fights.

"One night after I talked him into buying an oxygen tank some
guy faints. Those things were big and complicated back then. It
had three dials. I get it over to the guy and turn everything on.
Mushy's right behind me turning everything off. We're screaming
at each other, it looks like a comedy routine and this guy's turning
blue. We took care of him, he was all right.

"People knew how to enjoy themselves back then," Fisher said.
"They were more carefree. Today it seems people are drinking to
forget. There's an edgy, desperate manner in the way people drink
these days.

"I remember lawyers in here playing Liar's Poker with dollar
bills and keeping score on our white tablecloths. One night, late, a

couple of them came back in after an argument over the score and made me go into the laundry and get their tablecloth. They took it home with them.

"We had a few incidents in here over the years, but in 28 years I could count on one hand the ones that came to anything. We were good at heading off trouble before it began. Every night I'd walk around the bar greeting everybody and giving them a little pat on the side to see who was packing. That way I knew who to look out for," he said.

"There was a guy named Spats; nice guy, lousy thief. He got caught at everything he ever did. One night he comes in with a girlfriend and has another one sitting two tables away. These two go at it, pulling hair and kicking. One of them has a wig on, which goes flying across the room and lands right on my head. That's the kind of stuff I'll never forget."

I wrapped up the interviews and headed back to my office to sift through this hoard of history and hairy stories. I looked through my notes, read some of the files from the morgue and perused a Theatrical menu. The case of the Theatrical was going to be one tough nut to crack. I just couldn't seem to get a handle on it.

After a little swift dictation I sent Bunny home for the day and decided to cruise the Flats and see what the competition was up to. Something Morrie Fisher had said was bothering me and I didn't know why. He had told me that there were two generations of kids out there who didn't know the Theatrical existed, who didn't know what going to a classy restaurant was all about. Granted, it seemed the Theatrical hadn't done much to cultivate this crown, and changing the menu or putting in new carpet was too little too late.

Then again, what about tradition? The Theatrical represented a golden era of sorts. It had witnessed World War II, and, the rarest of all things, an Indians' World Series. The Theatrical was a passage back to a more simple time. The problem was trying to attract a crowd that had no memory of that time. What, if anything, could be done about that?

I was as guilty as the rest. Before the invest I had been as ignorant as anyone from my generation about that bustling period of Cleveland's past. I made my living assisting people who were continually trying to reinvent the culinary wheel. I was no archaeologist.

I stood on the banks of the Cuyahoga watching the Flats Brats, the juiced and moussed, nattily attired in their neon sports shorts, staring glazedly through their rainbow-tinted Oakley racing shades. Those hip sippers of Corona and Amstel Light; sockless groove thangs; daylight drinkers who couldn't imagine a beer without a boat or a Rum Rickey without a river to ruminate upon. Could it be explained to them that things weren't always thus? Would it matter if I could?

What if I told them about a time when decadence ran toward the shadows and the imbibing of alcoholic libations was mainly a manly art, that there was a kingdom of characters they would have loved to know? Would they believe this was when gangsters, not savings and loan officers, robbed banks? When you had to drive downtown to a burlesque theater to see a woman of questionable virtue in various states of undress instead of just flipping on MTV? A time when men were guys and women were dolls, when booze was illegal and you could get cocaine from the corner drugstore. When the flagpole got more attention than the flag and gambling was about bust-outs betting a few beans, not Charlie Hustlers doing time for tax evasion. It would be a crime, I thought, to let that epoch fade away.

Then it hit me like a load of linguini. Crime! That was the Theatrical's special allure, crime and criminals. That's what made it sexy. That's where most of the great stories and memories came from. That's who the most memorable characters were.

The problem was that the Theatrical's selling point was usually only whispered about after hours. Mushy Wexler, Milwaukee The Book, Squeaky Hilow, Race-Horse Richard, Mustache Mike, Fuzzy Lakis, Heigh-Ho Silver all may be gone, but they don't have to be forgotten. If people knew what a treasure-trove of hilarious history was ensconced in that glittering grotto between 9th and 6th, they'd beat a path to the Theatrical's door. But there would have to be something there for them to see when they did.

Buddy Spitz had said to me, "If only these walls could talk. Could you imagine? I can imagine. And those walls *could* talk. It would take some interior revamping and a bit of a PR campaign, perhaps a grand reopening, but it could be done.

First thing you do, name all the booths after these characters with plaques or pictures bearing their names. The beloved harlequins on the wall will have to go. You replace them with the Theatrical's real harlequins—namely giant, old blown-up (excuse the pun, Shondor and Danny) photos of these guys lining the walls. You could do the same with old newspaper clippings.

If you really wanted to soup it up a bit, you'd hang violin cases on the walls and betting slips and racing forms. Get rid of the multicolored window in the back and replace it with old photos of all the great jazz combos and performers who passed through those doors. Another wall could house pictures of the sports legends who drank and danced up those aisles.

Instead of just talking about the past, the Theatrical needed to celebrate it loudly with music and pictures from its infamous eras. It could be a Hard Rock Café of Crime, A Movie-Tone Newsreel of Entertainment, A Baseball, Football and Horse Racing Hall of Fame.

The old customers would come back to marvel in the memories and new customers would come to learn about the past. Rename the offerings on the menu after the famous people who ate there, just like the Carnegie Deli in New York. Then the restaurant would start living up to its name. Then a meal there would truly be a *Theatrical* experience.

I went back to the office and got on the horn. "Shorty," I said, "Your worries are over."

"J.J.," he said. "You're aces, kid."

September 23, 1990

SAVING CENTRAL

Councilman Frank Jackson fights to rid ward 5 of drug dealers, prostitutes and 'neglect by design'

Cleveland Councilman Frank Jackson is sitting in his ramshackle headquarters at East 55th and Central late one cold and sunny Saturday afternoon, explaining how much meaner the mean streets of Ward 5 have become since the days of his youth.

"Back then if people were doing drugs, they were smoking marijuana. Now people smoke crack. Back then if there was a fight, it might be two dudes who . . . " Jackson pauses as he looks out the window across the street at the Carver Park housing project.

"Oh my," he says, reaching for the phone he keeps in the top right-hand drawer of his desk. "Somebody's getting stomped out there."

Outside, a half-block away, a pack of eight or so teenagers has come out of the project yard and descended viciously upon two men. One man lies unconscious on his back in the street, while the other tries helplessly to fend off a hailstorm of whipsaw kicks and punches.

Jackson is on the phone talking with EMS. "I'm telling ya," he insists, "the man needs help."

Moments later Jackson is on the street, one of a small crowd gathered to help the fallen man whose swollen face is bleeding from the nose and mouth. The teenagers have dispersed, running back into the labyrinth of buildings that make up Carver Park.

Cuyahoga Metropolitan Housing Authority police and the Cleveland police are there in minutes, followed shortly by an ambulance. Once the police arrive, more and more onlookers appear, including small children who gather around the bleeding men. Unimpressed, they move on, following Jackson who is busy talking to people, trying to find out what caused the attack.

Back at headquarters 15 minutes later, Jackson is reminded he was discussing the neighborhood and how it has changed.

"Well, case in point," he says, gesturing out the window.

The councilman adds "Youth Gang Task Force" to the list of phone calls he has been trying to reduce all afternoon. Every time he makes a call, someone else stops by with a request. But Jackson never flags. He serves his constituents whenever and however he can. And in Ward 5, home to the largest number of Cleveland's poor, roughly 24,000, the need for service is never ending.

During that Saturday, Jackson spoke with a woman whose year-in-the-restoring house had been robbed of every antique vestige. He helped a man decipher a letter about his Social Security. He talked with two constituents about drug activity in their apartment buildings. He spoke with a recovering alcoholic who had been through rehab and was doing fine. A young woman who had been drinking came in and asked for $2. He gave her one. Another young woman wanted to get on a list to be considered for a summer job. A young homeless man wanted to get on the waiting list for a CMHA apartment. A "strawberry" (a young crack-addicted woman) came in and offered to mop his floor for $5. Jackson just kept adding names and numbers to his list, making more calls when he got the chance.

"These streets today are very unforgiving," Jackson says. "Used to be you could make a mistake out there and recover. Now you smoke crack once, and it's your life. You have sex with the wrong person once, and you have AIDS. You cross the wrong person once, and you're dead. You fall through the cracks in the system once, and you're homeless."

With his distinguished graying beard and almost perfectly coifed corona of buoyant black hair, Jackson could pass for a Roman senator. But he talks quietly and thoughtfully in the slow cadence of someone well-versed in the vernacular of the inner city.

"A lot of people consider these folks lost. But I can't do that. When I took office, I was sworn to provide for the safety, health and welfare of the people in my ward. I take that oath seriously.

"People think that housing and jobs and medical care are some kind of special favor," he adds. "These are things the people of Cleveland rightly deserve. They are entitled."

And Jackson, who chairs the council's Health and Human Services Committee, says he will work to see that they get them. Inevitably, when asked where the money will come from, he has a ready answer: "I always say, 'Look at Gateway.' Gateway is the No. 1 lesson you should learn about this city. Cleveland can do anything it wants when it has the will. When the political, corporate and civic lead-

ers of this city make up their minds to do something, they make it
happen, you see.

"It's all a matter of where the priorities are. And when you look
around, it's obvious that their priorities have nothing to do with
improving the lives of the people of Cleveland. We see billions in
tax incentives and development, and the people of Cleveland get
none of it."

With two years as a councilman behind him, Frank Jackson has
made an impression on both colleagues and constituents. At a time
when respect for political officeholders is at an all-time low, when
the mere mention of the word "politician" brings to mind over-
drafts, padded expense accounts, patronage, theft, sleaze, slime
and cynical indifference, Frank Jackson is a paragon of political
virtue. His only observable vice is eating barbecue and pizza late
at night. While reporters who cover City Hall will imitate his slow,
soft-spoken speech, make jokes about his beat-up Ford Tempo or
scoff at what they see as his unrealistic solutions, none questions
his sincerity or depth of commitment.

"You don't get too much sincerity in politics," says Roldo Barti-
mole, Cleveland political pundit and tireless City Hall watchdog.
"What he is about is what he can do for the people in his ward.
He follows Mike White on the major issues and then trades those
votes for things his ward needs. He has such horrific problems in
his ward, I can't blame him for doing what he can."

The 45-year-old Jackson is a study in contrasts. At council
meetings, he speaks only when he has something to say. Yet he also
keeps a very high profile as far as drugs and prostitution go. He's
not at all shy about holding news conferences in front of hotels that
cater to prostitution or cruising drug houses at night to let dealers
know he knows who they are and what they're doing.

One of the ways Jackson has hurt the drug and prostitution business has been to go after those who come in looking for it. He discovered his ward had been turned into a marketplace for drugs and
sex for people from the suburbs. In the last two years, 1,000 johns
have been arrested for soliciting sex in Ward 5. Jackson would like
to see potential drug customers treated the same way.

"If people from my ward were cruising Pepper Pike, they'd certainly be stopped by the police," he says. "Why can't we do that
down here?"

While Jackson will not abide the sale or use of drugs, or pimping or prostitution, he neither judges nor condemns those who do. He abhors the crime, not the criminal.

"Not many survive the conditions that make up neighborhoods like the ones in Ward 5," Jackson says. "That's why I can't judge these people. I don't think I'm in any way superior to them and they know that. I made some choices and I was lucky. I can't take credit. I'm not where I am today because I'm wise or by my will. I didn't get here on my own."

How Jackson did get there has a lot to do with his family, who lived first at East 83rd and Kinsman before moving to East 38th and Central 30 years ago. He still lives there, next door to his mother, with his wife of 17 years, Edwina, a social worker. (Jackson's father died in 1977.)

The Jacksons had four boys and one girl. George Jackson was a factory worker and his wife, Rose, a homemaker.

Jackson doesn't brag about his upbringing, insisting it was nothing out of the ordinary.

"We didn't go without, there was no hatefulness in our family," he says, adding, "My parents were strict. There was no cussin', fussin' or fighting. But there wasn't a lot of talk about it, either. We weren't big churchgoers. You just knew what to do."

Jackson's scholastic career was somewhat less than exemplary. He failed third grade three times and maybe another year as well. He's lost count. But what he does remember, is being 13 in the sixth grade and 20 as a senior in high school. He even got a rare high school deferment for the draft.

"I never thought anything I did or didn't do would keep me from passing. And there were lots of kids in the same position. I was bored most of the time and would just work on the things that interested me, like history. My mother used to say I must have been dropped on my head as a child," he says.

"Actually, Frank was dropped on his head," says Jackson's younger brother Anthony, now commander of Cleveland's 4th District police station. "We always like to kid him about it. But Frank was the level-headed one in the family. He thought about things before he spoke. He was not impulsive. He was quiet until he knew what he wanted to say."

Jackson was drafted shortly after his graduation from Max Hayes High School in 1966. He spent 18 months in Camranh Bay in Vietnam working in a supply depot safely out of reach of the fighting just across the bay. The lesson he learned there was about people.

"I really learned that people are the same all over the world. They all want the same things. No matter what culture, no matter where you go."

After coming home from Vietnam, Jackson knocked around at a few jobs, then ran the streets for a year or so until he realized his options were winding down to four: get strung out, go to jail, die or go to school on the GI Bill. Jackson got an associate degree at Cuyahoga Community College, double-majored in urban studies and history at Cleveland State University and got his master's at CSU in urban studies. He earned money while at CSU's law school, working in the clerk's office at Cleveland Municipal Court under Zeke Forbes. He later became a hearing officer for the Parking Violations Bureau. After three tries, Jackson passed the bar and then-Chief Prosecutor Patricia Blackmon hired him to work in the Cuyahoga County prosecutor's office.

"She said that she ought to hire me because no one else would," says Jackson.

Blackmon, now a judge in the Ohio Court of Appeals (8th District), remembers Jackson as being "very controlled, methodical and deliberate in his work. He surprised me by being so thorough. Initially I thought he was naive, but he understood the process much more than I knew," she says. "As a politician, he's honest and truthful and sad as it is to say, there's so few who are. . . . In a neighborhood that the world has forgotten, he builds people into his scheme. He doesn't write them off. I have a lot of respect for him."

It's a Tuesday night in March and Jackson is riding around Ward 5 with CMHA commissioner Dwayne Browder, a friend and colleague who has lived in public housing for 20 years. They have just left the Lonnie Burten Recreation Center on East 46th Street, where Browder has been training some kids for the Golden Gloves finals that week.

The two stop to thank a social worker who has helped them with a public housing family's drug-related problem. Then it's over to the house of another family who Jackson helps wade through a sea of bureaucratic red tape regarding their utilities. Along the way, they drive by the six major housing estates that hold some 5,000 public-housing units. The average income in Ward 5 is $4,500 a year. Jackson points out that his ward has the most vacant land

in the city, something he believes should make it attractive to de-
velopers who would like to push the poor out and put highways
through.

"The reason I ran for City Council," Jackson says, "is that I could
see the scheme to get rid of public housing. For years, these neighborhoods have suffered from deferred maintenance, a kind of neglect by design, you see. Then the political, corporate and civic
leaders can come down here and say the neighborhood isn't viable.
I couldn't sit by and let that happen. If I did, I might as well go sit
down for the rest of my life."

Gazing west toward downtown, Jackson surveys the night sky-
line and what he feels is the impending approach of doom for his
ward.

"Look at the new Convocation Center, look at Gateway; it's all
moving this way. I ask for more money for these neighborhoods
and they'll give me just enough to fail. Then they feel like they've
proven their point. They say the neighborhood's not viable, you see.
Their solution to getting rid of poverty, of crime of neglect, is to
get rid of the people. I say if you want to point to poverty, let's talk
about jobs. If you want to point to crime, let's talk about law enforcement. If you want to point to health and safety, let's talk about
drug treatment."

Jackson gets about as angry as you'll ever hear him. He doesn't
get louder but sounds weight-of-the-world weary, as if overbur-
dened by the banality of repetitious wrong. It's always the same
thing.

"They just don't want to spend their resources on poor black
people. That's what it always comes down to. As if these people
aren't worth spending the money on. If you take care of the services, Central will take care of itself."

It's 10:15 when Frank and Dwayne stop at Webb's restaurant for
some takeout barbecue. The owner, a man with a .38 tucked in
his pants, tells Jackson about some drug dealers who shot out his
windows and offers his restaurant's services for any more Habitat
for Humanity house-raisings. The barbecue gets cold as Jackson
delivers a City Council proclamation to a constituent whose sister
died that week. Jackson heads home at 11. Just another 16-hour
day in Ward 5.

The people populating the upper echelons of Cleveland's decision-making mountain have nothing but respect for Jackson.

Mayor Michael R. White puts it like this: "Most people believe the P in politics stands for political, but for Frank Jackson it stands for people and that's increasingly important today in the bump and grind of political office. He's a hard-working, service-oriented councilman who speaks to the issues that concern his ward."

But all the personal accolades in the world won't get decent housing, or jobs, or a crime- and drug-free environment for the people of Ward 5. On April 1, Jackson and Councilwoman Fannie Lewis, D-7, walked out of a meeting in Columbus on the General Assistance cuts after only four minutes. "It was some folks telling us how the cuts were actually going to benefit people. I decided I'd rather be outside with the people raising hell." When asked if he was unmoved by Gov. George Voinovich's tears on television that day, Jackson said, "There's plenty of tears without his."

Friday night. It's getting late at Jackson headquarters. The neighborhood folks have left the street, and are being replaced by the drunks and the drug-addicted. As nighttime creeps in, out come the freaks and Central begins to get scary. A young girl comes into the office with six or seven young children in tow. One child complains of cold feet, and the others ask the councilman if there will be a street carnival in Ward 5 this summer. After sending them on their way, Jackson talks about how he finds the strength to carry on against discouraging if not surpassing odds.

"I set certain goals for myself that I would like to see accomplished," he says. "I know I'm not going to change the world. I see myself as a person in time. In my time I'm going to do what I can. I think every black person has a duty and a responsibility to give back to where they came from. Compassion burnout is the philosophy of the heathen. Only artificial compassion can burn out. Does your love for your child burn out?

"I always think of a story in the Old Testament where this guy was all alone rebuilding a temple. All his friends came by and said, 'Come on down from there and party with us. Let's eat, drink and be merry.' He just looked at 'em and said, 'But the work is not done.' So I don't think I'm being noble. I feel like I owe. What right do I have to stop the work?'

May 10, 1992

MEDICAL DRAMA

Life and death in the emergency department

It's a full-moon Saturday night in February in the Emergency Department at MetroHealth Medical Center on West 25th Street. If lunar lore holds true, what used to be called the Emergency Room should live up to its name.

Earlier in the day, a man, his face opaque-pink and puffy from burns suffered in a grease fire, is Life Flighted by helicopter from University Hospitals. The Metro Life Flight crew, Dr. Karen O'Neill and nurse Anne Parker, sometimes referred to as "The Chicks In Charge," accompany the man from UH. As they wheel him to the elevator, the man wants to know where he'll be flying to next.

"You're here, sir," says Parker. "This is the place."

The place. The place you never want to be. But when there, enormously grateful. Where sometimes modern medicine mixes with miracles. And where other times, there's nothing left but a heavy shake of the head and a quiet breath.

It's the place where so many bad ideas—drinking and driving, handguns and Seconal—turn into physical calamity. It's the Shrine of the Second Chance, where "dead on arrival" is also known as "diagnose and adios." It can be the first stop for intense medical intervention or the last stop for the pulse. It's the place, all right. A vortex often spilling over with disaster and deliverance. You never want to be here. You hope.

Which is why some people in the medical community are drawn to just this kind of work. It might be said that these people are enticed by the excitement, the pressure, or the wide variety of medical experience an Emergency Department provides.

Emergency medicine, as a board-certified specialty, began in the late '70s. Before that, Emergency Room work was something every doctor, resident and some nurses had to do as part of their regular training and/or job. The hours are long (12-hour shifts are not uncommon), and the patients often obnoxious, if not dangerous.

As a doctor, it's your job to quickly differentiate between the dying, sick and stupid. Not to mention the guy who's looking for a free cup of coffe and a cab voucher to a homeless shelter. The atmosphere can be unnervingly chaotic. It's difficult to imagine a Norman Rockwell rendering of the modern-day Emergency Department at full-tilt boogie. Surreal illustrator Ralph Steadman's black-ink, slop-horror style would be far more appropriate.

Nurse Kathy Chohaney is one of the many Emergency Department afflicted. "It's the adrenaline," she says. "There have been times in the summer where I've been in the Trauma Room for six hours straight. You go from one to another. It can be draining."

The upside? "The variety is appealing. Every shift is different problems, different challenges. And then there are the homeless people we see again and again. They provide the continuity."

MetroHealth's Emergency Department, which saw 62,000 patients last year, is actually a block or so off of West 25th. But you can't miss it—if you make the turn. The big white letters spelling EMERGENCY against the red background hit you as you come around the corner. On this bone-chilling night, everything is quiet outside—and in. People sit and sleep in the reception area. A television is on for those willing to watch repeat episodes of *Star Trek* as they wait. It's kind of appropriate.

Once you get past the locked doors to the Inner Sanctum, it's not that different from the helm of the Enterprise. There's a large half-circle counter where patients check in and behind which the staff gathers and operates the Big Machine.

Divided into two sections, acute and non-acute, the place could easily pass for a spaceship bent on life-and-death exploratory adventure. They have the space-age machinery, the high-tech lingo ("234 has been trached and intubated, where's the Haldol for 236?"). They wear uniforms even though they lack the military cuteness found on *Star Trek* or, say, in Michael Jackson's closet. But there's nothing fictional or especially fantastic about this set.

Acute could mean anything from a gunshot wound (GSW) to a motor vehicle accident (MVA) to a heart attack or stroke. Non-acute sees a lot of children with everything from sniffles on up. It all goes on the big board, which lists who's in, what they're in for, who's attending to them and what their degree of emergency is ("1" means impending death, while "4" is sniffles).

Thanks to advanced technology and increased knowledge of

Emergency Department staff members, you're less likely to die here. On the other hand, because of automatic weapons and the proliferation of drugs and drug use, your chances decrease. The solution to that equation? Stay healthy.

Clinical Assistant Lisa Marko states it quite succinctly during her dinner break. "People are living longer," she says. "And meaner."

It's two weeks later, a Friday night, and Dr. Norman Christopher is looking at the X-rays of an elderly woman who has suffered a massive cerebral hemorrhage.

"It's not good," he says. "You can see here that the blood has spread almost completely though her brain. At this point, there's very little we can do. We have her on life support, but beyond that it will be the family's decision."

Her family is there—husband, sons, wives, grandchildren—and a priest. An hour later, the woman dies with her family gathered around her in a small room just off the center of the department. There are tears and embraces. A team from the coroner's office has come for the body. Before leaving, one son, his eyes red and wet, manages a smile as he thanks a nurse for her help.

But many situations that bring patients to the Emergency Department are not that dramatic. And the origins of street conflicts are often questionable. Dr. Greg Fedele, a second-year resident, explains "The Two-Dude Syndrome."

"A patient will come in banged up and drunk at 2 a.m. We ask what happened and the response is, 'I don't know, man, there I was minding my own business when these two dudes came out of nowhere and jumped me.' There are the patients who come in at odd hours with horrible infections, swollen limbs, contusions, lacerations and many other potentially life-threatening ailments. When asked how long they've been in that condition, the response is often, 'Oh, about two weeks.'

And then there are people who use the Emergency Department like a free Doc-in-the-Box. The word they seem to have trouble understanding is "emergency." A cold is not an emergency. A sprained toe is not an emergency. A headache, under most conditions, is not an emergency. Rashes, coughs, hangovers and bad-hair days do not qualify as emergencies. Yet the staff at MetroHealth sees all that and more on any given day or night.

While some patients have a problem with that first word, the staff has had problems with the second: department. Up until the late '70s, it was known as the Emergency Room. It may seem like a trivial question of semantics to outsiders, but to men and women who have been board-certified in emergency medicine, it makes a difference.

"It's really about respect," says Dr. Nick Jouriles. "It's not just a room and we're not doctors who just happen to be here. In the same way, they don't call it the Pediatrics Room or the Intensive Care Room, this is a department that has highly trained people who have specific skills that are suited to this area of medicine. But there are people who work here who still call it the E.R. It's just out of habit."

"Basically, our job is to evaluate and stabilize—quickly," says Dr. Jeff Pennington. "The trend among medical students is to specialize. Children, knees whatever. They concentrate specifically on one area. Emergency medicine requires that you know a lot about a lot of areas. Everything from serious trauma, gunshot wounds or motor vehicle accidents, to neurology, dermatology. That doesn't appeal to everyone. We have a limited amount of time in most cases to diagnose and treat. It's rare that we get to follow through with one patient. On the other hand, the experience you get here with the volume of patients gives you an amazing education."

The question of job burnout is one that comes up often. How long can a doctor or nurse take the frantic pace, the long hours and the regular percentage of patients who are abusive and disorderly? Some say 12 years, some say five. But others say that burnout was more of a problem before emergency medicine became a specialty.

"Emergency medicine attracts people who like excitement and edge work. They're also people who love to learn and have a low tolerance for boredom," says Dr. Brent Morgan. "I love the nurses here. They don't take shit from anybody. They walk that line between being compassionate and tough."

Nurse Chohaney agrees. "I always tell my mother she should have named me Mary Frances, the way I get called a 'motherfucker' by some of the patients who come through here.'

At 5 a.m. on a Friday night/Saturday morning that seems uneventful by Emergency Department standards, things take a quick lurch toward activity. Dr. Karen Villalba, the attending physician, is alerted by the Life Flight dispatching crew that two patients, one

an intoxicated male from Amherst who fell through the ice of a
creek, and another man, also intoxicated, from Sandusky, who was
beaten up in the Flats, will arrive soon.

Another call comes in. EMS will be bringing in a male with a
gunshot wound to the abdomen. He is characterized as violent.

A team of surgeons, doctors, nurses and radiation technologists
gather in Room 242, also known as the Trauma Room. Since two
of the arrivals are intoxicated and the other is considered violent,
everybody dons maximum surgical gear, which includes gowns,
gloves, head and shoe covers as well as plastic face masks to guard
against the possibility of HIV-infected blood splashing into eyes,
nose or mouth.

The male from Amherst arrives first. The information that's
been gathered indicates he had been drinking, had a fight with his
fiancee and walked out of his house to relieve himself in a nearby
creek. He walked out on the ice, fell through up to his waist and
was there for two hours before being discovered. The immediate
concerns of hypothermia and frostbite are alleviated as his temperature is near normal.

He bypasses the Trauma Room and is taken to an "acute room"
in front of the main desk. Even though the patient has not taken a
drink for several hours, he still is drunk and extremely belligerent.
Security is called to help transfer him from the EMS gurney to the
hospital bed. The tangle of his intravenous bag, oxygen mask and
the leather straps that secure his arms and legs make this a difficult
maneuver. Not to mention that the man is resisting the doctors,
nurses and security men with all his inebriated might. There is a
large tattoo on his left arm. In Emergency Department lore, the
more tattoos a patient has, the better his chances of living.

Back in Room 242, the gunshot-wounded male has been brought
in. He's also bound in "leathers." Once security has him tied to the
table, the doctors ask him questions. A nurse sits nearby recording
information for his medical record.

"What's your name, sir? Do you know where you are? Have you
been drinking? What else have you taken? Have you taken any
drugs? How old are you?"

As the questioning continues, the man's clothes are cut off with
scissors and his pulse is taken. There are gunpowder burns around
the bullet entry wound, but he is not bleeding badly. When his
clothes are thrown to the floor, two hollow-point .38-caliber bullets

fall out of his shoe. They're given to the policemen who accompanied him to the hospital.

"Do you know who shot you?" asks one doctor. Because of the face masks, it's hard to tell who is talking.

"Myself," says the patient.

"You shot yourself?"

"Yes."

When asked why he had shot himself, the patient says that he had been thinking about it for some time.

The man is either very lucky or meant to be. The bullet entered his lower abdomen, traveled a short distance just under his skin and exited without hitting any organs. The doctors tell him they are going to put a catheter into his penis and a tube down his nose into his stomach. The patient says he refuses. They do it anyway.

A report comes into the Trauma Room. Two cars have collided head-on, and the three individuals involved are on their way in. One victim reportedly has a broken leg.

There are four operating tables in 242. Two are in use. The car-crash victims should arrive in 10 minutes.

Meanwhile, the intoxicated man from Sandusky has arrived. He's pretty high but in a passive way. The word is he was beaten up at 9 p.m. in the Flats, drove home and was found unconscious and bleeding by his sister, who took him to a hospital from where he was flown to MetroHealth. The doctors check the severity of his head wounds.

"Can you tell us what happened, sir?"

The man mumbles something about an altercation with a couple of guys. It's "The Two-Dude Syndrome."

And the EMS drivers arrive with the first of the car-crash victims . . .

March 28, 1993

CLEVELAND: A CITY DIVIDED?

East Siders dream about moving to Manhattan;
West Siders dream about moving to Parma

According to ancient Scandinavian lore, the name Cleveland (from the Latin clevus, meaning to separate), was bestowed in 1066 by the Viking explorer Eric The Very Lost, who somehow found himself at the mouth of the Cuyahoga on his way to Greenland. Because the river cut the city in half, he cursed it, saying, "The land cleved by the crooked river shall always remain a city divided."

OK, so I made that up. But how else do you explain the weird polarity of the East and West Sides of Cleveland? They're like different cities. A friend from Cleveland, now living in Manhattan, recently remarked that when he meets someone claiming to be from Cleveland, the second question always asked is, "East Side or West?" Otherwise they probably grew up somewhere near Akron and are just trying to pass as Clevelanders.

And what about Cleveland to the south? You know, Strongsville, North Royalton, Parma, Seven Hills. Why is it that those suburbs never merit any mention? Are they so bland and lacking in personality as to be beyond any perceptible identity? Well, yes, quite frankly.

At least we can put that question to rest.

The two sides of Cleveland carry a lot of stereotypical trademark-type baggage. We all know that stereotypes are bad and wrong. They promote ignorance and ill will. I'm going to list them anyway.

The East Side has culture, in its museums, orchestra and avant-garde movie houses and coffeehouses. Even their garbage is gift-wrapped. The West Side has, well, bars. Hundreds and hundreds of them. Which I suppose constitutes an alcohol culture of some kind. Which might be considered better than no culture at all.

The East Side is home to Cleveland's largest Jewish and black communities. The West Side has the lion's share of Catholics and WASPs.

The East Side is known for its wealth, intellectual community and its colleges and universities. The kids there are so privileged they're breast-fed by caterers. The West Side has its undying devotion to the Browns, Indians and Cavaliers, as well as major participation in intramural softball, bowling and hockey leagues.

The East Side offers fine dining in a variety of styles. It's easy to spend lots of money, be treated badly and walk away underfed. An East Sider's idea of bravery is to eat in a restaurant that hasn't been reviewed yet. The West Side has hot dogs and pizza. (The hot dogs aren't all that bad.)

The East Side is home to Cleveland's professional community: doctors, lawyers, CEOs and the various aligned and non-aligned leftists in the Coventry area. The West Side is the blue-collar belt: union guys, skilled craftsmen, carpenters, plumbers and way too many politicians.

The West Side is basically conservative. East Siders are generally liberal, unless they're behind the wheel of car.

West Siders talk about their auto mechanics, East Siders their psychiatrists. Entertainment on the East Side is the orchestra and art museum. On the West Side, it's fishing and golf.

A big event on the East Side is a mansion fund-raiser for a Cleveland Play House play that no one will attend. What draws a crowd on the West Side is a VFW Hall beer bash and reverse raffle for Judge Mularkey's re-election campaign.

On the East Side, people play polo. On the West Side, they play pool. On the East Side, they read the business section and society page. On the West Side, those who can read, read the sports page.

The East Side is pricy nouvelle cuisine. The West Side is Ponderosa All-You-Can-Eat $9.95.

The East Side nuclear family is a divorced couple with 2.3 children. On the West Side, it's a couple who should have divorced 10 years ago but can't afford to because they have 11 kids and one on the way.

East Siders dream about moving to Manhattan. West Siders dream about moving to Parma.

If the TV show *Cheers* were set in Cleveland, Sam, Woody, Norm, Cliff and Carla would be from the West Side. Dr. Frasier Crane and his wife, Lilith, would be from the East Side.

If you were looking for representative leading men and women from Hollywood, Richard Gere and Barbra Streisand would be from the East Side, and Bill Murray and Roseanne Arnold would be from the West.

People from the West Side don't go to the East Side if they can help it because it's too easy to get lost and the people over there drive like maniacs. People from the East Side don't go to the West Side simply because there's no reason to go there.

East Siders drive Volvos and Saabs. West Siders drive "Catholic sports cars" (also known as Ford minivans).

East Siders speak a second language fluently. West Siders are struggling with English, which is their second language.

East Siders vacation in Europe. West Siders send money to Europe so the rest of their family can join them.

Though the resistance between these two seemingly implacable sides of town has remained strong for decades, there have been some meager signs of cultural exchange. Sports bars can be found on the East Side and, conversely, an Arabica coffee shop has opened in Lakewood as well as a sushi restaurant in Rocky River. Some years back, an art-film movie theater was attempted in Lakewood but that failed. Who wants to see a movie you have to read?

Perhaps one explanation for Greater Cleveland's lack of unification has to do with the fact that people here, for one reason or another, tend to stay firmly planted in their own neighborhoods. It's a source of amusement to people from Los Angeles, who think nothing of driving 30 minutes for a pack of gum, that people in Cleveland consider the other side of town a prohibitive distance to drive for anything.

Maybe the answer can be found in Cleveland's history.

"It's a good question," says Peter Gail, former associate professor of urban studies at Cleveland State University, "but it's not one that's easy to answer. You have to look at where people settled originally. People who settled west of the Cuyahoga tended to move west and those who settled east moved east. But even when you find the same ethnic groups on different sides of the river, they tend to stay in their own communities. For example, the East Side and West Side Irish don't mix generally. And this is true of the Eastern European communities as well."

Gail now operates Goosefoot Acres Field Study Centre, which introduces people to the resources of Northeast Ohio. He runs classes, workshops, tours and gives slide-show-illustrated lectures on the secret treasures of Greater Cleveland. He points to the Ohio

City wars of 1836 and 1850, in which the founders of Ohio City didn't want people crossing the bridge to spend their money in Cleveland, as an example of the city's divisive history.

But, Gail says, "the very wealthy in Cleveland have always tended to move East. First, it was from Tremont to Millionaires' Row, then on to Cleveland Heights, Shaker and Beachwood. This kind of separation in a city can't help it, but what can you do about it?"

Karl Bonutti, professor of economics and director of ethnic studies at CSU, admits he has no easy answers either.

"I'm as puzzled about it as anyone. The river certainly divides the city, but look at all the bridges that connect the two sides. There's no solid reason for it. The history of Cleveland is that small ethnic communities have always created corridors for themselves. The West Side has always been residential because it's close to jobs for people. All the major cultural institutions are on the East Side because that's where the people who donated the money for them live or lived."

But Bonutti also says that the city, during the last 20 years, has changed in the way and frequency with which people move. This is bound, he says, to bring change.

"This is a society of continuous change. I have heard it said that Cleveland is one of the most racist cities in the country, but there are bigots everywhere. The only place where there is no bigotry is where nothing has ever changed. We live in a nomadic society, and the more things change, the more we'll see our cities as testing grounds for the future of humanity. Cleveland is no different in this respect."

Dick Feagler, commentator on all things Cleveland, grew up on the East Side and attended John Adams High School but now lives in Lakewood. He sees the division as something that always was and probably always will be. And says that's not so bad.

"When I lived on the East Side as a boy, the only thing I knew about the West Side was that the sun set somewhere over there. It might as well have been Alaska. When I went to the (now-defunct) *Cleveland Press* and we happened to cover news events over there, luckily there was a photographer who drove. I always thought the West Side was a little Beaver Cleaverish. Now when I return to the East Side, people treat me like I'm in from out of town."

Feagler believes that some of the East Side snobbery is rubbing off on the West.

"The East Side has all the culture and the attitude that goes with it. But the West Side is catching up. People from Bay Village will tell you they live in WEST Bay and people from Rocky River just call it 'River.' And you'll see those bright pink and green clothes out there, too,' he says.

"But it's really a matter of one side having something the other side wants. The East Side has the museums and orchestra, but the West Side has what the East can't get. And that's all that Lake Erie water."

So maybe this east-west division is just as it ought to be. Maybe we should simply celebrate the difference instead of continually asking why it's there. Instead of asking why the glass is divided in half, why can't be glad there are two sides to drink from? We've got two cities in one here. And despite what people tell you, you don't need a passport to cross the Cuyahoga. All that's required is an open mind and a sense of adventure.

For all that is good and bad about the two sides of Cleveland, at least it shows a vibrant diversity and gives us a constant source of conversation.

There are even signs that, with the help of education, the rift is healing itself.

Gail, whose livelihood depends on Clevelanders' curiosity about their city, says business is good.

"What I do in my classes is introduce East Siders to the West and West Siders to the East. I haven't had to advertise. People are interested in learning about the tremendous resources and diversity we have here."

As the English philosopher Dr. Samuel Johnson once said, "So much are the modes of excellence settled by time and place, that men may be heard boasting in one street of that which they would conceal in another."

THE JOKES ON US

West Side: A West Side guy is granted three wishes by a genie. "I'd like a bottle of beer that is never empty," he says. Genie says, "Kazaam," and a bottle of beer appears in the guy's hand. He brings it to his lips, drinks it all down 'til it's gone. He brings it to his lips again and it's full. "This is great," he says with wild enthusiasm. The genie asks him about his other two wishes. "Two more of these," he says without hesitation.

East Side: What did the East Side guy who crashed his car say when he noticed his severed arm on the other side of the road? "My Rolex!"

TOP 10 QUALIFICATIONS FOR LIVING ON THE WEST SIDE:
1. You've never been drunk, just overserved.
2. You own a collection of ceramic Elvis bourbon decanters.
3. You own three or more cars, two of which are lawn ornaments.
4. Bill Cosby is the only black person you feel you really know.
5. You were surprised to find out that Mayor White is black.
6. You can swim.
7. You think Woody Allen is one of the "Little Rascals."
8. Your idea of art is the fountain at Westgate Mall.
9. The last book you read was the eighth in the Time-Life series on Home Repair: Do It Yourself Plumbing.
10. You think lox is something you buy at the hardware store.

TOP 10 QUALIFICATIONS FOR LIVING ON THE EAST SIDE:
1. You like children—other people's.
2. Your front lawn looks like the 18th fairway at Augusta, and it ought to. You have the same grounds crew.
3. You voted for Bush, felt guilty and made a donation to Amnesty International.
4. You have a cellular phone, fax machine and billiards table—in your car.
5. You wouldn't drive through Lakewood on a bet.
6. Your idea of ethnic food is dinner at Giovanni's.
7. You thought Mayor White was black.
8. Your idea of wilderness backpacking is shopping in Chagrin Falls.
9. You never drive to Cleveland Heights without 50 pounds of quarters.
10. You think Chief Wahoo is a soft drink.

May 9, 1993

GOING TO BLAZES

The sleepless knights of Engine 41

The C shift of the Cleveland Fire Department's Engine Co. 41 is on duty this slow Wednesday night. All four guys have known each other for years, but there's little conversation. Some watch cable. Others talk on the phone or just relax at the half-century-old station house on E. 116th St. north of Kinsman. The atmosphere isn't exactly what you'd call tense.

At 12:38 a.m. a dispatcher issues a call: "Male. Shot in the head. E. 98th and Elwell." They man the truck. The call is a "first response" so no firefighting gear is needed. All they need is to arrive quickly and stabilize the victim until an Emergency Medical Service ambulance can get there.

Once inside the Tele-Squrt pump engine, whose 36,000 pounds of metal carries 500 gallons of water, the men snap on latex gloves. There will be blood at the scene.

With sirens blaring, the truck pulls out of the station and turns left on 116th. It roars down the street to Buckeye, where it turns left again. Two minutes later, the crew, all in regulation blue T-shirts and trousers, has arrived at the scene, a dimly lit street corner. The firefighters find a young man lying face down on the sidewalk, in a crimson puddle. Several neighbors have gathered and are leaning over him.

With the arrival of Engine 41, the neighbors back off. The driver stays with the truck.

Seconds later, an EMS team arrives. With the firefighters' help, they move the man onto a body board, a sheet of hard plastic with handles is used to move the man from the ground to a stretcher. His pulse is taken. He is handled delicately by the firefighters as they get him ready to go to the hospital. The police arrive and move the neighbors farther back.

The only light are beams from the pulsating fire truck, EMS truck and police cars, and a nearby street lamp. But even in the eerie intermittent darkness a bullet hole in the back of the man's head is easy to see.

The man lives in the neighborhood, and within seconds police have determined he is 19-year-old Marvin Rox. A young man makes his way to Rox's side. He begins shouting, "My cousin, my cousin. They shot my cousin." He tries to hug Rox, and police gently usher him away as he wails in pain.

Firefighter Sean Hodges 26, a five-year veteran of the department, nods toward the crying man.

"I went to school with him. We go back to first grade."

Rox is loaded into the ambulance and it is decided that Firefighter Carlos Jordan will drive the ambulance to nearby St. Luke's Medical Center so that the EMS technicians can continue to work on Rox. The remaining firefighters stay at the scene to talk with the police and offer information about what they saw when they arrived minutes before.

When they are finished, the crew drives over to St. Luke's to pick up Jordan. There they are ushered into a tiny room off the emergency room holding Rox's body.

He was pronounced dead on arrival. And now, with the firefighters watching, the doctors point to where the 9mm bullet entered near the base of his skull, and then to where it exited on his right side under his armpit.

"He never had a chance," says the attending physician.

Quietly, the firefighters file out of the room."

"You just get tired of seein' it, tired of hearin' it. Shootings, stabbings, that kid's life had just begun," says Sean Hodges later. "You try to block that stuff out, but some days it just accumulates. It can get to you. I tell you what, we do it all on this job: from fires to parades to stuff like that."

From "fires to parades to stuff like that," Cleveland's highly regarded 939-member Fire Department answers an average of 4,000 calls a month. But increasingly, the department's members are responding to "stuff like that." Gone are the days when a firefighter's job could be romanticized to include a shiny pole, a Dalmation and a fire. Today the job often includes being first on the scene for a violent crime or auto accident.

In August, for example, Engine 41 was ranked first in the city in the number of alarms answered (1,975). Of that number, 1,090 were first response calls—more than any other engine company.

And with a staff of 21 men working 24-hour shifts, Engine 41 also
was the top company in number of hours worked on actual duty
(864.50). Those numbers hold fairly steady over the year.

Life at Engine 41, in some ways, accurately represents what
being a firefighter has come to mean to the city of Cleveland. And
in big cities all across the country. At this station, the changing role
of the firefighter is clear: The job requires the skills of a firefighter
some of the time, but those of an emergency medical technician
almost all the time.

But no matter what the nature of the call, the station is always
a second home for these guys. In a 30-year career, a firefighter assigned to Engine 41 will have spent 10 years actually living at the
house. Engine 41 even has its own motto: "Another sleepless knight
at Engine 41." The motto is being printed on T-shirts with an illustration of a firefighter fighting flames in the fashion of a medieval
painting of St. George and the dragon.

"What's unique about Engine 41?" asks visiting Capt. Ray Masirik with his typical deadpan delivery. "It's like working out of a
cave." The fire station is dark and cramped. The ceilings are falling
down in some places and much of the tile flooring, where there is
tile flooring, is coming up.

A tiny kitchen with an ancient stove is used by the resident cooks
to serve up mass quantities of baked rigatoni with garlic bread,
Parmesan chicken, lasagna and sometimes fresh perch with twice-
baked potatoes and brownies. The officers' quarters are hardly better than the crew's six-bed dormitory, a 15-by-30-foot room in the
rear of the building. The station is plagued with mice. It also has
no back door and no trustworthy security, which precludes anyone
bringing amenities from home to improve the conditions.

"They like the work here," says Masirik of the dank surroundings. "Work" is a firefighter's euphemism for a fire. "One year at 41
will give you six years of experience," he adds.

Or, as another firefighter put it, "We have a saying here: 'What
else can they do to us? We're already at 41.'"

Fifth Battalion Chief Bashir Rahman, who oversees 41's B shift,
and aide Kariem Hasan are having lunch one afternoon in the little
kitchen of 41. The conversation is light as Ed Rubensaal, a retired
lieutenant in the Cleveland Fire Department, walks in.

Rubensaal says hello and is offered a cup of coffee. Rubensaal spent 33 years as a firefighter, 15 of them at 41. The chief asks the visitor how he is doing. Rubensaal pauses.

"Had a loss recently," he says finally. "My wife died last month. It took us all by surprise."

"My condolences," says Rahman.

"Yeah," offers Rubensaal. "It's kind of tough. Physically, I'm all right. But otherwise . . . " His voice trails off.

After a pause, he continues. "Anyway, I wanted to see if any of the guys were around." He asks after firefighters Rick Jenna, Lavelle Davis, Darryl Sharp and Neville Lee, who are off that day. "I just wanted to thank them. I didn't know they had any idea about my wife. At the funeral, as I was leaving the church, I look up and there they are wearing their dress blues. I just burst into tears all over again. I was just so happy to see them. I dropped by because I wanted to thank them again. That was something else," he says. He smiles.

"At 8:38 p.m. a call blares over the house system. "Box alarm. 12301 Watterson." The A shift rolls. A box alarm means a fire.

They're into firefighting pants, jackets, air tanks and helmets with a silent, unruffled speed. The truck, with four men on board, roars from the station less than 10 seconds after the call comes in.

Lt. Tony Plute, visiting from Engine Co. 4, sits up front with the driver. Two cadets (first-year firefighters) sit in the back, fastening their jackets. "Come on, man. We got to get in there first," says John Ramsey to Pat Monar. Monar is silent. "Come on. Come on."

Lt. Plute interrupts with assignments. Ramsey will take the tip in. Monar will hang back. Lavelle Davis navigates the truck through evening traffic. The reaction from oncoming cars is sluggish. "We're lucky nobody flipped us off," Davis says with a laugh. That happens a lot.

Engine 41 arrives at the scene in under two minutes, but it is not the first. Two companies are already inside the flaming wooden house, which is abandoned. Neighbors have gathered on their lawns, fearful for their homes.

Forty-one's crew heads inside, and the silence is broken as the firefighters begin to smash windows with their metal hooks. Beams that might have burning embers are brought crashing down. Every so often the sound of old-fashioned telephone bells is heard, which tells firefighters they have five minutes worth of oxygen left in their 15-minute tanks. Five minutes later, everybody is still in the building.

Masks are ripped off and the men "suck smoke," sticking their heads out of windows for fresh air or grabbing breaths of trapped air between layers of clothes.

Thirty minutes later, the second floor is a mass of charred wood, ashes and smoking rubble. The fire is mostly out, but the chopping, hacking and spraying continues just to be sure. Nothing is left to chance.

In August, Engine 41 responded to 29 fires. Last year, the entire department responded to 5,626 fire alarms. Twenty-seven people lost their lives in fires last year. So far this year, 22 people have died. Only two firefighters have lost their lives in the line of duty in the last 15 years. One of those deaths was an alcohol-related accident this year."

"Fire is a weird thing, man," says Lt. Greg Perrin at the station after dinner one evening. "Think about it. If you're in a room with a fire, both of you need oxygen to exist. In a way, you're both fighting for the same thing. You got to put it out before it puts you out. It can start one place in a building and show up somewhere else.

"A lot of the houses in this neighborhood are those old pre-World War II balloon frames without fire stops. A fire can start in the basement and run up into the attic without burning anything in between at first. It's weird."

Perrin is a 13-year veteran of the A shift. A poster of the 1991 movie *Backdraft* hangs on the wall over his shoulder.

"The worst thing you could say about a fireman," adds 13-year veteran George Redcross, "is that a guy didn't like fires."

Perrin says he "loves this job"—a job that pays $31,612.19 the first year. Sitting in 41's kitchen with Tom Diamond, a first-year firefighter, Perrin talks easily about why he does what he does.

"This is the greatest job in the world. Only a fool would blow it. You get paid to be a hero. You work with great guys, there's public recognition. There's a real satisfaction in knowing you put a fire out. You can't imagine the feeling when people say thank you for saving them or their house. It's pride and joy.

"That phone rings," Perrin adds, nodding to the dispatch phone on the kitchen wall, "and your heart starts beatin'. You wanna know, whatta we got? Is it a first response, an MVA [motor vehicle accident], or is this The One? Lives may be in danger, people in pain right now. You begin to prepare yourself mentally."

LOCAL TROUBLE

"The squealing of brakes and the crunch of metal has sent Firefighter Al Jordan out of Engine 41 into the early evening light. Some 50 feet from the station, a half-dozen young men are dragging 19-year-old Wally Adams along the street.

Jordan pushes his way into the group and wrestles Adams free. Adams throws his arms around Jordan's waist even as two of his assailants continue to pull at his body. The tug of war continues even as Jordan is joined by his brother, Carlos, and Sean Hodges, both firefighters at 41. They stand at Jordan's side.

Adams is being roundly cursed as Jordan works to calm the crowd.

"Are you the police?" someone demands as the Jordan brothers and Hodges try to gain control of the situation. By now, the crowd of young men has grown to a dozen.

Through the yelling the firefighters make out that only 10 minutes before, Adams—high on cocaine and PCP, doctors later determine—ran a stop sign and smashed into a car driven by a young woman. Another young woman as well as several children were in the car. The women emerged from the car seemingly unhurt, and began to scream at Adams.

Fearing for his safety, Adams got back in his car and tried to flee. But his front axle was so badly bent that he careened into another car, a new Toyota 4-Runner parked on 116th. When Adams saw what he had done, he got out of his car and ran down a side street adjacent to Engine 41.

The young men, including the Toyota's owner, chased Adams. The mob caught him just as Al Jordan came out of the station.

The commotion attracts others. Now more than 100 people are screaming for Adams to be released into their hands. Adams is accused of killing babies and stealing a purse by members of the now-enraged mob, who are being provoked by some local thugs who want nothing more than to see a good fight.

"Call the police," Al Jordan urges. Firefighter George Redcross radios police from inside Engine 41. Engine 41 had been on a routine call just a few minutes before. Returning to the station, the firefighters happen upon the scene just as it threatens to worsen.

Three calls, all increasingly anxious, are made to the Police Department. Ten minutes later, a black-and-white unit arrives, but the patrolmen, who are responding to a different call, leave without getting out of their car.

At Engine/Hook and Ladder Co. 36, on E. 131st St., the dispatch calls made by 41 are heard on the radio. Like the cavalry charging over the hill at just the right moment, Engine 36 responds with truck lights flashing and siren screaming. Five men—in full fire gear and axes in hand—jump off the truck. The crowd quiets immediately. Shortly after, four police cars arrive, joined by a police helicopter with a spotlight illuminating the scene from overhead. Adams is cited for five traffic violations and taken away in a squad car.

Sighs are heard from Engine 41's crew. Thanks are spread all around for the crew from 36. There is laughter and a great feeling of relief.

"After leaving St. Luke's, C shift returns to the station for some much-needed rest. But no luck.

At 2:30 a.m. the house phone rings. It is homicide detectives telling C shift that they have completed their investigation at the scene of Marvin Rox's murder. Engine 41 could now return to Elwell Ave. and finish up.

A few minutes later, Sean Hodges stands under the street light on Elwell and uses a fire hose for something it was never intended: washing the blood of Marvin Rox off the sidewalk, into the gutter and down into the sewer.

November 20, 1994

IN THE VALLEY OF THE LOST BOYS

They thought the party would never end

"It used to be that the only way a guy would leave the valley would be if he died, joined A.A., or got married," says Mark Sage sadly, standing on his back porch watching John Deere backhoes and bulldozers roll ever closer to his upstairs apartment. The house Sage lives in was torn down in early August as were three adjacent rentals to the north, right on the Rocky River, making way for expensive homes on some of the most valuable property in Cuyahoga County.

"If this house could talk," cracks Sage, 46, "it would be really hung over."

The demolition marks the end of an era. Sage is one of the last of a long line of valley boys who inhabited various units in the four houses over the last 25 years. These hardcore partiers were also legendary playboys who made a religion of avoiding adulthood. Avowed enemies of serious work, marriage, or any kind of daily routine that didn't involve malt beverages, games of sport or chance, and the close company of amorous young women, they dedicated their lives almost exclusively to the pursuit of pleasure.

"When [my son] Terry moved down there in 1989, he was there with all his high school friends. They were all bachelors and they all partied and played all the time. I always called them the Lost Boys, from *Peter Pan*," says Jan Galvin. Terry, 42, is now executive chef at Rattlesnake Island, the private retreat.

Mike Miller, also 42 and former owner of Wilbert's Café, had his own apartment in Sage's house and has since moved in with his old high school buddy Pat Carney in a house across the street.

"It's like that show *Survivor*," says Miller. "We got voted off the island."

There was no better place in Cleveland to carve out a wild life-style than down on South Island, a road that runs from under the Rocky River Bridge out to the mouth of the Rocky River just west of the Cleveland Yacht Club.

Not only were the Lost Boys paying laughably cheap rent, (Sage was coughing up $175 a month when his place was torn down) but they were living on the water in a vacation-style community that offers one of Cleveland's most beautiful vista of trees, water, sky and high-priced boats surrounded by million-dollar homes. Along with low monthly payments and shimmering natural surroundings, the Lost Boys also initially had free dockage. The people across the river paid thousands of dollars for dockage every month.

And there was no greater irony than these professional ne'r-do-wells reveling in their lives of leisure just across the river from captains of industry, corporate CEOs and self-made millionaires. The Lost Boys would rather live like millionaires than actually be them. The contrasting philosophies were not lost on Yacht Club members. There was no shortage of animosity between the two groups. Former Lost Boy Parnell Egan, 49, now manager and part owner of The West End Tavern, called it: "The Blue Bloods vs. The Buttheads."

Herb Brough, 67, owner of Herb's Tavern in Rocky River since 1963, has been a member of the Yacht Club for 26 years. He knows people from both sides of the river. "There were complaints [by CYC members] over the years. Mostly about loud music. But those guys would only tease them, turning up the music all the louder," he says. "Those guys could really party. People who call themselves partyers today don't know what they are talking about. Those guys were amazing. They all used to drink here [at Herb's]. It was kind of a Golden Era. Just thinking about it brings back a lot of good memories."

The Lost Boys were like a funhouse mirror reflection of their betters across the water. And they loved rubbing it in. If the Yacht Club had a regatta, a sailing party complete with a formal dinner and dancing, the sounds of Benny Goodman wafting through the night air, the Lost Boys put on a counter regatta.

The west bank, known as South Island, would be the site of a party consisting of 10 or 20 kegs of beer, iced in the back of some rusted, red '64 Ford pickup, a weenie roast and men and women in various states of undress smoking anything available and jamming to the Rolling Stones blasting at full, ear-bleeding volume. This would go on until 3 or 4 in the morning.

"Our parties were successful because we always offered three things: All the free beer you could drink, Beatles, Stones and Motown music, and all the good looking women in Cleveland," says a 54-year-old former Lost Boy and current sports handicapper who goes by the name of Will Cover.

If Yacht Club members called the Rocky River police because the Lost Boys' music was too loud, the Lost Boys would complain that the Yacht Club dance band was too loud. Turnabout was fair play. And those guys *loved* to play. On at least one occasion the police came back in street clothes off duty and joined in the fun. Some Lost Boys were even known to cross the river under the cover of night, swim in the Yacht Club pool after hours and pilfer booze from the bars on the big fancy boats.

But the Lost Boy lifestyle was more than a class war with the Yacht Club set. There were South Island neighbors who found the summer long bacchanals a bit much. Betty Skryzmosk has owned two houses just west of the Lost Boy properties for 50 years. And she has not suffered the fools quietly.

"I'm an American and when I see something wrong, I say something about it. They had parties every weekend, hundreds of people, 30 barrels of beer, loud music. They'd moon me. I come home late at night from work and there's people having sex in my driveway," she says. "I took pictures. I wrote down all the car license plates, all the boat licenses. Then I'd complain to the cops, to the mayor, to city council and find out they were all *at* the party."

Dan Wiest, 54, retired from the Rocky River Police Department this January after 26 years on the force, was called down to the valley often over the years.

"I was down there a number of times mediating disputes between the Yacht Club and their neighbors across the water. Sometimes Pat Dailey would be playing at the Yacht Club and some of those guys [across the way] would come over to hear him. Then as they were leaving, they would call the police *from* the Yacht Club to complain about the noise there, just to bust their chops," he says.

"But those were good guys down there on South Island. A lot of those parties raised money for people who were hurting or down on their luck. I was at a few of them. And they could get out of hand. When you have parking space for three cars and 300 people show up, there are going to be some space problems. It could be a bit of headache. Just like any graduation party in any suburb.

"I had to be good cop and bad cop all rolled into one because I knew those guys. But they were essentially harmless. In all those years I don't recall a single fight. Those guys just like to have fun," says Wiest.

It wasn't much fun for neighbor Skryzmosk. "All those parties were put on by those protégés of [their landlord] the Cookstons."

All four rental properties were owned by the late Ray and Dorothy Cookston, longtime members in good standing at the Yacht Club. Dorothy handled the rental properties and is revered as a saint by the Lost Boys. She never raised the rent on a tenant. Rents increased only when someone moved out of one of the units. Even then, they were ridiculously affordable.

The first Lost Boys were Tim Kopp and Bill McKnight. They went to Cookston's house in Bay Village to interview for the house in 1976 and won her over with their charm and good manners.

"We wore ties to the interview," says McKnight, nicknamed "Hossy" because of his resemblance to *Bonanza* actor Dan Blocker. "I remember because I had to borrow mine. I didn't own one. We fixed up the house. Painted it, put in new carpet. All Mrs. Cookston wanted us to do was keep it clean. Which we did—for a while." McKnight says smiling.

Both Kopp, 46, and McKnight, 48, have since married and moved out of the valley. They are founding Lost Boys, as is Sage, and are regarded as elder statesmen by the generations who followed.

"We had it all figured out back then," says Kopp who now owns and runs Ohio Valley Supply and Maintenance Company, a successful commercial cleaning supply company. "We had as much fun as you could possibly have on $125 a month. There used to be a restaurant up the hill in the Westlake Hotel called The Silver Thorn that featured a prime rib special for $3.95. We *lived* on that. We had all the angles covered."

Kopp had a 1950s 16-foot Glasstron outboard dubbed *The Tuna*. It was a source of great amusement for the Lost Boys. They used to love to ride by Yacht Club parties, naked, waving to members.

"One day, me, Will Cover and some other guys were out on the boat fooling around over by the Gold Coast and Pier W," Kopp says, referring to the lakeside restaurant in the Winton Place apartment building in Lakewood. "That night Will Cover had dinner at his mother's house. She mentions that while she was having lunch at Pier W. some boys came by in a boat and pulled their pants down. He didn't know what to say," Kopp says laughing.

Just up the hill from the valley was a Victoria Station restaurant. It quickly became a Lost Boys haunt. Victoria Station Manager Parnell Egan got to know the boys and soon became a valley resident, moving in with Sage and McKnight. Kopp moved into another house and each year more guys would move into one of the eight units in Cookston's four rental homes.

"We would walk up the hill to Victoria Station and later come rolling back down," says Cover. "I extended my fraternity days by 19 years living in the valley."

Cover isn't the only former Lost Boy who looks back warmly on days and nights in the valley. Egan shares the nostalgia.

"Remember the very last scene in *The Flintstones* television show where it's night and Fred is shouting for Wilma to let him in the house and you can see all the lights in Bedrock coming on one by one?" asks Egan. "That's what the valley would be like after the bars closed at 2:30 [a.m.]. Everybody would come back down to the valley with the girls they met, drink more beer, crank up the music, light the grills and get some food going. Then the boats would start going out on the lake. Naked boating and other festivities ensued. Things would wind down around 6 a.m. and people would crash. Then we'd wake up and do it again the next night. This went on and on," says Egan, who now lives in Lakewood.

Second only to drinking, are the Lost Boy tales of sexual shenanigans. The Lost Boys had no shortage of cads, rakes, rogues and bounders in their ranks. Pat Carney, a relative newcomer to the valley, has heard about the legendary bad boy behavior.

"I don't want to name names," he says. "But one night this guy meets a girl at Victoria Station. If you didn't have a car that's where you went. He brought her back down to the valley for a romantic interlude, or whatever. Now he feels like he's stuck with her all night. So he tells her he's called for a pizza. They're up in his bedroom when they hear the car pull up. He says he'll go down and get it. In reality he had called a cab. He just got in the car and left. A classic Homer Simpson move."

But the most famous story of all involves a midnight tryst that took place in the winter. No one claims to remember this woman's name, but she was famous in the valley for being a *lot* of fun. One night after a big party she left one of the houses at 8 in the morning and got in her car to go home. No one knows if she was disoriented from drink or the way the lights played off the frozen river, but she got her directions turned around and drove her car off the ease-ment onto the ice. Luckily, the river wasn't very deep, so her car went nose first through the ice, where it stuck into the river bed. The back of the car stood straight up in the air. She got out of the car screaming, ran back across the ice and was never heard from again.

Mike Miller described the aftermath. "The next morning there was this car sticking through the ice. The driver's door was open and there was a trail that led across the ice back to the street. There was a lipstick, a hair brush, a pack of cigarettes, some gum, one of those make-up things with the mirror . . . It was a sight."

If day-to-day life and impromptu behavior in the valley sound outrageous, it was nothing compared with the planned and orga-nized parties that occurred two or three times a year. The parties reflected the cultural events of the times. The 1975 heavyweight boxing championship fight between Muhammad Ali and Joe Fra-zier, "The Thrilla in Manila," would later inspire a series of annual autumn valley parties known as the "Thrilla at the Villa" because they were held at the Villa Apartments just north of the Lost Boys.

There was a 1978 toga party honoring the one in the movie *Animal House*. There was a Jonestown party that featured plas-tic trash cans full of a 100-proof purple concoction called Guyana Fizz. There were Hat Parties that ended with hundreds of people wearing only hats. There were Blender Parties where each person brought a bottle of rum and his favorite fruit. No less than seven of the kitchen appliances hummed through the night.

Mark Sage is unique among the original Lost Boys—he re-mained single and a valleyite long after his contemporaries had moved on with careers and marriage. Sage graduated from Bay High School in 1972. He moved to Florida for a while, fished, came back to Cleveland, moved into the valley and worked for a carpet cleaning company.

From 1977 to 1981 he was a prison guard at the Justice Center in downtown Cleveland. Then it was back to Florida for some con-struction work. He came back to the valley in 1983, cleaned some more carpets and got a job tending bar at the Coast Guard Club. He retired from the Coast Guard Club in 1997 and bought the Rich-land Café (Motto: Warm beer, bad food, good people) on Madison Avenue in Lakewood. He also works part time as a baggage han-dler for Continental Airlines which allows him heavily discounted travel privileges.

While not every unmarried man who ever lived in the valley was a party animal, Sage typifies the kind of carefree soul who has grav-itated to the valley for the last 25 years. Clinical psychologist Dr. Joseph W. Rock, co-author of *Let's Face It, Men Are #*#$@%*@,* has had a lot of experience with Lost Boy types. In his book he calls them "Eternal Teenagers."

"To some guys, life consists of four events," says Rock. "You're born, you get married, have kids and you die. If you're married and have kids, your life is three-quarters over. Why wouldn't someone want to prolong their adolescence? And it's also easier to do today than ever before. People are getting married much later in life than they used to. Guys like this tend to be both loved and reviled for the lives they lead. Who wouldn't want to lead a fun-filled carefree existence," he asks.

"On the other hand, some women call them Peter Pan and say they're immature and in denial. They can be frustrating to women, who see potential in them, because they never change. They attract women because they're fun, high-energy people. They are hard not to like. They're not tortured souls," says Rock.

Peggy Ziegler lived in the valley for a time. She met and married her husband, Paul, an attorney, there.

"My husband talks about the valley as if it was the happiest time in his life. I moved out after three years. I went all the way to Shaker to get away. I mean you can only watch *Caddyshack* so many times," she says of the classic Bill Murray movie.

But Rock sees them as essentially harmless goofballs.

"One thing I will say on their behalf is that there's no deception in the lifestyle. These guys are very upfront regarding what they're about. They're not like guys who get married and cheat on their wives," says Rock.

"If they have even a modicum of ambition, they can have suc-cessful careers," says Rock. "They often make great salesmen. As long as they can make their own hours."

While the Lost Boys might have been the original ambition-impaired, protoslackers, there were noteworthy achievements, however dubious, over the years.

Former Lost Boy Mike "Redman" Foley, 48, now a major account executive for BFI trucking, brought honor to the valley by winning the 1980 Agora-sponsored Air Guitar contest. The price was $1,000 and assorted smaller gifts. Foley won the day, arriving with an empty guitar case, and performing The Grateful Dead's *Alabama Getaway*. He had a little help on the applause-o-meter from 50 or so Lost Boys who tipped the needle in Foley's favor. But Foley wasn't a complete shoo-in.

"After I won the semifinals they told me if I came to finals as high as I was then, they would disqualify me. So I had to tone it down a little," says Foley, who admits having been overserved at the time but who has been sober since 1983.

In late June, Sage and his remaining valley housemates threw a final valley party inviting back two decades worth of Lost Boy alumni. The majority have "matured out" of the lifestyle as they say. But they were back in force on that sunny Sunday, some with wives and kids in tow. It was a festive but uncharacteristically sedate affair. After they polished off a keg, three large coolers full of beer survived untouched.

Eleven-year valley veteran Rob Waldheger, now 50, emphasized the communal aspects of life in the valley. "There was an open-door policy in the houses, borrowing beer on the honor system. There were community pets, Sage's cat, Ray, and Buster, the dog. My cat Flanagan. These guys were true neighbors in times of need. When I broke my leg, people brought food by every day. There was a camaraderie and closeness, not just to each other, but to the lake and river and the local watering holes. It was an ideal and idyllic lifestyle."

There was laughter as they passed war stories back and forth, construction equipment sitting idle in the background. Someone mentioned the time a beer truck piled high with kegs on the way down the narrow valley road took out all the electrical wires. And the sight of Redman Foley standing in the river waist deep in water directing boat traffic with one hand and a martini in the other. Then there was the morning-after practice of guys sitting out in the yard along the river wearing bathrobes and cowboy boots, drinking coffee, and discussing the previous night's adventures while reading the sports pages.

Jim "Popeye" Ward, who put in 10 years in the valley after his divorce, says he will remember the routine aspects of the valley more than the parties. On one afternoon during his last week in the valley he sat in his Adirondack chair looking north down the river, taking in the tranquil scene. "When I think of the valley, I think about how beautiful life was every day down here. Just getting up in the morning and looking at all this. The water and sky. There were a lot of parties. But everyday life was pretty good, too," Ward says.

Mike Miller has tried to be practical about recent events.

"We all knew this was coming. Anybody who ever lived down here had that feeling they were getting away with something. Life down here has always been too good to be true," he says.

Sage strives to be philosophical about giving up life on the water. "I always thought that if I won the lottery I would build a 40-room hotel, staff it with a 24-hour kitchen staff and let all my divorced friends live in it for free."

As the party winds down, someone asks Sage where he is going next.

The King of the Lost Boys looks into the setting sun on his last evening as a Rocky River resident. And he almost cracks a smile.

"To hell probably," he says. "Where I belong."

August 20, 2000

THE THRILL OF THE CHASE

Grand River Hunt involves riders, hounds,
'buckets of tradition' and a very crafty fox

An hour and a half into the fox hunt, it all came into a sharp, almost mystical focus. What originally seemed nothing more than rich people with too much time on their hands playing dress-up on horses unfolded like a living, breathing pastoral painting.

I was standing next to a pickup truck on the high side of a seasonally spent field of brown cornstalks, looking down on a pack of 20 white-and-brown hounds leading a procession of 17 riders on horseback. They rode regally in and out of the woods against a fiery splash of red, orange and golden autumn foliage. The scene was soul-stirring.

Seeing the circle-of-life link between man and horse, horse and hound, hound and fox, fox and the earth all played out against an unspoiled bucolic terrain was like looking clearly through 200-year-old eyes. The chill up and down the spine wasn't just from the cold, early morning air or dewy mist. It was from the sensation of feeling out of time, experiencing the grandeur of nature from a bygone era. This must have been what our ancestors saw and thought and felt on their one day a week away from heavy rural labor.

For all the pageantry and decorum involved with fox hunting, some find it a cruel and barbaric activity popular among upper-crust snobs and British wannabes. The debate is an international and extremely emotional one.

A recent study by a fox expert in England purports to shoot down the theory that fox hunting keeps that population in check. Researcher Stephen Harris reported that a 10-month ban on fox hunting had no effect at all on foxes.

The Masters of Foxhound Association of America, established in 1907, has published The Code of Hunting Practices, which insists that foxes and coyotes be hunted in their natural habitat and forbids any practice or activity "contrary to the best traditions of the sport."

Late last month, my guide, Steve Peplin, graciously agreed to give me his unique take on the Grand River Hunt. We pulled into the driveway of Fox Chase Farm in Parkman, Ohio. It was 7 a.m. Sunday. There was a low, slate-gray sky overhead. Rain threatened.

"Basically, you're taking 20 dogs for a walk in the woods without a leash," Peplin said.

Heidi Van de Motter, who owns the farm with her husband, John, was in the kennel selecting 19 dogs from their 40 for the hunt. The couple also breed chocolate Labradors. The barking of dogs eager for the hunt was deafening. Heidi Van de Motter knew each brown-spotted, white dog by name.

"And another thing," Peplin said, "you never say dogs. They're called hounds. This is a very terminology-heavy activity. For example, you don't say 24 dogs. You say 12 couples of hounds. They're counted in couples. Don't ask me why. It's all tradition. Buckets of tradition."

My guide isn't a fox hunter. Peplin owns a metal stamping plant, and his hobby of choice is sailing. He's merely a longtime observer of the sport. His girlfriend is a fox-hunting enthusiast from her youth. Peplin and I were "hilltopping," following the hunt in a truck driving from one high vantage point to another, keeping in touch with the riders by hand-held radio. In England, people still pay good money to sit in their cars and watch the chase from afar.

The opening of the formal fox-hunting season brings with it some extra activity. From August to October, fox hunters call what they do "cubbing," that is training the younger hounds to hunt and the less experienced hunters to ride. The attire is slightly less formal during cubbing season, partly because the weather's warmer and also because it's preseason.

But on this day, the gear was out in full regalia. The riders wore black velvet riding helmets and matching black, knee-high leather boots, with jodhpurs, white shirts and ties with gold stock pins. There are two kinds of melton fox-hunting coats. Red and black.

"Don't call the red coats red," Peplin told me. "The proper term is pink, supposedly after the guy who first designed them. The riders wearing the pink coats are also called 'whips' and are in charge of keeping the dogs together by cracking leather whips."

At the farm, horses were loaded into one trailer and the hounds in another. Two people were involved in counting the hounds. "Getting an accurate count is important," Peplin said. "You want to come back with the same number of hounds you left with. Nothing is more annoying than having to spend two hours after the hunt driving through the countryside looking for stray hounds. Or getting calls from farmers telling you your hound is in their corn."

Once all the trailers were loaded at Fox Chase, they were driven 10 minutes to a hilltop field where the blessing of the hounds and the Stirrup Cup toast took place. The Rev. Richard Savage of the Twin Oaks Baptist Church in Brunswick read the prayer of St. Hubert, the patron saint of foxhounds and fox hunting.

As he read, we could hear the jangle of bridles and the squeak of leather boots on leather saddles.

"Oh, mighty God, on this glorious day we thank thee for thy creation, for field and forest, for wind and rain and animals large and small . . . you have given the fox his cunningness and speed, the hound his love of the chase and keenness of smell, the horse his sureness of foot and strength of body, and to man the zeal for life and of high adventure."

After the prayer came the toast. Though traditionally the Stirrup Cup is a hot punch served before a hunt, the Van de Motters prepared two dozen small plastic snifters full of the mixture of Canadian Club whiskey and maple syrup. These and plates of small pastries were distributed to the riders. There was apple cider for the children.

I was looking around waiting for the fox to be released and for the hunt to begin when Peplin corrected another common false impression.

"They don't 'release' the fox," he told me.

The dogs roamed until they pick up the scent of a fox or a coyote. The Van de Motters, the co-masters of the hunt, followed the dogs into the woods. The rest of the riders, called "the field," rode in a single-file line careful never to pass the hunt masters and to follow their cues.

From our perch on the top of the hill, we saw the riders following the dogs, with "pink" coats riding horses on either side down into a ravine where they momentarily disappeared from sight. The morning silence of the brown fields and multicolored autumn tree line was shattered by the barking of the hounds and the bleat of the horn. They were obviously onto something.

"You don't call it 'barking,'" Peplin said. "They say the hounds are 'speaking' or in 'full cry.' "

For the next hour, we drove from ravine to hill, catching glimpses of the hunt as it traversed the hills and fields, always careful to stay out of local farmers' corn and beans. The farmers were gracious enough to allow their land to be used for the hunt. The riders were careful to respect the land.

The field circled a wide area through thickets and hills, pursuing an animal the dogs could smell but no rider ever saw. The assumption was that this was a fox. Foxes are territorial and tend to stay within certain boundaries. Coyotes will take a hunt far afield.

Back at Fox Chase Farm at the lunch following the hunt, the riders talked excitedly about the animal that led the hounds and horses for more than six miles back and forth through the woods. The hounds eventually lost the scent at a beaver's dam in a nearby creek. None of the almost 20 riders could remember ever catching a fox.

"There may be reason to hate fox hunting or fox hunters," Peplin said. "But animal cruelty isn't one of them. They never catch a fox. Foxes are too quick and smart. There are too many places where they can, as it's called, 'go to ground.'

"That's why it's called a fox hunt," he said. "Not a fox kill."

November 3, 2002

LIFE AND TIMES

MARY COWAN'S
TRACE EVIDENCE LAB

Death by misadventure in Cuyahoga County

You've heard that dead men tell no tales. Don't believe it.

At least it's not true of the 3,118 cases handled by the Cuyahoga County Coroner's office in 1991. The dead men, or women, who wind up at the Trace Evidence Lab on the fourth floor of the coroner's office often tell a life story—but more importantly, a death story.

The first question you want to ask Mary Cowan, who supervises the lab, is, "What's a nice girl like you doing in a place like this?" She laughs. She heard that question some 50 years ago in 1939 when she left her medical training at Mount Sinai Hospital to work for the coroner.

And she truly is a nice person. She could pass for anyone's grandmother. It's just that she doesn't do what most grandmothers do.

Cowan spends a great number of her waking hours supervising and working with a team of medical technicians to try to determine how the most unfortunate, violent and often most gruesome deaths in the county occurred.

While some dead men do tell tales, it's not easy to get Cowan to flap her jaw specifically about the work she does. She's been known to tell reporters that, if she isn't reading from the official record, she doesn't want to be quoted.

"People always ask me what's the most interesting case I've ever had," she says. "And I always say, 'The one I'm working on now and I can't talk about it.' And then she gets that sweet smile and a sparkle in her eyes. But little else.

There is one case, however, that she will talk about. That's because it illustrates the meticulous work the lab is expected to do at the drop of a body.

It happened in 1984. The Cleveland police had heard that a man was bragging in bars about having killed someone. And, in fact, the man in question had been reported missing. The police had a problem, though: They had a possible murder and a suspect to that murder, but no body.

The plot thickened when it was learned that the suspect worked at the Case Western Reserve University furnace where road kill and other dead animals were incinerated.

The Trace Evidence Lab was called in. The furnace was shut down and the lab's med techs began to sift through pounds upon pounds of ashes. Experts from the Cleveland Museum of Natural History were brought in to help identify and separate the bird bones from the dog bones, the squirrel bones from the cat bones. Soon after, positive identification was made on some human bones.

And, as if that wasn't enough evidence, among all that dust they also recovered a .38 caliber slug. The suspect confessed to the crime, and the case never even went to court.

"We're lucky to be where we are," says Cowan, referring to the location of the coroner's office just off Severance Circle. "We've got specialists from the hospitals, museums and universities all around us. We have a wealth of expertise right here in the neighborhood."

The Trace Evidence Lab is unique in other ways. As part of the coroner's office, which also has a pathology department, a toxicology department and medical advisers who handle odontology, anthropology, radiology and computers, the Trace Evidence Lab is not part of any law-enforcement agency. Unlike the Bureau for Criminal Investigation (BCI), which is headed by the state attorney general, the Trace Evidence Lab is available to assist defense attorneys as well as prosecuting attorneys. It has a kind of scientific independence that other BCI labs don't.

"We're not here to prove the state's case," says Cowan. "Our job is to come up with scientific facts, and facts are just skeletons. Detectives will come to us with rumors, hunches and theories about crimes. Sometimes we prove their theories are right, other times we knock them down. We have the luxury of being purely scientific about our work."

Without attention to scientific detail, the margin for error could be great. Numerous forms of death require an examination of the body by the coroner's office. Chief among them are homicides, but others are considered reportable. They include: sudden death on the street, at home or your place of employment; death under unknown circumstances where there are no witnesses; death following accidents sustained at work like caisson disease (the bends), industrial infections, concussions, abrasions, fractures, poisonings; death where attending physician cannot ascertain cause of death; or death occurring 24 hours after admission to a hospital unless the person was sent there because he or she was expected to die anyway.

Then there's the category of accidental death, 20 last year, including all deaths arising from blows or other forms of mechanical violence; burns and scalds; death from fallen objects; cutting or stabbing; drowning; electric shock; explosion; hanging and strangulation, among others.

It is a Thursday morning, and a class of Police Academy cadets are in the basement of the coroner's office being lectured about the ways death may intersect with their job—and what to do when it does.

Cuyhahoga County Coroner Elizabeth K. Balraj explains the importance of protecting evidence. She stresses bagging the hands of victims so tests can be made with chemical sprays to determine if a gun has been fired. Fingernails, she says, can hide blood and hair that may be relevant to the case. Examining the clothes for bullet holes and powder burns can reveal which direction a shot came from and from what distance. She tells a story about a hit-and-run accident, which was solved after traces of car paint found in the victim's clothing led police to the car's driver.

New DNA testing and genetic markers are both controversial and increasingly important in criminal trials. The autopsy, she says, is one tool available to the coroner, and 40% of the bodies brought in rate one. There are many questions that accompany every corpse. Cause of death, time of death.

"An autopsy can reveal a lot," she says. "A small meal, say like a hot dog, will be digested in two hours. A large meal, four to six hours." Slides are part of the presentation, and while they're less than lovely, they tell the cadets a lot.

The cadets are, for the most part, a young and lively group. Fresh-faced and funny, most haven't seen the street close-up from the inside of blue uniform yet. But they're willing, and that's what counts. They're like something from a cute-but-earnest B movie. It's obvious some of them come from long lines of law-enforcement families and have heard what to expect, while others have driven for EMS. But still, they seem new to this death stuff.

A forensic toxicologist speaks to the cadets about the work being a blend of science and art. A combination of intuition and luck, he tells them. You make the best use of what's available, and what's available is always dependent upon good police work at the death site. The toxicologist talks about testing methodology and complicated scientific techniques.

But he hits home with a story about the day three people at Thistledown racetrack had heart attacks. Toxicologists were called in to check for a link between the incidents. Something in the coffee, perhaps?

As it turned out, it was just coincidence. Two of the victims had a history of heart disease, and the third . . . well, who knows. Maybe he went down holding what he thought was a winning ticket after a 15-minute jockey's objection. Thistledown is a great place to jump-start your heart.

Then Mary Cowan takes the stage to explain the essence of the service performed by the Trace Evidence Lab. The cadets listen raptly to this small senior citizen quietly on fire with a love of science. The possibilities of exactitude, the elimination of error, the pocket of tangible facts in what is usually a messy, obscure and often loathsome situation. She brings elements of intellect, precision and common sense to bear on scenarios commonly charged with white-light rage and random madness.

Cowan explains modes and manners of violent death. Blood prints and bullet holes. "The vestige of something once present," she tells the group, "are the clues by which we track the truth." It's pure poetry. At least as poetic as science gets. And then the announcement comes.

Some bodies have just been brought in. The cadets will get their first opportunity to see how the system works, and what they may be in for each day. There's a surge of excitement and repulsion in the air; a weird blend of curiosity and fear. Enough of this hypothetical stuff. The real deal has arrived. It's literally time to look into the face of death.

There are jokes among the cadets, the nervous kind. The class is too big for everyone to see at once. Half of the lecture room leaves. The rest wait, and there's more forced humor. One cadet produces a small jar of Vick's VapoRub and receives considerable ribbing for applying it to his nostrils.

When the first half of the class returns, the look on their faces gets the little jar moving quickly around the room. This is no time for histrionic bravery. Death isn't pretty—or aromatic.

Two corpses have been brought in. The cadets move toward the window separating them from the deceased. The two attendants on duty sit calmly while the cadets, some covering their mouths and noses, others merely wincing, take a look. The dead are bloated, covered with maggots and their blood has settled close to the skin due to gravity and inertia.

The Trace Evidence Lab will later determine that both deaths were suicide by drug overdose.

When you first meet Mary Cowan in her office, it can be a bit unsettling. Important things happen here (not life and death, more like death and death), and they happen around the clock, at a moment's notice. But maybe you just caught her on a good day. Just outside the door, serious-looking people are congregating over who knows what.

"Defense attorneys," she says, emphasizing the non-partisan role of the Trace Evidence Lab.

Cowan is a farm girl—of sorts. Many years ago, *Cleveland Press* reporter Jim Flanagan wrote a story about her in which the headline read: FARMER'S DAUGHTER WHO NEVER MILKED A COW. Her parents owned a dairy farm, but she's a self-proclaimed "spoiled brat" who fought the sexist bias of the day and pursued her love of science. She admits having read all the Sherlock Holmes books early on but says they were not a driving force. Fiction, she found out later in life, couldn't come close to reality.

"Imagination can't conceive of things that happen in real life," she says. "But there is great tragedy in what we see. I'll never forget talking to a 25-year detective who had just dealt with the death of an 11-year old girl. He said to me, 'You'd think I'd be hardened to this by now.'

Beyond the scientific side of things, Cowan sees a lot of the bad side of humanity. She has another life. She has traveled all over the world, has family, cats and a home of her own. But so much of her work revolves around ugliness and violence. She doesn't know how she feels about capital punishment. She explains it this way:

"So many of these cases revolve around bad tempers. There, but for the grace of God, go I."

THE ILLUSTRATED LIFE
OF HARVEY PEKAR

Who is Harvey Pekar?

Only followers of the Cleveland writer's darkly autobiographical alternative comic book *American Splendor* know anything about this 54-year-old who works as a file clerk at the Cleveland VA Medical Center.

For instance, his middle name is Lawrence. He has been married three times. He once collected jazz records. He has a reputation for being cheap. He has been on *Late Night with David Letterman* eight times, antagonizing the host to the point of being banned more than once. And, yes, he has a tendency toward obsessive-compulsive behavior. He even mooches doughnuts from doctors at the VA hospital.

All this and more can be learned about the man by reading his comic books, his singular art. He presents the trials of his unglamorous life in a format best known for its superheroes. And strangely, it's funny. And ironic. Is Pekar trying to say we're all superheroes and that each life, no matter how media-neglected, is worthy of thoughtful examination and appreciation?

It's not that easy.

Pekar, not unlike comic Jerry Seinfeld, is greatly amused and aggravated by life's little things. But where Seinfeld finds humor, Pekar finds horror.

This month, *American Splendor* readers will discover Pekar's anything-but-ordinary battle with lymphatic cancer in a new book-length comic strip narrative called *Our Cancer Year*. Pekar co-wrote the book with his wife, comic book journalist Joyce Brabner. It is illustrated by Frank Stack, an art professor at the University of Missouri.

Publishers Weekly, the trade publication, has called the book "By turns amusing, frightening, moving and quietly entertaining. . . . Pekar's cancer treatment and suffering will take your breath away."

R. Crumb, Pekar's first and best known illustrator, calls him "the soul of Cleveland."

"He's passionate and articulate. He's grim, he's Jewish. It's a good thing he has stayed in Cleveland all his life. That place would be forgotten in the soup of history without him. Life ain't all beer and Skittles. I appreciate the way he embraces all that darkness," Crumb says.

For anyone who has read all 17 of Pekar's comic books, meeting him is a bit like stepping into a movie you've seen many times. A great number of Pekar's stories are the result of conversations (and overheard conversations) with hospital patients and employees. And while Pekar has been envisioned by a dozen illustrators, the real-life sight of his dark, large-eyed, I've-looked-into-the-abyss stare and ensemble of frayed jeans and faded blue work shirt are unmistakable.

"The theme of my work is about staying alive," he says. "What it takes to stay alive. Getting a job, finding a mate, having a place to live, finding a creative outlet. And more recently, health."

When it is mentioned that he has all of the above—a recent medical exam found him cancer-free, he's happily married to Brabner, they live in a house they bought in Cleveland Heights, he has held his file clerk job since 1965, and the new book is just out—he frowns.

"Life is a war of attrition," he explains. "You have to stay active on all fronts. It's one thing after another. You get one situation settled and you have to deal with another. I'm kinda old to change. I pretty much have the same fears I've always had. I've always tried to anticipate everything. I've tried to control a chaotic universe. And it's a losing battle. But I can't let go. I've tried, but I can't."

He speaks with a feverish anguish, rethinking each response as he speaks it. Even his pauses carry a weight. He is self-deprecating to a fault, and quickly finds a number of arguments to check the slightest praise. When the tag of "working man's hero" is brought up, he's ready.

"Working men certainly don't read my stuff. They don't need to. They have enough of their own lives. They don't need mine. But people with a certain bent, in certain intellectual circles, read me. Not to say only Ph.D.s read me, ya know. But people who are interested in the alternative scene."

When asked about the apparent contradiction between his fear of a cruel and unforgiving cosmos and his ability to go on national television and handily dispatch America's favorite talk-show host, or survive a year of debilitating chemotherapy/radiation treatments and then surgery to replace his disintegrated hip, he comes back quickly.

"In a way, courage is almost a meaningless word," he says. "Who can say what or why you'll do things under certain conditions. With Letterman, what did I have to lose? His audience isn't mine. People give me credit for surviving cancer. What choice did I have? And besides, I fell apart that year."

And where many survivors of cancer have found a renewed belief in God or an appreciation for life's simple pleasures, Pekar can't call up those emotions quite so easily.

"I'm a lot more fearful than I used to be. And I worried and obsessed before the cancer. Every day was so miserable with the chemo. I was so weak I was barely able to move. It was terrifying. I know I have to concentrate on other activities and short-term goals. But I still have a lot of gloomy thoughts. Sometimes life seems like a cruel joke. What does anything matter? I know I'm not the only person to have gone through this, but I think of that saying 'I'm sick of living and scared of dying.'"

But it's exactly this bleak realism that underscores the compelling nature of Pekar's writing. His refusal to look away from the void, his interest in finding epiphanies in the uneventful work of life and his uncanny eye and ear for humor have provided a body of work that, while not widely known, has found singular praise.

In 1989, Joseph Witek, an English professor at Stetson University in DeLand, Fla., wrote *Comic Books as History*, which examines the work of alternative cartoonists Jack Jackson, Art Spiegelman and Pekar. Witek sums up Pekar's style succinctly: "Harvey Pekar specializes in comic book stories which present his own life in all its ordinariness and which examine his often prickly personality with all its annoying, frustrating and disagreeable traits. Pekar tries to balance each issue of *American Splendor*, mixing short, humorous pieces with long autobiographical stories and philosophical reflections, and his own moods in those stories range from angry paranoia about his personal frustrations to (relatively) cheery optimism about his life as a writer."

But appreciation for Pekar and his work is not limited to academia. At last summer's comic book convention in San Diego, Kim

Thompson, the publisher of Fantagraphics Comics, the best known among alternative publishers, paid a debt of gratitude to Pekar.

"Harvey is absolutely crucial to the industry," says Thompson. "He was the first person to write autobiographical comics and, for better or worse, the alternative field has followed him ever since."

Alternative comics make up only about five percent of sales in a market where superheroes reign supreme. Yet Pekar has supporters among industry mainstreamers. Tom Linn, of Capital City Distributors in Madison, Wis., one of the largest distributors in the country, says, "He goes back to the original generation of alternative cartoonists. He depicts his inner life very honestly. That takes courage. His stints on *Letterman* are classic. I think they've brought new readers to comics."

Pekar, while grateful for the kind words, eschews any credit.

"I wasn't sure what exposure on *Letterman* would mean for me. I was not optimistic to begin with. And it hasn't changed my life. My name is a little more well known, which has made it easier for me to get freelance writing jobs. And the issues of *American Splendor* with Letterman on the cover have sold at a slightly faster rate than ones without. But overall it hasn't made that much difference. At least not enough to make me be nice to him,' Pekar says.

Another Pekar admirer is *Village Voice* cartoonist Stan Mack, whose "Stan Mack's Real Life Funnies: All Dialogue Reported Verbatim," shares a style and sensibility with *American Splendor*.

"I'm a fan of Harvey's. We have a similar approach but get different results. He has a format which has not been much explored beyond Art Spiegelman's *Maus*. I see myself as a kind of reporter. What Harvey does is more akin to autobiographical short stories. He's taking literature into a different place. The way he uses different illustrators is like a movie director using different cinematographers,' explains Mack.

He adds, "The marriage of ideas to words to pictures is a continuation of the writing process. He uses stream of consciousness, interior monologues, narrative dialogue. He's breaking new ground with the cancer book. That could be the road of the future for other topics and for other writers."

Pekar was born Oct. 8, 1939, to Saul and Dora Pekar, working-class Jewish immigrants from Bialystok, Poland. (Both are now dead. His younger brother, Allen, is a chemist and classical trumpet player in Indiana.)

Saul Pekar owned a small grocery store on Kinsman, where he worked 80 hours a week, spending evenings studying the Talmud. Dora was a politically active non-religious Jew who believed you should always expect the worst so you'd be surprised at the good.

Her pessimism was not lost on Harvey, who graduated from Shaker Heights High School in 1957. The years that followed were full of anxiety, as he worked one menial job after another. He attended Case Western Reserve University for 1 years with his eye on a history degree. He did well, but then became paralyzed with anxiety about the pressure to succeed and eventually dropped out.

After a brief stint in the Navy, another succession of minimum-wage jobs occurred. His hobby was buying jazz albums, and he pursued the avocation like a demon. (At one time, he owned 15,000 records.) He also read voraciously—fiction, history and politics.

In 1960, while employed by the old Carling Brewing Co., he married his first wife. The marriage lasted 12 years.

In 1962, he met Crumb, a fellow jazz fanatic and struggling artist from Philadelphia. Three years later, Pekar got his job as a file clerk at the veterans hospital.

The year 1972 was marked by two big events: Pekar's first divorce, and the publication of his first comic strip, which was illustrated by Crumb. Pekar was intrigued by the format he found deceptively simple yet with endless possibilities.

Eventually writing overtook the collecting of jazz records in Pekar's private battle of obsessions. In 1976, Pekar self-published *American Splendor* No. 1. The following year he married again. The marriage lasted 3 years.

For the next 15 years, Pekar's life, when he was not at his file clerk job, consisted of writing the strips, haranging illustrators and publishing each year's *American Splendor*.

It was a labor of love. Pekar expected to lose money on each project and he did for the first 10 years. But he garnered a national cult following and critical acclaim. In 1983, he married Joyce Brabner, a woman he had met through correspondence. By 1986, with the help of Brabner's organizational and public relations skills, Pekar began to turn a profit on *American Splendor*.

In 1990, Pekar was diagnosed with cancer, just after he and Brabner had bought a house. The ensuing 48 months or so are chronicled in *Our Cancer Year*.

While that's the Harvey Pekar data, much of the history, body and soul of his life can be found in *American Splendor*, issues 1 through 17. And Pekar continues his life's work.

"It's an autobiography written as it's happening," Pekar says, attempting to clarify just what it is that he has been doing for 22 years. "God, I don't know. . . . I'm not trying to take literature into a new place. . . . If anything, I'm trying to reinvent the comic book. The form has been ignored by all but a few serious writers. . . . And thank God, that leaves so much more for me to work with."

Pekar and Brabner live in a kind of cluttered American splendor. Their four-bedroom house is full of books, records and mementos gathered by two people who have devoted their lives to art, politics and popular and world cultures.

Over a dinner of takeout food in foil tins, they repeatedly interrupt and finish each other's sentences with the good-humored aggravation that only people who are committed to one another for the long haul can abide.

"Joyce," Pekar says with a rueful smile, "you saved my life and you're gonna be the death a' me." He picks up envelopes from the dining room table.

"See, here's a letter from a kid from Brazil. Loves *American Splendor*, wants me to look at his artwork. Here's another from a guy in Kansas City. You would think I'm really famous, but that doesn't translate into book sales. A lot of people seem to know me, I get stopped on the street in Toronto, but I still need my job at the VA."

Harvey Pekar may well be Cleveland's most well-known unknown artist. In 1989, the *New York Times Book Review* said that "Mr. Pekar's work has been compared by literary critics to Chekhov's and Dostoevski's, and it's easy to see why."

Perhaps nobody knows Pekar better than Brabner, who serves as his manager and adviser.

"We just fit," she says. "I give him stability and focus, and he gives me fluidity to stay at home and pursue my own work. When I first met him, I thought, 'Finally, someone who can keep up with me.'"

But what about the infamous Pekar persona? The violent grouch, the chiseler, the obsessive-compulsive nut of *American Splendor*?

"He's a generous person and collaborator. He's tender-hearted, supportive. He's very interesting and has amazing smarts. I mean, you can imagine my impression just from seeing Crumb's depictions of Harvey. I was delighted to find out he didn't smell bad," she says, laughing.

So who is Harvey Pekar?

"I'm just tryin' to get along like everybody else," he says. "Doin' the best I can."

October 2, 1994

CLEVELAND'S HOTTEST CHEF

Iron man Michael Symon rises to the top

Michael Symon, by all accounts Cleveland's youngest and most talented professional chef, knew what he wanted to be as a kid. He found his field of endeavor at age 7, and through commitment, discipline and sacrifice, dedicated his life to it for the next 11 years.

He wanted to be a high school wrestling coach.

How he wound up being Cleveland's hottest star on the ever-burgeoning cuisine scene is another story entirely.

The 25-year-old Symon, voted "Most Likely To Succeed" by classmates at the Culinary Institute of America in Hyde Park, N.Y., when he graduated in 1990, has since been the major creative force in the kitchens of four of Cleveland's top restaurants. While he is praised outside the food world for his accomplishments as they relate to his age, those in the business laud his talent, hard work and passion without mention of his tender years.

Symon most often is credited with taking the art of fine dining to new levels of appreciation and adventure. At his current job as chef at the Caxton Cafe on Huron Rd., he has created what he calls a New World cuisine, which combines foods and flavors from an international spectrum and presents it with highly stylized flair. His friends in the restaurant business simply call it "cool food."

In short, it looks good, tastes good and is good for you. And you've probably never seen anything like it.

Susie Heller, 44, is a nationally respected food consultant. She began 16 years ago in Cleveland in the catering business. She has written extensively about food and restaurants, been hired to test cookbook recipes and has produced TV cooking shows for world-renowned chefs such as Julia Child and Jacques Pepin. She now is back in the service end of the industry with her own Cleveland catering company called Food Fanatics.

"I like Mike," she says. "Some chefs tend to stay in that comfort zone. They find something they can do well and that's it. Mike constantly wants to grow. He likes to change the food. He's known for stretching the boundaries. He really cares about learning as much as he can. He's done a lot in a short period of time and that takes a kind of self-confidence you don't often find in someone his age. He's a risk taker, and in this business that takes courage. It's not an easy profession. He has tremendous energy and creates a lot of excitement."

To look at Michael Symon you might not guess right off the bat that he was an exalted luminary in the shimmering night sky of Restaurant Cleveland. He jokes that when he leaves the kitchen to schmooze with customers they sometimes wonder why the dishwasher is asking them about their meal.

At 5 feet 11 inches tall and 195 pounds, he is sizable but not intimidating. And despite his shaven skull and mustache-free goatee, which create a kind of Amish punk-rocker look, Symon has the explosive, killer smile of someone almost too happy to be alive.

When he is up, that face, that smile, radiate a rare kind of uncut joy that is instantly winning and that draws those around him closer. Then there is that laugh. The hyper-silly two-tone vocal salute reminiscent of an asthmatic bull-goose. This kid is the great chef? The culinary artiste? Well, yeah.

He eschews the toque, the classic tall white hat of chefs, in favor of a turned-around brown-suede newsboy's cap from the Gap and has been known to sport sunflower cooking pants as well. On Saturday nights in the Caxton's tiny 12-by-15-foot kitchen, Symon and sous chef Willie Guzman like to "burn and turn" to a radio station that plays hits from the '70s.

Though Symon is a hard-core modern rocker whose taste in music runs to bands like Nine Inch Nails and Fishbone, he gets an ironic twentysomething nostalgia kick from these tunes. Songs that were hits when he was 5 years old.

Symon likes to call himself a rock 'n' roll chef. When asked what that means exactly, he is surprisingly literal.

"The prep work is like the sound check," he says. "You make sure everything necessary is there and in working order. Ready to go. The menu is the song list. The reservations are the house. You hope it's a sellout. Cooking is like a four-hour show. You give it everything you've got. When the show's over, you walk out into the dining room exhausted and hope there's applause. It's a rush. Then you do it again the next night."

In case the musical metaphor is lost on you, check out a couple of Michael Symon compositions. The Caxton Cafe menu offers these two entrees among others:

Grilled salmon wrapped in Swiss chard (a big, hearty spinach-like leaf), on a bed of wild mushrooms (shiitake, chanterelle and oyster mushrooms sauteed in white wine, chervil and shallots) on top of al dente asparagus.

Two veal chops resting on a Gorgonzola risotto cake, which is held together with arugula and sage pesto and topped off with frizzled leeks.

While these dishes are an earful when read aloud, and certainly a mouthful while being eaten, what's missing is the visual presentation. And the visual is one aspect of Symon's cooking that sets him apart from others. Symon builds a plate vertically. It is his trademark. He has been called a frustrated architect, but his dishes have a distinct tendency to go north. They have a stunning look. But according to the rock 'n' roll chef, it is more than special effects.

"My food is about tastes and textures," he says. "I use ingredients from around the globe put together in a modern fashion. The reason I stack the food is so people will eat them together. The traditional plate has your meat here, the vegetable there and a potato on the side. I'm trying to get people to eat it all together, because when I do it, it's together there for a reason."

The reason Michael Symon is stacking salmon and veal chops instead of pursuing his first love, high school wrestling, is a mysterious and fateful one. And no one had a closer seat to the action than his mom, Angel Symon.

Judging by her size—4 feet 8 inches tall and maybe 90 pounds—you would never guess they were related. But all you have to do is look at her face and see the Greek-Italian eyes, all that flowing coal-dark hair and that smile. Michael's mother for sure. She manages Petite's by Tangerine, a women's clothing store in Westlake. Did she ever imagine her son would become a highly regarded chef?

"Never in a million years. He was always into that tough, macho stuff. Wrestling was his life," she says.

"But even as a little kid he would sit and draw by himself. We didn't know where that came from. But once the wrestling started, that was it. When he was wrestling in high school, at St. Ed's, he would come home from practice and his meal for the day would be this much water," she says, showing four inches between her thumb and forefinger, "and a Lean Cuisine frozen dinner. We'd eat early and open all the windows so the smell of food would be out of the house by the time he got home."

Michael Symon recalls those days with an ironic smile.

"There's my mom making all this great food—spanakopita and lasagna—and I can't eat it. I was wrestling at 105 pounds. Then I broke my arm."

It happened during a practice session at St. Ed's. Symon's right forearm required a plate and 10 screws. He wore a cast for eight months and was told he would never wrestle again. Determined to pursue his lifelong ambition, he started wrestling and a year later broke the same arm again. For Symon, any illusions about athletics were as shattered and torn as his arm. It was a tough reality to face.

"To be told at that age that the only thing you wanted to do was out . . . that was hard for me. It was so final," says Symon.

His mother remembers the time well. Here was her son, the happy, bright, charismatic kid, a leader among his friends, who suddenly turned bitter and angry.

"I was worried about him then," says Angel. "He was angry at God, angry at me. He felt everything had been taken away from him. But I always felt things happen for a reason. He had always worked, so he took a job cooking at Geppetto's [the local rib and pizza chain]. Then one day he called me and asked me to come down and meet him at the restaurant. He said he wanted me to see his kitchen. That's when a light went on in my head."

Michael Symon, whose first job at Geppetto's was as a broiler cook, enjoyed the energy level. The rush. That no no suit and tie were required. And that Geppetto's owner Mike O'Malley drove a Corvette . . . that was cool.

After graduating from St. Edward in 1987, Symon spent one quarter at Cleveland State University, taking requirements and contemplating a degree in architecture. The contemplation was short-lived. When the quarter was over, he had something to tell his parents. He wanted to go to cooking school.

"To tell the truth, I didn't think it would last," says Dennis Symon, Michael's father, a supervisor at the Ford Motor Co. in Brook Park for 25 years. "I thought it was a stab in the dark and would last about two weeks. I was glad when he started cooking at Geppetto's, because he had been just devastated when told he couldn't wrestle.

It was the end of his world. Life was over. We were very concerned. Geppetto's was something for him to do. A place for all his energy and disappointment over wrestling. But who knew what it would become? We do now."

The Culinary Institute of America is considered one of the finest cooking schools in the nation. Symon earned an associate's degree in culinary arts, spending 10 months in class, eight months at an internship at Sammy's in Cleveland, and another 10 months in class.

"It was very demanding," says Symon. "But I learned a lot about the fundamentals of cooking. It gave me a good base. Each class was three weeks long, eight hours a day. We had a final every three weeks. They taught you everything from butchering meat to doing your books to waiting tables. Restaurants are basically math and cooking. They covered it all."

Symon graduated in the top 5 percent of his class and gave some thought to staying in New York. He had been cooking at a place called Melrose in the West Village in Manhattan on the weekends to earn extra money. He had received a taste of the good life and the fast lane that big-city restaurants can offer. And it made him think twice about staying in New York.

"There was a lot of cocaine and a lot of partying in New York in the restaurant world," says Symon. "It can easily become a part of the life. I thought, 'If I stay here, I'll never make it.' I knew somehow I had to get out of there. It probably would have been good for my career but not for my physical state. I saw it destroy people. The place was packed every night and still went out of business. I'm sure the drugs were part of that, too.'

So he moved back to Ohio and in with some friends who were living in Kent and attending Kent State University. Not long after, he applied for a job at Players restaurant in Lakewood, which was owned by Mark Shary and his now former wife Julie.

Shary and his wife had come up with a unique and promising concept. The 40-seat restaurant sold primarily gourmet pizza and pasta. Customers could pick among highly specialized add-on items for their meals. Along with pepperoni and mushrooms were sun-dried tomatoes, smoked rabbit and fontina cheese. Since pizza and pasta are universal favorites, Shary was free to be more flamboyant with the specials and appetizers without fear of alienating the clientele.

"I was looking for kitchen help at the time," says Shary, 39, who now works at Edible Arts catering. "But I was not enamored of CIA graduates. Generally I found them to be arrogant and inflexible. I'm a self-taught cook and I was looking for someone who shared my enthusiasm and ideas. I didn't think I'd find it in Michael."

The 20-year-old Symon knew he wanted to work there right away. In his opinion, Players was the first place in Cleveland to serve great food in a casual atmosphere. Like places he had seen in New York. He wanted this job.

"We had a beautiful interview," says Shary. "Michael was very charming. He knew he had a lot to learn. More importantly, he was willing to learn. I hired him right at the interview and soon found out he was very, very talented. He had skill, technique and creativity. He had a real passion for the food. He's both an artist and a craftsman. By craftsman I mean he keeps working at it. I gave him a lot of responsibility. Total freedom over food development. And we went wild. I just hope he stays in town."

Two years later, Shary was getting ready to sell Players to restaurateur Gary Lucarelli and Symon was ready to move on. Carl Quagliata, the owner of Chanterelle Catering and several restaurants, including Giovanni's in Beachwood, was interviewing for his new downtown restaurant, the 120-seat Piccolo Mondo. Symon was offered the second-in-command position of sous chef. He took it.

It would be four months before the restaurant opened. And the project was behind schedule. So there was plenty to do. Going from a 40-seat restaurant to one three times that size was going to be a new and challenging experience for Symon. More challenging than he ever imagined.

One week before Piccolo opened, the chef quit. This is equivalent to losing the leading man in a large production of an Italian opera. It spells disaster. General manager Tim Bando offered the job to Symon.

" [Bando] kept saying to me, 'Can you do this, Mike?' I'd say, 'I can do this.' It went on like that all week. 'Can you do this?' 'I can do this,' says Symon, laughing.

Symon did do it, but not long after the restaurant opened, Bando quit. Doug Petkovic, who knew both Symon and Bando, and who had been flying in on weekends from his restaurant job in Chicago to help them open, came in and took over the job of general manager. He was there firsthand to see Symon come into his glory as a chef.

"When I first began working with Symon, he was skinny and had hair," says Petkovic, taking a friendly shot. "I saw him go from a completely disorganized, fairly inexperienced chef to an amazing machine in three months. His confidence kicked in somewhere, he began rewriting the menu and creating that thing he does with textures and height, and the place exploded. Carl created it, Mike took it to another level. We did $2.6 million the first year.

"Symon has something few people have," adds Petkovic. "He's an artist."

The 31-year-old Petkovic has been in the restaurant business since he was 12, when he began working at his parents' party center in Avon Lake. He knows the many ways in which a restaurant can go wrong.

"I've worked with a lot of chefs," says Petkovic. "A lot. Mike has natural talent. He expresses himself with food. He's not in it for the money. He does it for the love of what he's good at. He's a purist. No filler, no flour, no breading. He makes the stock and the sauces himself. He's not watching the other guys to see what they're doing. And he's not afraid to step out there and do something different."

In response, the 56-year-old Quagliata says, "I have to work hard. I don't have the brains. But I have a young mind. Michael's a very nice young man. He's aggressive, positive and talented. But these kids today, they're not frightened of anything. I was 30 years old before I would talk to anybody. Being a star chef is a media thing. The main thing you have to do is please the people to be successful. Michael learned a lesson at Giovanni's, but I was willing to give it a try."

In 1989, Joe and Allie Hadden Hanna had moved back to Cleveland from Manhattan. Allie was from Cleveland and Joe had been designing restaurants for an architecture firm in New York.

The Hannas opened their own 44-seat restaurant in the Caxton building in November 1992. Hanna favored the beaux-arts design of early Cleveland architecture. The room was informal but stylish. But there was one problem. The food was unremarkable and the place had seen two chefs come and go in a year. Joe Hanna got a recommendation on Symon from Marlin Kaplan whose namesake restaurant he had designed.

"Michael had a good reputation in the industry. He was up to date on what was going on in food, he was a hard worker. But best of all what he said he would do worked. We eased into it, but basically we bagged the whole menu and gave Michael the freedom to do what he does. And we've just had three record-setting weekends in a row," says Hanna, obviously pleased.

It is midnight on a Saturday at the Caxton Cafe. The staff is breaking down the kitchen and putting up chairs. Michael Symon is having a well-earned martini and talking about the restaurant business.

"I need to learn more about the front of the house," he says. "That's where I need improvement. In this business you can cook the best plate of food in the world, but if your waiter is lousy, it's all for nothing. People will go back to a place that has average food and great service, but not the other way around. Every aspect has to work to make a restaurant a success. And it has to work every day. Consistency is crucial."

Symon talked about the two parts of his personality: the athlete and the artist.

"In wrestling, my coach, Howie Ferguson, always insisted we give 110 percent. If you're not there to win, why even show up? I try to apply those ideals to my work. But I've always thought of myself as an artist. Even as a kid I would draw. Those two sides to me have just always been there."

That assessment is confirmed during a conversation with Maureen Arbeznik, Symon's second-grade teacher at St. Richard's School in North Olmsted.

"I remember Michael," she says. "He had that smile. He was the kind of kid who during recess would find a way to get in the middle of every fight on the playground and always come back to class totally disheveled. But he had the most beautiful handwriting I'd ever seen."

April 9, 1995

ALMOST FAMOUS

*The elusive, brilliant multimedia artist Ray Johnson was
called "the world's most famous unknown artist"*

On Friday, January 13, 1995, Ray Johnson checked into Room
247 at Barron's Cove Motel in Sag Harbor, Long Island. That evening, the 67-year-old artist drove a short distance out to the Sag
Harbor Bridge. It was a balmy winter day. Johnson climbed up on
the bridge's railing and jumped into the icy water below.

Was it suicide? Or just the final work of a man *New York Times*
art critic Grace Glueck called "the world's most famous unknown
artist"? Sag Harbor police said that on the day of his death, Johnson arranged his Long Island home so all of the hundreds of images inside faced the walls. From the front door there was only one
picture showing outward. It was a large color image of Johnson's
face.

Johnson left no will. All his money and property went to a dis-
tant cousin.

He had a preoccupation with the number 13, and the canvas of
his death seemed carefully chosen. It was on Friday the 13th. His
age added up to 13, as did the number of his hotel room. 247. The
time of his death: 7:15.

"Ray Johnson was a mystery inside of an enigma who should
have been wrapped in a bathing suit," says artist and writer Mark
Bloch.

"Picasso was the greatest artist of the first half of the 20th century. Duchamp was the greatest artist of the second half," continues
Bloch, who is working on a book about Johnson called *The Last
Mail Art Show*. "I think 50 years from now people will look back
and recognize Johnson as the next big influence."

Johnson was a painter, performer and collagist who was also
hailed as the father of "mail art." He is credited with helping to pio-
neer pop art and performance art. He knew and influenced artists

such as Andy Warhol, Robert Rauschenberg and Claes Oldenburg, to name a few.

Outside the art world, he was all but unknown. Within it, Ray Johnson was a legend.

"He was an idiosyncratic figure. He was very inventive. He's known for actually predating pop art with the use of subject matter before Lichtenstein and Warhol. But he is best known as the inventor of mail art," said portrait artist Chuck Close shortly after Johnson's death.

Johnson's mail art, the hand-crafted pieces he circulated to other artists in the United States and around the world, were generally small collages of mailing size that incorporated drawings, stamps, pieces of magazine photographs, words, pictures and other recyclable detritus combined for singular effect. He often mailed them with instructions reading "Add to and return to Ray Johnson."

His collages, or "moticos" as he called them (taken from the word "osmosis"), were coveted by art dealers, collectors and galleries. The intricate, meticulously crafted works combined kaleidoscopic whimsy with pop culture references, hand-drawn figures, letters and numbers.

Raymond Edward Johnson was born in Detroit in 1927, the only child of an auto executive, Eino, and his wife, Lorraine. His parents were of Finnish descent. Johnson's artistic talent was apparent at an early age. He attended Cass Technical High School in Detroit and enrolled in the advertising art program there. During the Forties, Johnson went to Black Mountain College in Black Mountain, North Carolina, where he studied painting under renowned artist Josef Albers. It was there that he first encountered Marcel Duchamp's radically iconoclastic ideas about conceptual art that would influence everything he would do.

At Black Mountain, he also became friends with painter and faculty member Willem de Kooning and fellow students Robert Rauschenberg, the multimedia artist, and John Cage, the avant-garde composer. All of them would go on to become giants in the art world.

In 1948, after graduating from Black Mountain, Johnson moved to New York City. He took an apartment across the hall from Cage and choreographer Merce Cunningham. He worked on art projects and socialized with many of his fellow free-thinking Black Mountain alumni. Johnson wanted to revolutionize traditional ideas about art. He renounced easel painting, buring some of his early pieces and cutting up others. Later he would use some of those fragments in his collages.

In New York, he became friends with Warhol. On June 3, 1968, the day Warhol was shot by deranged stalker Valerie Solanis at The Factory, Johnson was mugged at knifepoint by three men in lower Manhattan. The incident, combined with the assassination of Robert Kennedy two days later prompted Johnson's move to Long Island.

As cutting-edge pop artists, Warhol and Johnson shared trend-setting temperaments and new ideas about art. They were the next Big Thing following abstract expressionists such as de Kooning and Jackson Pollock.

Johnson was one of the first pop artists to create multimedia pieces incorporating pop culture references, photographs of movie stars and household commercial images. He used a photo of Elvis Presley in his work in 1957, seven years before Warhol became famous for his silk-screened *Triple Elvis*.

Johnson was an artist's artist. A radical visionary and purist. He believed art was more than a commodity valued only by dealers, collectors and gallery owners who profited when it changed hands. Johnson infuriated some in gallery circles by giving his art away. Mail artists like to say Johnson's art couldn't be bought or sold— only *received*.

Johnson did, however, sustain himself by selling his artwork— but in a fashion so unorthodox as to be comical. When wealthy art patrons (Marian Javits, the wife of former New York Senator Jacob Javits, and literary agent Mort Janklow are two) sought to buy Johnson's work, he put them through strange rituals that would test the resolve of any reasonable person. Johnson's friends tell about how he would arrange to meet collectors at predetermined rest stops on the Long Island Expressway. He would arrive with a suitcase full of unframed collages and show them in a precise fashion, telling the prospective buyer which pieces would be available, in what order, and for what price. Any deviation from Johnson's prescription for viewing his work could nix the sale.

Johnson tried to be in control of every aspect of his life and art.

Galleries displaying, promoting and selling his work faced even more exacting rigors. Johnson would confound them with complicated demands. Everything from the printed invitations to the way the work was hung had to conform to Johnson's specific design in excruciating detail. Time and again, often at the last minute, he would cancel and exhibit. Johnson didn't merely hinder his career, he torpedoed it.

Johnson once approached his friend Sandra Gering, a Manhattan gallery owner, about selling a piece of his work. Johnson showed her a collage that involved a pornographic image taken from a *Playboy* magazine photograph, combined with other elements. He asked that Gering sell this piece—to Madonna. The Material Girl passed on Johnson's material.

Johnson considered art sacred. He abhorred the art world's rules. He told Bloch he wanted to paste his art on the side of railroad cars so only coyotes in the desert would see it. Johnson believed the *action* of making and sharing a creation is what made art *art*. His work was put in motion when he dropped it in the mail. his visually chaotic, yet physically pristine collages have been said to "resemble moments of meaning in life," according to longtime Johnson friend and archivist William S. Wilson. Johnson emphasized the communal, democratic aspects of the creative process and attracted a fanatical following of mail artists whose devotion to the medium still borders on the religious.

Johnson championed a life-as-art/art-as-life philosophy. His work dissolved the line separating the two. At the same time, Johnson was a maddening obscurist, a joker and trickster who delighted in layering on hidden meanings and non sequiturs in his work. Where composer John Cage and his disciples created *Happenings*, Johnson called his performances *Nothings*.

Johnson once gave a lecture at the Rhode Island School of Design in which he unsuccessfully tried to push a piano across the stage. His humor could be camp, cruel and petty, but never lacking wit. When informed the actor Ed Harris was to play the lead in the movie about Jackson Pollock's life, he replied, "Ed Harris is going to play [Pollock's wife] Lee Krasner?" Some women considered him a misogynist because he often objectified the female form to comic effect. Jill Johnston, former dance critic for *The Village Voice*, said Ray Johnson "frightened" her."

Johnson was famous for being bizarre and unpredictable. According to Bloch, he was once invited to the home of famed Fluxus artist Alison Knowles to look at her paintings. Dozens of pieces lined the wall of one room that led to the kitchen. Johnson spent some time looking carefully at each painting before movig on to the next. When he was done, Johnson told Knowles that they were very nice. "But this," he said patting her refrigerator, "is *really special.*"

On September 15, the day before a Wexner Center panel discussion about the life and art of Ray Johnson, 35 mail artists from the United States, Canada, Belgium and England spent the day at the home of Mark and Mel Corrato in Delaware, Ohio. They were there to celebrate the opening of the Johnson exhibit. Bloch dubbed the event *The Fake Ray Johnson Weekend.*

Those gathered represented the radical fringe of the art world.

Many of those who honored Johnson were not full-time art professionals. They were art world outlaws. They didn't quit their day jobs because being a mail artist didn't require it. They didn't participate in "legitimate" art shows, yet their work was seen by thousands. Ray Johnson was, and is, their leader, their liberator.

The mail artists commemorated the Wexner exhibit by enjoying the Corratos' endless hospitality. Most were scheduled to be on the Ray Johnson panel discussion the following day.

During a 10-year "relationship," the Corratos met Johnson only once, while attending a wedding in Long Island. Of all the mail artists there, Bloch and Clive Philpot spent the most face time with Johnson.

Philpot had traveled to Ohio from his home in London, where he's also writing a book on Johnson's life. Philpot first came into contact with Johnson while working at the Museum of Modern Art in New York, where he was director of the library. The two began corresponding and eventually collaborated on two books containing Johnson's artwork.

Sitting on the Corratos' front porch, Philpot shared Johnson stories with mail artists BuZ Blur and Picasso Gaglione. "Anything you could say about Ray Johnson, the exact opposite was also true."

Mark Corrato and his wife, Mel, originally from Youngstown, also found Johnson enigmatic. They began corresponding with Johnson in the late Eighties. Johnson used to dispatch mail art pieces to the Corratos requesting they send them on to other artists such as Yoko Ono, Chuck Close or Christo. His practice of using other artists as intermediaries was one of his hallmarks. He also phoned these correspondents frequently to discuss whatever happened to be on his mind.

"Ray invented the concept of six degrees of separation," says Mark Corrato. "He developed the Internet without computers. He was always looking for connections and creating relationships. He seemed attracted to me because I lived in Youngstown, which he drove through from New York when he visited his parents in Detroit," Mark Corrato says.

"Our relationship with Ray was like an ongoing dialogue, whether over the phone or through the mail," Mark Corrato says.

Bloch, who moderated the Wexner Center panel discussion, discovered Johnson's work in 1978. As a weird form of tribute, Bloch began appearing as Johnson at art events and even sent mail art to people who though it was coming from Johnson. Johnson eventually found out about Bloch and admired his stunts.

"I think he saw the humor in what I was doing," Bloch says. "He started sending me invitations asking me to go places and impersonate him. Every piece of mail he sent was tailor-made for each correspondent. My mail from Ray contained unexplained references to Fifties socialite Elsa Maxwell and the actor Dana Andrews. He never told me why.

"Sometimes his letters came on the back of photocopied articles about himself. Some were recent, some were 40 years old. I left like this was his byzantine way of revealing his biography to me," he says.

Johnson spent his life spinning a huge web of communication among artists around the world. One way he kept the wheel turning was to engage people in a series of oddly juxtaposed words, ideas, and images. Bloch describes his phone conversations with Johnson as being works of art.

"He'd begin a conversation with some odd topic like, 'Did you see Molly Ringwald's gums on *Arsenio Hall* last night?' From there the banter would escalate into this swirl of name-dropping and punning that would reach magnificent heights. I used to use the nickname PAN, which stood for Postal Art Network. One time he left a phone message calling me 'Mr. Wok.' Later I asked why and he said because it rhymed with Bloch and it was a kind of pan. These kinds of triangulations were what made Ray tick. I was always honored to be part of the gyroscopic puzzles," Bloch says.

"But, when Ray was talking to you on the phone, you'd hear the sound of him sanding something. He was always at work on his art. It was all about the art," Bloch adds.

Two high school girls walking on the bridge on that Friday the 13th in 1995 were the last to see Ray Johnson alive. They heard his body hit the water at 7:15. Running to the railing, they saw him swimming the backstroke out to sea. The following day, Sag Harbor Village Police Chief Joe Ialacci discovered Johnson floating face up, his arms folded across his chest. Ialacci described him as looking "peaceful."

Gallery owner Sandra Gering says she received a "Happy Death" card from Johnson in the months just before he died.

"I talked with him in November," she recalls. "He told me he was at work on his most important performance. Even with that and the card, I never picked up on it."

Johnson's unexpected demise took many of his friends, fans and correspondents by surprise. Initially, people were reluctant to talk about their relationships with the artist out of respect for the privacy he cherished.

"Ray Johnson was unique and fiercely independent. I feel his death was his last work. We all miss him," Yoko Ono says.

"I've always thought that if everyone who ever got a piece of mail art from Ray would bring them all together, they would complete one giant jigsaw puzzle," Bloch says.

Bloch views Johnson as a direct descendant of the father of conceptual art Marcel Duchamp, who died in 1968.

"People thought Duchamp had retired from art, and when he died they found this piece he had been working on for 20 years," Bloch continues, referring to the installation called *Etant donnes* at the Philadelphia Museum of Art.

"Ray and I used to talk about that [Duchamp piece] all the time. I asked what we would find after *he* died. All he said was, 'Don't think I'm not working on it.'"

Clive Philpot sees it another way.

"I think he simply retired in January 1995."

December 3, 2000

ONE LOVE, TWO WORLDS: PACKY MALLEY'S GOOD VIBRATIONS

On the night that Toots and the Maytals are to play Peabody's nightclub, Packy Malley has a big problem: *He can't find the band.*

Outwardly, the promoter is calm enough to take in an early show at the Rock and Roll Hall of Fame and Museum. Former Rolling Stone Bill Wyman is performing with his band, the Rhythm Kings. But inside, Malley is worried because Jamaican reggae legend Toots and his 12-man band are driving in from a concert in Winnipeg, Manitoba, some 1,200 miles away, and he hasn't heard from them all day. This is not good.

Cell phone in hand, Malley heads to the Rock Hall bar just before the 8 p.m. Wyman show. To take the edge off, he orders a gin and tonic, the cocktail preferred by his grandfather, Mike Malley, the founder of Malley's Chocolates in Cleveland and his inspiration.

The place is crowded, with a mainly older and sedate group. Patrick "Packy" Malley, the 36-year-old veteran promoter of more than 100 shows, most of them reggae, nervously snaps the rubber bands that help him grip his cell phone, willing the phone to ring. It's not uncommon for reggae bands in Jamaica to go on at 2 a.m., or whenever the band decides to play. Malley's shows start before midnight and on time. He fines bands $100 for every 15 minutes they're late.

"When I tell bands about my policy, they say, 'Oh, Meesta Beezness-mon!' But I don't care. People gotta go to work in the morning. I know *I* do."

Malley's place of business is Malley's. He is the director of retail operations and oversees 12 stores. In 1998, when he joined the family firm, he already was established as a concert promoter. His parents, Bill and Adele, chairman and president, respectively, of Malley's, worried that his reggae shows would interfere with selling candy.

"We had a formal sit-down at my parents' house to talk about my job and what was expected," he says.

It's now 8:45, and the band is still missing. Malley doesn't know what to do. There's little he *can* do.

A week earlier, at the Mid-West Reggae Fest, Malley has no such worries. The sky is Caribbean blue, the music is jamming, and revelers dance deliriously in front of the elevated platform to the Jamaican beat and rhythm of the band Stagalag. Two hundred-foot-long purple and yellow streamers wave in the wind on either side of the stage while Frisbees share the air with the indigenous birds of rural Huntsburg Township, 20 miles east of Mayfield Heights. Malley's 10th annual reggae extravaganza is in full, sun-splashing swing at Meadowridge Farm.

More than 1,500 people have paid $25 each to hear six bands perform at this 140-acre farm. Most promoters would kick back and congratulate themselves on a job well done. Not Malley.

He's introducing the next band, checking the take at the gate, socializing with friends, moving from one task to the next with a smile and handshake.

Out on Mayfield Road, cars continue to pour into the farm. Malley's brother Mike directs traffic, brother Dan minds the beverage sales. His parents sell tickets under a white tent. Adele rips the stubs, Bill counts the cash. They've missed only one of their son's Reggae Fests in 10 years.

"Every day of the year for Packy is the best day of his life," says Adele of her youngest son and the fourth of her six children. "Every party is the best party he ever went to, every band is the best band he ever heard. He has a real talent for fun."

Packy Malley is a human dynamo who works seven days a week at four businesses and sits on a handful and a half of civic and charitable boards. His social life would waste most teenagers.

"Packy has no 'off' button," says his college friend industrial-oven salesman John Doherty, who rarely misses a Packy Malley happening, be in a concert, a party or Malley's Sunday night bartending shift at the Treehouse in Cleveland's Tremont neighborhood.

He's as serious about having fun as he is about the family business.

The socially insatiable chocolate retailer/reggae promoter/disc jockey/bartender is simply his parents' son. He inherited his entrepreneurial spirit from his dad and grandfather, and his organizational skills and love of people and social activities from his mother. He developed his cosmic and comic worldview over the years following the music and hippie philosophy of The Grateful Dead and Bob Marley while laboring under the Jesuits at St. Ignatius High School.

The cosmic and comic are both evident in one of his favorite jokes. "Know what the Zen master said to the hot dog vendor? 'Make me One with everything.'"

Malley is a master of synergy, arranging work and play so they feed off one another, overlapping until the lines that divide them disappear. The one consistent element in all his activities is that he brings people together for fun and profit—be it for a concert, a wedding, a beer or a hot fudge sundae.

"My brother celebrates the differences in people," says Bill Jr., known as "Bee." "I'm a white, West Side Irish Ignatius grad and most of my friends tend to be white, West Side Irish Ignatius grads. Packy's friends are all different, and he loves getting them together all at once."

Malley's gregarious nature is deceptive. He's a hard worker who takes the business side of his shows seriously. He's forever handing out flyers and pounding posters into telephone poles to get the word out about his events. His old-fashioned, do-it-yourself approach to concert promotion recalls the free-spirit *Zeitgeist* of the late Sixties. But his devotion to reggae music has won him a reputation in the United States, as well as in Jamaica, as a true believer.

"His taste in music is impeccable," says Roger Steffans, an internationally known reggae author, lecturer and archivist from Los Angeles. "As a promoter, Packy breaks the mold of those you generally see putting on reggae shows around the country. He's a real amateur, meaning he *loves* the music he presents. After a good show he always has a big grin on his face whether he's turned a dollar or not. He delights in giving exposure to acts that are sometimes obscure even to a reggae audience."

Malley admits that his musical taste is anything but mainstream. "Nothing makes me happier than being able to say I brought the 'Nigerian Elvis Presley' [Majek Fashek] to Cleveland," he says. When asked how the 1995 show at the Agora drew, he says, "Not well," and erupts into his trademark staccato laugh.

9:10 p.m. Malley paces behind rows of Cleveland's rock cognoscenti who are listening to Wyman play. His cell phone rings.

It's the manager at Peabody's. There are 500 people waiting for Toots and the Maytals, who are scheduled to go on in 50 minutes. The band is nowhere in sight.

Malley is sweating now. He tells the manager to have The Mighty Levites, the opening band from Akron, play two more songs.

"Where are they?" he says to no one in particular. "I wouldn't *want* to do this full time. This way it's a hobby and something I love. This is a perfect way for the reggae and the candy to co-exist."

The candy is Malley's Chocolates, the family business with headquarters at Brookpark Road and West 130th Street. During the week, Packy Malley can be found there or visiting one of the retail stores. On this day, he is conducting an informal tour of the production facility. Candy makers on the floor greet Malley cheerfully.

"We're always talking about the business," Malley says. "I know some people must come home from work and have a beer to forget about their jobs, but we talk about it constantly; how to improve things, how to grow and expand the business."

Later, over lunch next door at Bob Evans, Malley talks about the privilege and the responsibility of being part of the Malley family empire.

"People assume that because you're a Malley you're rich. This is a tough business. There's a lot of overhead people don't think about, a lot of upkeep of facilities and wages. We've had slow years where we [family members] all took pay cuts. It's a seasonal business; there are limits to sales."

When a waitress notices the Malley logo on his shirt and asks for some candy, he feigns polite laughter. It's a question he hears all the time.

"My parents opened the Brookpark facility in 1990," he continues. "And they're not kids. So there's a lot of planning, hard work and sacrifice that goes into this that the average person doesn't see."

"Only 17 percent of family businesses make it to the third generation," he adds. "I am that third generation. I think that's cool and fun."

9:43 p.m. Malley leaves the Rock Hall lobby while the band's still rocking. It's time to deal with the Peabody's crowd just blocks away at East 21st and Euclid.

"This is the kind of stuff that makes you crazy," says Malley, shaking his head and laughing nervously.

Malley's introduction to reggae music occurred in 1982, on a camping trip to West Virginia with his brother Mike. The vacation was marred by rain, and Malley passed the time in a tent listening to the cassette tapes of his brother, who is now the publisher and editorial director of *Hotel & Motel Management* magazine, based in Cleveland.

It was in that tent that Malley first heard reggae legend Bob Marley.

"The album was *Rasta Man Vibration* and I was like, 'Whoa. What's this?' I listened to it over and over again. It was so cool. I still find it endlessly intriguing. When I got home, I bought more reggae music and just immersed myself in it," he says.

"I'm attracted to lyrics that deal with social and spiritual issues. They make you think. It's rebel music. Bob Marley was a revolutionary. People find it amusing that I'm an Irish guy into reggae, but I see a connection between the Irish music about political struggles and reggae songs about social and political oppression."

One year later, Malley was an Ohio State University freshman, majoring in economics and minoring in Latin and astronomy. He was on the eight-year plan. It allowed him to work as a bricklayer during the day, earning tuition money, and take his economics, Latin and astronomy classes at night.

"All three subjects are pretty much worthless when it comes to finding a job," says Malley today.

Ever a man of the people, Malley ran for student body president. His campaign consisted of a series of concerts at the Mirror Lake amphitheater adjacent to the school commons. His shows—reggae, country and blues—attracted massive audiences of 3,000 students. The parties won Malley a large following.

But Brian Hicks, a more serious-minded candidate, defeated Malley. Packy was particularly upset because he was convinced that had the school counted the write-in votes for Patrick *"O'Malley"* he would have won. Shades of Election 2000.

"I think Packy had the right idea about the kind of campaign to run," says Hicks, who is chief of staff for Ohio Governor Bob Taft. "Packy was a spirited and entertaining guy. Those concerts put the importance of the election in proper perspective."

Malley continued staging concerts. Organizing and executing the events became habit-forming. Malley loved the rush of producing big shows. The Mirror Lake concerts became larger and more popular until Ohio State authorities grew uncomfortable about their size and the security and insurance issues they raised. Malley was told he would no longer be allowed to stage the events. But he wanted to do one more with his favorite reggae band, Identity.

One night, after a few beers, Malley took a boom box to the amphitheater and plugged it into an outlet. To his amazement, the electricity was on. He realized he could put on a show anytime he wanted.

Malley proceeded to do just that. By the time the campus police came by to complain that the show wasn't authorized, the band was playing and thousands of kids had turned out. Deighton Charlemagne, Identity's lead singer, remembers the concert as a huge success. And he still admires Malley's pluck.

"For de love of de music, Packy Malley will bend de law," Charlemagne says in his heavy St. Lucia accent.

The following week, Malley was informed by mail that he was suspended from Ohio State for one academic year.

He later reapplied, deciding it was time to focus on graduating and join the real world. He received his economics degree in 1991 and moved back to Cleveland, where he briefly worked as a stockbroker for Dean Witter and then A.G. Edwards from 1995 to 1998.

Malley found the stock market a tough business. Even with his high energy and natural charm it was still difficult to get established in the world of high finance. He was discouraged when constant cold-calling of potential clients failed to yield success. He continued to produce shows and became better known for his entertainment ventures.

Malley vividly remembers the day he realized he'd lost his desire to do battle with the bear and bull.

"I was sitting in my glass-enclosed office on East 9th and St. Clair one morning making my cold calls when I noticed the window washers setting up their scaffolding. At the end of the day they had washed all the windows in the building and were packing up. I had made 187 unsuccessful calls. I thought to myself, 'Those guys did some work today. What have I done? Nothing.' That's when I took my reggae posters off the wall and resigned," he says.

9:58 p.m. Malley grimaces and slams his palms against the steering wheel of his 1995 aqua-blue Chrysler Sebring convertible (License plate: JAMAICA). He's weighing his options regarding the missing Toots. He could have the Mighty Levites play even longer. He could make an announcement and ask the crowd to be patient. But it's two minutes to showtime and he still hasn't heard from the band.

Malley has promoted shows that were failures, even disasters, before. His Psychedelic Sock-Hop at Upper Arlington High School near Columbus in 1988 cost him a $5,000 college loan. His 1993 Country Music Fest—at Meadowridge Farm—set him back $20,000 when fewer than 100 people showed up.

Malley stops on a side street near Peabody's and dials the band one more time. No answer. He lays his head against the steering wheel. On the floorboards are two cassettes: *Reggae Jamfest,* a collection of classic reggae hits, and *Bringing Out the Leader in You,* Dale Carnegie's motivational tape.

His cell phone rings. It's Toots' manager.

"Where are you?" Malley shouts into the phone, a squint of uncertainty on his face. It's clear he is almost afraid to hear the answer. Then a smile crosses his face. It turns out the Maytals' tour bus is four blocks away, sitting in front of Peabody's.

Packy Malley laughs wildly as he puts his cell phone in his pocket and puts the car in gear.

"You are looking at one happy dude," he says, heaving a sigh of relief.

September 23, 2001

FATHER'S DAY

Prosecutor's dedication born of his father's death

The remaining few "It's a boy!" cigars lay on the kitchen counter. Neighbors entered through the side door, carrying casseroles. The phone rang with congratulations for the beaming dad, Brendan Sheehan, still wearing a plastic wristband from the hospital.

Sheehan, Cuyahoga County's 35-year-old boy-wonder assistant prosecutor, smiled and hugged his two daughters after returning home from seeing his son. In the living room, 5-year-old Erin and 3-year-old Makayla were having a kiddie birthday party to mark their little brother's birth.

But one Sheehan family member was absent. He was represented by an old photograph, prominently displayed on a living-room table. It wasn't the only birthday Timothy Sheehan, Brendan's dad, missed. On Aug. 27, 1982, he was due home from work to take the family out to dinner to celebrate his only son's 15th birthday.

Timothy Sheehan never came home that day. His murder by serial killer Frank Spisak, a nebbish neo-Nazi tormented by his desire to become a woman, resulted in one of the most bizarre trials in Cleveland history and forever intertwined the lives of Spisak, Prosecutor Donald Nugent and young Brendan Sheehan.

Timothy Sheehan was a model of Irish immigrant success. He was the oldest of six children and the only one to cross the Atlantic in search of a better life. Sheehan's wife, Kathleen, was also a native of Ireland. She immigrated first in 1954. He followed in 1962. A year later, they married.

His first job in Cleveland was running the warehouse at Higbee's downtown. By 1980, he was superintendent of the physical plant department at Cleveland State University. He was a hard worker, devoutly religious and a devoted family man. He rode the bus every day to save money for his children's education.

Tradition dictated that one or more members of the family greet Timothy Sheehan at the bus stop each evening when he returned from work.

That's where Brendan and his mother were on Aug. 27, 1982. Shortly after they gave up waiting and returned home, a Fairview Park police car rolled ominously into their driveway.

Timothy Sheehan had been found dead, shot four times at close range in a basement men's room at CSU. It looked like a robbery/homicide, police said. His watch, wallet and beeper were missing. There were no suspects. Timothy Sheehan was 50 years old, leaving behind his wife and four children.

"Within an hour, the house was full of people," Brendan said. "Relatives, neighbors. The parish priest was there. There was a lot going on. We were all in shock."

In the pain and confusion of the next few days, Brendan found a way to deal with his father's death. He insisted on writing and delivering the eulogy.

"Our father was someone who . . . guided and inspired," Brendan said at the funeral Mass. "His heart was a treasure of kindness and strength, of manliness and honesty. Daddy is someone whose love we will cherish forever. For no one can ever take Daddy's place."

The last man who saw Timothy Sheehan alive was a 32-year-old neo-Nazi with a history of problems.

"Mr. Sheehan looked at me when I shot him," Spisak said months later. "I was a little disturbed by that. He looked right at me. He looked at me with eyes that didn't comprehend. No fear or anything. He looked at me with an absolutely blank look. One minute he was looking at me, and the next minute I shot him."

Spisak was picked on and bullied as a boy. At age 8, he said, he recognized the desire to be female. He found refuge from his personal torment in the hatred espoused by white supremacy groups. After high school, he had difficulty staying employed. When a brief marriage ended, he began experimenting with homosexuality and cross-dressing. He once was arrested for prostitution while dressed as woman.

Four months after Sheehan's death, Cleveland police followed up on a complaint that someone was firing a gun from the window of a second-floor apartment at East 53rd Street. They arrested Spisak and seized a .22-caliber automatic and three other guns. He was released on a $200 bond, but after police received two anonymous calls linking him to other deaths, he was rearrested.

Officers soon discovered Spisak had been on a rampage. Sheehan's death was one of three murders and two attempted murders.

Spisak also was indicted for the murders of the Rev. Horace Rickerson, 57, and Brian Warford, 17, and for the attempted murder of John Hardaway, who was shot five times but lived. Spisak also was charged with the attempted murder of CSU chemistry lab assistant Coletta Dartt, who fended off an attack by Spisak.

The city was relieved. A very scary character was behind bars. The pending trial would show just how scary.

The four-week trial, which began in June 1983, turned into a racially and sexually charged public spectacle, at times bordering on the theater of the absurd. Spisak grew an Adolf Hitler-style mustache and carried a copy of Hitler's book *Mein Kampf.* He said he was an agent of God in a war against blacks and Jews.

Spisak clearly loved the attention.

"When I walked in the courtroom and all these TV cameras were in there and all the bright lights were shining on me, that was the most exciting thing that ever happened to me in my life," he told a reporter. "It was like being Hollywood, you know. I couldn't resist the temptation to really ham it up. The whole town was interested in a bad guy, and I showed them a bad guy."

Center stage was Nugent, then the assistant county prosecutor and now a federal judge, who handled the Spisak case along with Patricia Cleary. Nugent and Spisak's attorney, Thomas Shaughnessy, were both hard-chargers. Nugent baited Spisak, calling him "Frankie," his feminine name. Shaughnessy repeatedly asked witnesses about his client, using half a dozen slang synonyms for the word "crazy."

The Spisak trial was a momentous undertaking for Nugent. The jury examined 240 exhibits of evidence and listened to 60 witnesses testify for the state. Judge James J. Sweeney ruled the defense didn't provide sufficient evidence to allow the jury to consider Spisak's plea of not guilty by reason of insanity.

"We showed that he knew right from wrong, and that he was able to refrain from committing the acts," Nugent said.

Brendan Sheehan sat through some of the trial. "You go to a trial like that to see the guy who shot your dad. You've got questions, and you want answers. Why would a person do something like that? And all I see is this squirrelly punk. And worse than that, he seems to be enjoying the attention."

After the jury found Spisak guilty of all charges, Sweeney sentenced him to die in the electric chair. Spisak responded with a two-minute tirade about white supremacy, ending it with a vigorous "Heil Hitler" salute.

On July 21, 1983, Brendan's sister Catherine called from the courthouse to tell him the jury had recommended the death penalty.

"I remember getting that call and feeling a great sense of relief," Brendan said. "It was a demonstration that the justice system worked, and it helped put that long, ugly and painful chapter of my family's life behind us."

After the Spisak trial, Nugent, a Jesuit-trained former Marine, became a mentor and father figure for Sheehan.

"Nobody succeeds in this life without the good works and help of others," Nugent said. "Legendary prosecutor Charlie Laurie helped me out. I wanted to do the same for Brendan. Because he showed interest."

Sheehan graduated from St. Edward High School in 1985 and went on to Baldwin-Wallace College, where he double-majored in business administration and communication. He was president of his senior class in 1989.

Two years after the trial, Nugent ran for common pleas judge. Sheehan volunteered for Nugent in the campaign, helping him win the election in 1984. During college summers, Sheehan worked as a clerk in a law office. He was a "runner" at the firm, and his travels took him past Nugent's chambers daily.

When Sheehan expressed an interest in law school, Nugent recommended he work at the courthouse and attend law school at night. Brendan followed Nugent's advice and, with a letter of recommendation from the judge, found a position as scheduler. In 1991, Nugent needed a bailiff and hired Sheehan.

"I missed out on doing the things kids do with their dad," Sheehan said. "Playing catch, going to Browns games. But what I really missed was his advice about what to do with my life. Career advice.

"That's where Nugent was so great. For someone looking to be a lawyer, who could be better? Who would know more about showing a young person the ropes? I was really fortunate to know him and be his friend."

Sheehan passed the bar exam in 1994. The following year, Nugent was appointed a federal judge by President Clinton. Sheehan wanted a job in the prosecutor's office, but Stephanie Tubbs Jones wasn't hiring. Nugent brought him on as a law clerk.

"Researching and writing briefs made my head feel like it would explode," Sheehan said. "The training was great, but it was like law school times 10."

Sheehan made $50,000 a year as Nugent's bailiff and $80,000 a year as his law clerk, but what he really wanted to be was a prosecutor, even though assistant county prosecutors start at $34,000.

After Bill Mason became Cuyahoga County prosecutor in 1999, he ran into Brendan Sheehan outside the Justice Center.

Sheehan immediately asked him for a job. And soon the boy who had sat through the trial of the man who murdered his father would be trying capital cases of his own.

DEATH ROW

Spisak lives on Death Row in Mansfield Correctional Institution. His petition for a writ of habeas corpus was recently denied by U.S. District Judge Solomon Oliver. Spisak and his attorneys argued ineffectiveness of counsel during his 1983 trial. The appeal will move to the U.S. 6th Circuit Court.

He arrived for an interview wearing a prison-issue white jumpsuit. His feet and hands were shackled. His gold-rimmed eyeglasses looked like those from 20-year-old trial photographs. He carried a stack of documents relating to his case and talked openly about his crimes.

"I'm very sorry for what I've done, and I have to say I'm ashamed of what happened," he said. "If I could talk to the families of my victims, I would tell them I'm very, very sorry. I never meant to hurt them. At the time when the crimes were committed, I didn't know what I was doing. My illness caused me to do those things. I would like those people to forgive me, but I don't know if they can."

Spisak said he has renounced his Nazi beliefs and insisted his criminal behavior was the result of frustration regarding his gender-identity issues.

"My lawyers didn't tell the jury that I suffered from a mental disorder. Transsexualism is a mental disorder. Gender dysphoria is a mental disorder. It's listed in the Diagnostic and Statistical Manual of Mental Disorders, which is the American Psychiatric Association's guidebook."

Spisak also said he has sorted out his problems.

"I think I've learned who I really am. For many years, I was confused. Other people always tried to mold me to go their way. I didn't have the freedom to be myself. Since I've been locked up, I've had to confront a lot of these things. I want hormones and surgery, absolutely. I just got a stronger sense of who I am now.

"I'm Frances Anne. That's who I am."

Spisak may have forever altered Brendan Sheehan's life and career. But criminals in Cuyahoga County are worse off for it. He tries twice the cases of the average assistant prosecutor and his conviction rate is better than 80 percent.

He is motivated by the murder of his father.

The affable, baby-faced lawyer drinks way too much coffee. Sometimes 10 cups a day. He'll go out and get a jumbo-size one after the kids go to bed. All that caffeine fuels a furious attention to detail. He gives his home phone number to witnesses and reporters. He returns all calls. He prides himself on being thorough, working every angle and reading every piece of paper. His witnesses show up. There is no mistaking his high-pitched voice and the energy behind it. What Sheehan lacks in courtroom presence he makes up for with shoe leather and sweat. It's how his dad did it.

His persistence was never more evident than in the case of the murder of roofer Robert Cutler, who was shot at close range three times in the head in Bay Village on Jan. 4, 2001. A suspect, Timothy Moulder, had been interviewed, but he had an alibi. The case was going nowhere until Sheehan discovered that Moulder had been indicted in the beating and robbery of Cutler the previous April, and that he had threatened to kill Cutler if he went to the police.

Further investigation by Sheehan turned up a videotape of Moulder at a Bay Village gas station when he said he was home sick. Phone records also put him at the murder scene. Moulder is currently serving life in prison.

Some of his colleagues gripe about Sheehan's showboat style and his flair for theatrics, like the time he brought an exotic dancer into a courtroom in an obscenity case against a bar owner. While Sheehan jokes, he can be a shameless self-promoter; he won't apologize for working hard. He knows what it's like to be a victim of crime. And it drives him.

"Prior to his job as a prosecutor, I wouldn't have told you that Brendan was a workaholic," said his wife, Michelle, an attorney and

partner at Reminger & Reminger Co. LPA. "But he became one
when he joined the prosecutor's office."

It's his way of honoring his dad, just as he did in the eulogy 21
years ago, which concluded:

In closing, then, my prayer is
That I may pass along
To my own children
As much nourishment of the soul, and
As much fulfillment of the heart
As he has given to Mom, the girls and me.

So as much as he loves his work, Sheehan knows what it's like to
miss sharing time with a father; he says he plans to spend as much
as he can with his two daughters and his newborn baby.

The son he named Timothy Sheehan.

June 15, 2003

WELCOME TO THE WEIRD: BROWNS LEGEND GARY COLLINS

It was quite a sight.

The 35 members of the 1964 Cleveland Browns championship team lined the north tunnel of Cleveland Browns Stadium at just after noon Sunday, waiting to take the field in their white jerseys. At the same time, the current players ran off the field following warm-ups and into the tunnel.

The two rivers of testosterone intersected with handshakes and high-fives. It was age handing off to youth, the present saluting the past. The air in that tunnel had an electric, almost cosmic quality.

You might say that the Browns' 20-3 victory over the Baltimore Ravens was sealed in that magic moment. You might, but Gary Collins wouldn't. The most valuable player from that '64 championship game is proud of the fact that he had a good day, catching three touchdown passes to help ensure the 27-0 victory over the Baltimore Colts. But he doesn't go in for that esoteric bullshit.

Never has. He's a just-do-it kind of guy for whom it's easier to find raucous humor in life than to endure tired honorifics from people who don't hold themselves to any other kind of standards.

Collins is a football legend who now works happily mowing lawns. He's a famous party guy who has quit drinking.

He takes pride in his athletic accomplishments but doesn't want them to define him. He's tired of talking to the media about the championship game yet allowed a reporter to shadow him for three days.

Like his former teammate Jim Brown, Collins doesn't conform to the stereotype of the legendary sports hero. He allows for his complexity and contradictions. If at times he's too blunt, so be it. He's not about to put on an act just to make people with unreasonable expectations comfortable. If you've ever dreamed about being a football hero, hang around with Gary Collins for a few days. It can be educational. And pretty funny.

Especially if you have an appreciation for the absurd.

"Welcome to the weird world of Gary Collins," he said as a warning before beginning three days as our guide to the championship reunion.

5:45 p.m. Friday

Gary James Collins was going deep. Deep in thought. The former wide receiver who was famous for hating practice missed the rehearsal for the "Browns Town" television extravaganza at Severance Hall celebrating the 1964 NFL championship.

He was on the bus with his old teammates and their families heading for the live taping. He knew he would be asked for his favorite memory of the championship game.

Collins, 64, is a little heavier and the hair is thinner than when he was 24 years old, 6-foot-4 and 220 pounds. He attended the celebration with his son Gary, 45, and granddaughter Alicia, 21.

Sitting in front of him on the bus were former quarterback Frank Ryan and his wife, Joan. Collins leaned over to Joan.

"So far this afternoon I've been called Frank, Harry, Barry and Handsome . . . I think half the guys on this bus are senile," he said.

She looked shocked until she realized he was kidding. Forty years later, same old Gary.

And he is still as direct as ever. His one reservation about attending this event was that he is tired of questions about the '64 championship game and about scoring the first touchdown in a *Monday Night Football* game.

"You know the Austin Powers character Mini-Me? I should be called Gary Two-Game. Fifty times a year people come up and ask me if I know I scored the first touchdown on 'Monday Night Football,'" he said. "I always say, really?"

Still, as the bus got closer to Severance Hall, Collins came up with his special moment of the championship game, just in case he's asked.

"On my last touchdown, I ran through the end zone and into the crowd waiting on the field. If you see it on film, I completely disappear into the crowd. I was absorbed by cheering fans. All those people grabbing and groping you. Now that's a good feeling."

6:15 p.m. Friday

At Severance Hall, after negotiating the red carpet lined with fans and autograph seekers, Collins ran into former offensive line-man and current Browns radio announcer Doug Dieken. They over-lapped in 1971, Dieken's rookie season. Dieken introduced Collins to his girlfriend, saying, "Gary, I know you have great hands, but could you keep them in your pocket for the next couple minutes."

Dieken and Collins hit it off right away in 1971.

"He was a slow, white wide receiver," Dieken said. "He was my hero. That's what I was in high school."

Collins waited backstage at Severance with Jim Brown and former lineman Dick Schafrath. As they talked, they could hear a muffled version of the tribute just on the other side of the wall.

"This is all bullshit. Why don't we just send Jim out there now. That's what everybody's waiting for," Collins said, teasing Brown.

"It's just like all our games. We'd be in the huddle. What should we do? Hmm. I know. Give the ball to Jimmy," Collins continued as Brown smiled and Schafrath laughed.

Brown begged to differ.

"I remember coming into the huddle on several occasions say-ing, we need to throw that ball *now*," Brown said.

"Remember that game against Dallas in '63? They made us stay out at the airport [because the team had black players]. They didn't need to do anything to make you more angry," Collins said. "You ran 232 yards that day. And it was hot. I said to Cornell Green. This is the man."

It was time for Collins to be introduced. He walked onstage as they showed the clip of him scoring that last touchdown and get-ting sucked up by the end-zone crowd. Then the live audience at Severance gave him a standing ovation.

Gary Collins looked pleased.

7:30 p.m. Saturday

One of the weekend's many lavish events thrown by Browns owner Randy Lerner was a dinner for the '64 team at the stadium. Collins was relaxed and talked about his past and his life today. It's fitting that Collins, a man who won acclaim tearing up foot-ball fields, still works on grass. He lives in Hershey, Pa., and works for his son's landscaping company. It's physically demanding work. Sometimes they mow 23 lawns a day. He doesn't mind. "It helps me keep in shape," he said.

After he was cut from the Browns following the '71 season, Col-lins coached in the World Football League and then was an assistant coach at a junior college. He raised horses, moved back to Pennsylvania and got into financial planning. He's the first to admit that he didn't transition well from pro sports to civilian life.

"It's a statistic that a high percentage of NFL football players divorce seven years after they retire. I got divorced exactly seven years out. I tried different things. I lost all my money. I'm OK now. My [second] wife just retired. We're middle class. Fame is fleeting. Money comes and goes. I consider myself semiretired. I still do a few appearances a year. I get a lot of fan mail. I'm happy. Faith and family. That's what's important."

11 p.m. Saturday

Collins joined many of his teammates in the bar at the Hyatt Regency Cleveland at the Arcade.

He was a carouser when he played ball. He helped organize the after-game parties. During summer camp, Collins was something of a scout. He'd find bars close enough to Hiram College, where the Browns trained, so players could pound a few cold ones in the hour between practice and dinner—places such as the Freedom Tavern that used frosted mugs.

"Those tasted so good after two-a-day practices in July," he said.

But not anymore. Collins said he hasn't had anything stronger than Diet Pepsi in 21 years. And he's been married to his wife, Carole, for 24.

"I married an Italian girl," he said. "They keep you in line."

12:15 p.m. Sunday

The former Browns ran out of the tunnel, onto the field and watched as a red veil was removed from a championship trophy that had been made specially for them.

Then announcer Casey Coleman interviewed a slightly confused Collins briefly for the fans while a clip of one of his catches played on the scoreboard screens above him. He saw the announcer's lips move but couldn't understand what he was saying because of the acoustics on the field.

"I couldn't hear his question. I just gave an answer I thought would apply to any question. I must have sounded like an idiot," Collins said, shrugging.

On his way back from the dedication, Collins signed autographs and chatted with fans. Later, up in a suite with former teammates

Charley Scales, Jim Ninowski, Jim Houston, John Brewer, and Sidney Williams. Collins enjoyed some old war stories.

The subject was former Browns coach Paul Brown.

Collins had everybody on the floor mimicking the way Brown instructed the team in the precise art of folding their game plans and placing them in their pockets.

Ninowski, the backup quarterback, wasn't afraid to rile the coach during practice.

"Remember the time Paul sent [equipment manager] Morrie Kono in with a play. I said to Morrie, 'I don't like that one. Go get me another one.' Morrie was scared to death."

"What about the Bolsheviks on the roof?" Collins said. "Remember during practice Paul saw some guys working on a roof, and he thought they were spying, stealing his plays? He sent Morrie over to check them out."

2:45 p.m. Sunday

At halftime, Collins left the suite to give television and radio interviews. Former quarterback Frank Ryan saw him in the hallway.

"Be kind to me," Ryan begged of his former receiver, acknowledging that his throws to Collins weren't always on target.

After the laughter, Collins talked about the weekend. "This was nice. It was good to see everybody," he said. "It's amazing everyone's alive but Lou [Groza]. The 50th reunion won't be like this. They'll need a much smaller room. That, and canes and seeing-eye dogs and interpreters. 'Cause none of us still around will know what the hell we're talking about."

Collins enjoyed the attention over the weekend but said the constant praise from strangers has a kind of numbing effect. "We're just football players," he said.

On the elevator back to his suite after the TV interview with CBS announcer Randy Cross, Collins pointed out the dichotomy between his life as a football legend and his real life.

"You know what the folks back home in P-A are saying after seeing me on TV?" Collins asked.

He paused for effect.

"Hey, that guy cuts my grass."

September 14, 2004

ROUNDING THIRD AND HEADING HOME

Casey Coleman fights cancer with 'no complaints, no regrets'

Casey Coleman was connected to Cleveland sports broadcasting for more than four decades. He agreed to share his struggle with pancreatic cancer with the *Plain Dealer* in a series of periodic reports.

'LUCKIEST GUY' IS STILL VERY MUCH IN THE GAME

On Monday, Oct. 10, there was a cobalt-blue Ford Escape in the driveway of the modest Cape Cod-style home in Rocky River. The letters on the license plate read LGITW, for "luckiest guy in the world."

Two media identification passes hung from the rearview mirror. One for the Browns and one for the Indians. The name and picture on both plastic cards: Casey Coleman.

Normally, at 10 a.m. on weekdays Coleman wouldn't be home. He would have finished his 5 to 9 a.m. "Wills and Coleman in the Morning" show on WTAM AM/1100. After the program he would be out at the Browns' training facility in Berea interviewing players and coaches. Or he would be at a Recovery Resources office doing counseling.

Instead, Coleman was home recovering from surgery during which half his pancreas, his spleen and eight lymph nodes were removed. He had been diagnosed with pancreatic cancer only a week earlier. Now, he faced seven months of intensive radiation and chemotherapy.

Coleman was told he has a 12 percent chance of living five more years.

Most people wouldn't feel very lucky to be diagnosed with an aggressive and deadly form of cancer. But Coleman still stands firmly behind the motto on his license plate. And while recovering from his operation at home with Mary, his wife of four years, he exudes a remarkable serenity.

"You know, 90 out of 100 people who get this aren't diagnosed in time to qualify for surgery. So I'm grateful for that," Coleman said.

"And even if the survival rate is 12 percent, somebody has to be in that percentile. Why not me?"

Coleman credits his peace of mind to seven years of sobriety, a 12-step program and an active faith in God.

"If you're worried, you pray. And if you're praying, you don't need to worry," he said.

"I'd miss having more time with Mary and my kids but the sum total of my life has been blessed. And if you look on the table in the other room there are literally thousands of printed-out e-mails from friends, and listeners, wishing me well and sending prayers. And even though this hasn't been exactly fun, it's been great for Mary and I just to have this time together."

A VACATION DETOURED, A LIFE FOREVER CHANGED

Coleman's early diagnosis was the result of a forgotten passport. Coleman and his wife planned a vacation to Chautauqua, N.Y., and Toronto during the Browns bye week in late September. As they approached the bridge to Canada, Mary realized she didn't have any identification. She had misplaced her driver's license the week before and forgot to bring her passport.

So they turned around and drove back to Rocky River. While home with time on his hands, Coleman finally told his wife about the pain he had had in his side for several months. He decided to go to the doctor. Coleman assumed it was a pulled muscle. Friends told him it was probably his gall bladder.

He saw the doctor on Wednesday, Sept. 28. He underwent a CT scan the next day. The results were due Monday.

On Monday, Oct. 3, Coleman gave a lunch speech at the Pro Football Hall of Fame in Canton. Afterward, he went with Mary to the doctor to learn the results. Dr. Jan Bautista was serious and direct. He told Coleman there was a mass on his pancreas. He said he couldn't be sure, but it wouldn't surprise him if it was cancer. Bautista said to hope for the best but prepare for the worst.

Coleman was stunned. He knew three people who had pancreatic cancer. None are alive.

The doctor gave him a list of surgeons and recommended he make an appointment right away. Surgery was scheduled for Friday, Oct. 7.

Coleman worked on Tuesday that week. Wednesday on the way to work the gravity of the diagnosis finally hit home. He was eye to eye with his own mortality. And it took his breath away. He composed himself with prayer.

At home, Mary tried to stay busy. Casey was so positive and calm. She wanted to be the same. But even when he was home she kept finding herself sitting on the stairs off the kitchen crying so Casey couldn't hear.

On Thursday afternoon, the day before his operation, Coleman sat on the deck behind his house, taking in the unseasonably warm weather. Mary joined him and in the course of small talk, burst into tears.

Coleman put his arms around her. He told her there was nothing to cry about and said they shouldn't worry about things they can't control. Coleman then reminded his wife that he had turned his life over to God a long time ago. It was all in His hands.

Mary said at that moment she felt a great weight lift. Her fear and sorrow evaporated. That night she and her husband went to dinner at Three Birds restaurant. They sat on the patio, had a long dinner, laughing and talking late into the night.

Mary could hardly believe their sense of peace.

'No complaints, no regrets' no matter the outcome

Coleman survived the surgery the next day, but was plagued with infections and high fevers that sidelined him for almost a month, including a five-day return to the hospital and a two-week quarantine at home.

For the time being, every day without a fever is a good one for Coleman. And the Browns' astonishing 22-0 shutout of the Miami Dolphins last Sunday was an emotional boost. So he remains thankful, if pragmatic.

"Say I get the worst-case scenario, I've got no complaints, no regrets," Coleman said.

"Who's had the kind of life that I've had? There's no one richer than me. Everything's gone my way. From the time I was a kid. I was captain of my high school football team, president of my senior class. I got to hang around my sports heroes, Ted Williams and Jim

Brown. I have two beautiful kids, a great career doing something I love. If I was given a month to live there isn't a list of 16 things I'd be running around doing. I can't think of anything I'd do differently."

Coleman still sounds a lot like the Luckiest Guy in the World.

November 24, 2005

HALF OF COLEMAN'S BATTLE IS KEEPING HIS HOPES UP

Casey Coleman is ecstatic that both his daughters, Kayla, 17, and Chelsea, 19, will be over for the holidays to help decorate the tree. Chelsea has been away at school in Denmark and hasn't seen her dad since August.

But he's disappointed that he will be under quarantine, especially susceptible to infections.

"I hate the idea of hugging them through a mask," Casey said Wednesday from his bed in the VIP wing of the Cleveland Clinic.

That's part of the frustration for Coleman in his battle against pancreatic cancer. One step forward and two steps back. Hope often muted by disappointment.

His wife, Mary, always at his side, has kept his spirits buoyed with her wisecracking sense of humor and an article she recently found, written by the late biologist Stephen Jay Gould. Gould was diagnosed with a rare, aggressive cancer and was given eight months to live. He lived 20 more years and died in 2002 from an unrelated illness.

"That's the kind of information Casey needs to hear," Mary said.

Otherwise, Casey has been typically blunt about his progress.

"This chemo's been kickin' my ass," he said.

He's lost 45 pounds since the sessions began. He says that the chemotherapy makes everything taste terrible.

The short medical definition for chemo is: "Treatment with drugs that have a specific toxic effect upon the cancer, usually interfering with cell production." Chemo causes cells to commit "cell-suicide," as one medical metaphor puts it. Another metaphor applies, too. Chemo is like burning the village to save it.

When Coleman was diagnosed with cancer in early October, doctors were eager to get the longtime Cleveland broadcaster through surgery that removed half his pancreas and into chemotherapy to eradicate any residual cancer cells.

But post-surgical infections in a 15-inch incision delayed chemo for a month and included a two-week quarantine that left Coleman fighting for his life on two fronts instead of one. Wednesday, Coleman was back in the Cleveland Clinic for three separate procedures deemed necessary after his second round of chemo kept him in bed for three days and brought on a fever of 102 degrees.

It has been tough from the start for the 54-year-old Coleman. He knew this fight wasn't going to be easy. But knowing and living it are two different things.

His chemo treatments showed early, if brief, promise. On Dec. 4, the Sunday after his first chemo session, Coleman felt so good that he drove to the game between the Browns and Jacksonville at Cleveland Browns Stadium.

"They let me park inside, under the stadium where the players do," he said. "I was invited to sit up in [owner Randy] Lerner's loge with Jim Brown, [team president] John Collins and [general manager] Phil Savage. When I got down there, I walked around the field before the game chatting with some folks. Somewhere in the back of my mind I'm wondering if this is the last time I'm going to be doing this.

"Then a weird thing happened. I noticed with my peripheral vision the camera guys were all shooting me from a distance. I thought, what's this all about? Then it dawned on me. B-roll [background film] for my obit," Coleman said smiling with a bit of gallows humor.

Later, Coleman made his way up to the press box.

"It took me 45 minutes to get from one end to the other. There were so many friends saying hi and wishing me well. It was really something. Just great. But by the time I got to Lerner's box, I was feeling very tired. Jim Brown said he enjoyed my recent description of him as 'vice president of scaring the hell out of people.' Not long after that, I started feeling like I was going to pass out. I had to hold on to my chair to keep from falling over."

It became increasingly clear to Coleman he wasn't going to make the 1 p.m. kickoff.

"They called ahead for my car. The security guard down there was so nice to me and such a sincere, sweet person, it was the first time all day that I almost choked up," Coleman said.

But in keeping with Coleman's demeanor, no story ends on a down note.

"Then the car rolls into sight with about $10,000 worth of fancy rims on it. It was the wrong car. It was right guard Cosey Coleman's car," he said laughing.

Coleman thought about keeping it. But it didn't have his LGITW license plate. It stands for Luckiest Guy in the World.

And that's still the diagnosis that he gives himself.

December 19, 2005

COLEMAN HEARTENED BY PRIEST WHO IS TRUE FRIEND

Casey Coleman and the Rev. Tim Gareau were already friends when Gareau heard Coleman give a talk at a Catholic men's retreat last year. Coleman spoke about his alcoholism and how the struggle brought him back to God and the Catholic Church in 1998.

"I turned my life over to God, and it got so much easier," said Coleman.

The priest was wowed by Coleman's story.

"It was a powerful talk, and it had a lasting effect on me," Gareau said.

Good friends now, Coleman and Gareau met in a roundabout way. In 1999, Cleveland Browns head coach Chris Palmer asked Coleman if he knew a priest willing to be a team chaplain. Coleman asked the pastor of his church, St. Raphael in Bay Village, who recommended Gareau, who was then at a parish in Fairview Park.

In 2000, Gareau became the team's Catholic chaplain and transferred to St. Raphael, where he and Coleman became friends.

"You don't have to spend more than five minutes around Tim to know he's special," Coleman said.

At times Coleman brought Gareau with him when he counseled troubled people at a drug-treatment center.

"It was something we did quietly," said Gareau.

But the priest had a bigger impact on Coleman than he knew.

"The thing about people who are addicts is that they often have both low self-esteem and big egos. I know that sounds contradictory. But Tim showed that to me once when we were talking with a woman who suffered from mental illness and addiction," said Coleman. "She had a long story. She couldn't forgive herself. He told her that if God had forgiven her, then she should be able to. It was like a revelation for me."

Given the friendship, Gareau was the obvious choice to celebrate the Mass Mary Coleman wanted said for Casey for Christmas last month. On Dec. 26, 150 family and friends of the couple gathered at St. Raphael. Several dozen of Casey's colleagues from the media and executives from the Browns' and Indians' front offices attended. In the choir loft at the back of the church, Denise Dufala and singer John Kassimatis poured out the Andrea Bocelli Italian duet "Prayer."

Mary wrote about hope in a card she put together for the service: "It will also guide us through this illness and probably the rest of our lives . . . please remember our friends who are fighting similar battles.—Casey & Mary."

Coleman is still fighting infections and, more recently, a hole in his stomach that has doctors puzzled. When low on hope, he draws on his memories of the church service.

"When I was a little kid, I had my First Communion in St. Raphael's church. Back then, the church looked like the biggest building in the world to me," Coleman said.

"When I came back to town in '87, it looked small, and I remember wondering how it could have shrunk so much. But on the day after Christmas at that Mass, I was like a little kid again. When I saw all those people, all my friends and family . . . it looked like the biggest building in the world again."

January 20, 2006

BELICHICK, COLEMAN TIES REMAIN TIGHT

After covering sports for almost 30 years, Casey Coleman has many big-league names in his Rolodex. Dozens of old friends have called to wish Coleman well during his battle with cancer. One of them is former Browns coach Bill Belichick.

That's right. Bill Belichick, aka Dr. Doom, the stone-faced, Super Bowl-winning coach from Planet Football 24/7. *That* Bill Belichick.

"In this business, people come in and out of your life because they move around so much. But Bill is one of those people, who, after he left in 1995, never stopped calling. We've always kept in touch," Coleman said.

The relationship was controversial. No coach in Browns history angered fans the way Belichick did in 1993, when he let quarterback Bernie Kosar go in midseason. No one in the media was closer to Belichick than Coleman. And when public anger boiled up at the coach, some spilled on Coleman.

"Bill's kids could no longer ride the bus to school, and I had to have a police cruiser parked outside of my house because of death threats. How insane was that?" Coleman said.

The two became friends when they began taping a weekly Browns television show together.

"We're almost the same age. We both grew up in the '60s. We both loved rock 'n' roll. We were both married and had kids close in age. We had a lot in common," Coleman said.

Belichick mentioned something else the two had in common.

"We both came from football families. We had both played New England prep-school football. His dad was a sports announcer; mine was a scout for Annapolis [the Naval Academy]. He grew up around the Browns' training camp at Hiram. My dad used to take me there, too, in the summers," said Belichick.

When Belichick coached the Browns, he and Coleman had a professional relationship that some people in the media looked at skeptically.

"Casey gave me a lot of good advice on a lot of things, including players, coaches and media relations, game planning and strategy. He understands the game and the personalities involved," said Belichick.

As a journalist, Coleman doesn't feel any need to defend his relationship with the coach.

"Look, if you're covering a football team and the coach opens up the door and offers you the kind of access I was [offered], I don't think you hesitate too long before you walk through that door. When he said to me, 'Let's watch some tape,' I didn't have to think real hard about whether I wanted to or not," said Coleman.

As for cutting Kosar, Coleman says he was the first to criticize Belichick.

"On our first show following the Kosar thing, I said to him point-blank on television that he had committed the cardinal sin of coaching—that he had neglected to put his team in the best position possible to win games. Bill defended his decision. And the next season the team went to the playoffs, and the defense set a league record for least number of points scored."

Belichick has no regrets.

"For me it was a football decision," said Belichick. "Despite the public criticism, I could live with that decision because I felt then, as I do now, that it was the correct one. You would have to ask Casey what that situation was like for him. Our friendship was strong before the Kosar situation, and we have built on it every year."

Coleman talks with Belichick by phone almost every week.

"We've always had an easy rapport. I've watched Super Bowls with him at my house when he was coaching the Browns. We talked football. We still do," said Coleman.

The coach regretted he wouldn't make it in town to see Coleman inducted into the Cleveland Area Broadcasters Association Hall of Fame Wednesday at Windows on the River.

"He is just a guy I admire," said Belichick of Coleman.

"He was always someone I could trust. Even though he was in the media, if I told him something in confidence, he'd follow through on that. Now he never complains about his condition, although I know he's been in a great deal of pain and discomfort.

"Casey has shown a tremendous unselfish attitude in his life. He continues to help and inspire others."

Meanwhile, Coleman, who said he is feeling the best he has since the ordeal began, has nine weeks of chemotherapy under his belt and said he has quit trying to figure out why one treatment works and another does not.

In late February, doctors found a malignant tumor on Coleman's liver. They removed it and found no other cancer cells. He hopes that by next month he can undergo radiation and turn a corner on the cancer.

"I feel terrific," said an upbeat Coleman. "I'm actually itchy and raring to go. I've cleaned out my briefcase nine times. The pencils are all sharpened."

March 16, 2006

CASEY ON THE MOUND IS OPENING DAY HIT

"The only difficulty was seeing through the tears. Very emotional," said Casey Coleman.

Coleman's home-opening first pitch, high and outside, had fans on their feet and cheering. Seven months into his battle with pancreatic cancer, Coleman was in fighting form and enjoyed the thrill of a lifetime.

"It meant the world," he said afterward.

Indians manager Eric Wedge caught the pitch and congratulated Coleman on the toss. Coleman, 55, chatted with players, coaches and media before the game. Bench coach Joel Skinner lent Coleman a warm-up jacket while he waited for the two teams to be introduced and for local *American Idol* star Scott Savol to sing the national anthem.

Once off the mound, Coleman was reminded that Opening Day first pitch honors are often reserved for presidents, governors and Hall of Famers.

"Well, when they realized that Bob Feller has pitched an entire game's worth of Opening Day pitches, that's when they decided to call me," he said.

Back upstairs in his suite, Coleman was congratulated by friends and family, including daughters, Chelsea, 19, and Kayla, 17.

All week long the 30-year sportscaster's main concern was getting the ball past, if not over, the plate. Various friends stopped by last week for games of catch so Coleman could get his arm in shape.

"If I was the weather guy, I wouldn't have been as concerned about my throw. But c'mon, I'm the sports guy. I have something to live up to," said an exhilarated Coleman.

Coleman is looking at the possibility of a June comeback for his radio show on WTAM. He has finished his first round of chemotherapy, and, after losing 80 pounds, he has finally put 3 back on. It's the direction in which he would like to keep going.

"I told Wedgie I was planning my comeback, the same way he does in spring training. I have every day of the calendar marked," said Coleman.

Coleman said he also appreciated the Tribe's front office maintaining the "Casey" theme throughout the home opener.

Casey Blake hit a grand slam and KC of KC and the Sunshine Band sang "Take Me Out to the Ballgame" during the seventh-inning stretch.

April 8, 2006

DESPITE DIRE PROGNOSIS, COLEMAN STAYS FOCUSED ON LIVING

Bay Village—"This is a glorious sight," Cleveland broadcaster Casey Coleman told a crowd of more than 900 runners and walkers Saturday morning.

Coleman was the celebrity starter of a 5K run and two-mile walk that raised more than $50,000 toward research into pancreatic cancer, which Coleman is fighting.

Coleman, who was recently given six months to live, told the crowd that pancreatic cancer is the ninth-most-common cancer but the fourth-leading killer because research into that type of the disease is the least funded.

"I thank you for your support and prayers for whatever time I have left," said Coleman, who is continuing treatment.

Among those attending were Coleman's former WJW Channel 8 colleagues Robin Swoboda and weatherman Dick Goddard.

Earlier in the week on a dreary Wednesday, Coleman was fishing off the Bradstreet Landing pier in Rocky River and talked about what it has been like facing a terminal illness.

"A jerk on one end of the line waiting for a jerk on the other," the 55-year-old sports broadcaster said ruefully. Coleman has spent his 30-plus-year career primarily in Cleveland on radio and television.

Coleman spoke of the six-month prognosis in somber tones.

"When I was first diagnosed, every step offered another reason for hope," he said. "I qualified for surgery. The operation went well. The chemo was working. I felt good. To suddenly hear the word 'inoperable' was a blow."

After baiting his hook, Coleman cast the line.

"I had to go back to what I believed when this started. That I've had a good life," he said. "I'm grateful. But it's been emotional. I had lunch with my daughter the other day and broke down. I told her I was sorry I wasn't going to be here for her."

Coleman was blunt with doctors when he received his bad news.

"I asked them how you die from this," he said.

"They said as the liver shuts down you become more tired, lethargic and sleepy," he explained. "With drugs they would manage the pain. And then you just slip into a coma until you die."

These days Coleman balances his optimism and realism.

"This chemo is no fun. It's chapping my face and it gives me insomnia for days. But if I can squeeze out a little more time, I'll take it," he said.

June 25, 2006

WTAM'S COLEMAN DEFYING ILLNESS IN RETURN TO SHOW

Veteran Cleveland sports broadcaster Casey Coleman, who has been off the air from his show "Wills and Coleman in the Morning" on WTAM AM/1100, returns today despite a 10-month battle with pancreatic cancer.

Doctors gave him six months to live in June, but Coleman has felt so good and excited about the start of the Cleveland Browns' training camp that his doctor gave him permission to return to the air. The show airs from 5 to 9 a.m. weekdays.

Coleman recently learned he will receive the National Academy of Television Arts and Science Silver Circle Award for 25 years in television, on Saturday, Sept. 9, in Westlake. The award will be presented to Coleman by former Cleveland anchors Kelly O'Donnell and Martin Savage.

Regarding his return to radio, Coleman trotted out his familiar sign-off.

"I'm rounding third and heading home," he said.

August 1, 2006

THROWING SEEDS

A casual tour of Casey Coleman's home yields a scattered array of awards, honors and gifts recently given to the longtime Cleveland sportscaster.

On the kitchen table is a large color photograph of Coleman with the current Cleveland Browns. The occasion was the recent naming of the Casey Coleman Field House, the team's indoor training facility in Berea. On the coffee table in the living room is an invitation to tonight's dinner at which Coleman will be inducted into the Cleveland Journalism Hall of Fame.

A painting by comedian/actor Martin Mull, a gift to Coleman, hangs on the wall over the fireplace. There is a letter from Recovery Resources, a 50-year-old Cleveland organization that treats drug and alcohol addiction, announcing the establishment of Casey's Fund to help underwrite the treatment of indigent clients.

But what means the most to Coleman is the DVD he pops into his home entertainment center. On Sept. 11, Coleman gave the talk he had given at 12-step meetings many times before. This time, however, it was recorded and will be shown to everyone who goes to Recovery Resources for treatment.

"So many wonderful things have happened to me this year. But this is the top," Coleman said, warming himself in front of the fire. "This is like throwing seeds, hoping a few of them take root and grow. And it will go on after I'm gone."

Coleman's story of addiction and redemption is familiar to anyone who knows the genre. His happy childhood was muted by a vague sense of not fitting in. The first flush of the alcoholic buzz in college was a liquid panacea to a host of dark, emotional discomforts.

The drinking increased over the years. The daily pint of vodka after work quickly became the daily quart, pounded down in the car on the way home from the radio station or television studio. A DUI arrest, later thrown out of court, increased his drinking while driving it further into the closet.

Laid off from his television job, sick and tired of being sick and tired, Coleman entered a Cleveland Clinic alcohol-rehabilitation program. The intake doctor told Coleman that he was a full-blown alcoholic and one of the most depressed people he had ever treated.

Once he was out, Coleman began attending 12-step meetings. The third step, surrendering his will to God, gave him problems. The Catholic nuns from his school days were the first to give his self-esteem a beating. His religious involvement since then had been negligible. A fellow addict told Coleman to simply substitute God for alcohol. The booze had controlled his life for years. Now give God a turn. Coleman was doubtful but willing.

A few weeks later, Coleman was home on a sunny Saturday when he happened to catch sight of his daughter making a bed in the next room. She was bathed in sunlight from the window. Coleman felt like he was having a vision. He was suddenly filled with an otherworldly radiance and joy. He knew at that moment that God had entered his heart. He gathered his two daughters, and they drove to a nearby church and attended Mass. It was Nov. 11, 1998, the day he celebrates as marking his true recovery.

On the DVD, a woman asks Coleman if he feels cheated by the diagnosis of his terminal illness. He tells her that he will miss people. He will miss his family but knows he will see them again. Someone thanks him for sharing his story. Coleman said whenever he gives a talk, he always leaves the room with more than he brought in.

The DVD is over, and Coleman is working on a pint. Now it's Haagen-Dazs black raspberry chip.

Coleman's doctor told him in June he had about six months to live. "The doctor's prognosis seems fairly right-on," Coleman said calmly.

"I'm feeling more frail by the day. I take a 12-hour pain pill in the morning and the morphine as needed. I have tumors in my liver, cancer in my pancreas and a hernia, so it's a three-ring circus of pain down there. I'm almost ready for the hospital bed in the living room. What I do every day is based on how I feel each morning. I'm hopeful to see January," he said.

"I'm still open to a miracle," he said. Doubtful, but still willing.

October 26, 2006

SAYING GOODBYE TO A SEASON AND A FRIEND

They call it a holy day of obligation.

Monday was the last day of the thoroughbred horse racing season at Thistledown. It's the day all the bust-outs and losers come back for one last chance to recoup their misinvestments, as it were.

Of course I was there.

Early that morning, I got the news we lost sportscaster Casey Coleman after his year of defying the odds on pancreatic cancer. The disease takes most people in three months or less. Casey was too strong in so many ways.

I didn't know if going to the track was the right thing to do. But then I rarely know what the right thing to do is these days. All I knew is that I wanted to be outside. It was unseasonably warm and mild for late November. Sixty degrees. The sun kept trying to shine.

When you lose a friend, it can feel claustrophobic. Like life is closing in. That's why the air felt so fresh and the horses smelled so good. Even the wafting cigar smoke was invigorating.

Casey and I were around each other almost all of our lives. When we were kids, he lived one street over. But he was five years older. That's a generation when you're young. Because my dad was a sportswriter and his dad was a sportscaster, we were often thrown together. Like at the Browns training camp at Hiram College during late summers in the 1960s.

I got to know him better decades later after we had both moved back to Cleveland following our respective job hops around the country. Then we spent even more time together when he married my high school friend Mary Ross.

And then in the last year and a half, Casey and I became close, in a fashion, when he asked me to help him chronicle what would become his excruciating, yet graceful, dance with death. I wrote a half-dozen stories about his brave gaze down that endless road. He was upbeat and good-natured about his bad luck and trouble to the very end.

Being at the track is all about time. So is life. You want to get there for the first race. You want to stay until the last. And you want to win. There are 18 minutes between races. You have to make decisions. You have to gamble. Time flies.

Time flies, unlike the horses I bet on that day. But Casey's passing made me want to make more of the time I have. All around me, I heard the horseplayers talking about Casey. "You hear about Casey?" They called him by his first name. Like they knew him. Because they did. He would have loved that.

I kept looking for horse names that would have some meaning for Casey. I wanted to honor Casey out there with a big win for my few dollars. I was hoping he was with me, looking down from that great press box in the sky.

Late in the day, I heard a losing bettor near the finish line say, "I follow horses who follow horses." It reminded me how funny Casey was. Off the cuff. Once I called him for rock star Michael Stanley's phone number. He said, "You know who I would call if I needed Michael Stanley's phone number?" I was hopeful. I asked who. "You," he said.

Before the last race, I met an ex-jockey named Bill Avalon. He rode for 10 years. He always comes out for the last day of the season at the Big T. He said it was always a bittersweet day. There's a celebration of the past season, but a lot of people are going separate ways.

"Some people don't come back," he said. "They go different places. Some you don't see again."

I continued to scour the program for some sign of Casey in horse names. In the very last race, I found the No. 11 horse, Chelsea's Boy. Casey's oldest daughter is Chelsea. I had finally found what I was looking for. All pumped up, with a fistful of cash, I went to the window.

"That horse has been scratched," said the betting clerk.

It was that kind of day.

December 1, 2006

CLEVELAND PAYS SPORTSCASTER FINAL RESPECTS

Casey Coleman had time to plan his own funeral, and he turned it into a celebration of his faith in God.

Family, friends and fans gathered yesterday at St. Angela Merici Church in Fairview Park to say farewell to the longtime Cleveland sports broadcaster who died Monday after a 14-month battle with pancreatic cancer.

The funeral Mass was concelebrated by the Rev. Tim Gareau, Auxiliary Bishop Roger Gries and retired Cleveland Bishop Anthony Pilla. In attendance were media members from Cleveland's television and radio stations as well as representatives from the front offices of the Browns, Indians and Cavaliers.

WOIO Channel 19 News anchor Denise Dufala sang several hymns as duets with her singing partner, John Kassimatis.

During Gareau's homily, he said Coleman might have selected the second reading from the book of Timothy—"I have fought a good fight, I have finished the race."—because it was the closest thing you could find to sports in the Bible. He also talked about Coleman's religious conversion eight years ago and his unfailing devotion to the virtues of faith, love and peace.

"We walked in faith, we walked in light," Gareau said of Coleman. "I got to know Casey from the inside out. Most people know him from television or the radio. I got to know him as a man for others. A man who knew the Lord."

WJW Channel 8 sportscaster and Coleman's longtime friend John Telich gave an upbeat and heartfelt tribute before the service's close. He talked about Coleman's endless knowledge about sports and how hard he worked to include it in all his broadcasts. He did an imitation of Coleman calling a Browns game: "Kevin Mack at the 30 yard line. He's at the 20. The 10! He's allergic to shellfish! Touchdown!"

Telich later said, "People will know that Casey stood for more than home runs and touchdowns, and that the only dunk that matters is in the waters of salvation."

On the back of the services' program was a list, written by Coleman, explaining why he felt he was the Luckiest Guy In The World, LGITW, being the letters on his license plate. He mentioned his faith and sobriety, his daughters, Chelsea and Kayla, and wife, Mary, the opportunity to work in sports, and the love and support of his friends.

The front of the program offered a variation on "Rounding third and heading home," Coleman's signature sign-off:

"Rounded third and safely home."

A GIFT FROM GOD

*Romanian born sculptor Ted Stroie carved
a new life for himself in the U.S.*

"These things, good Lord, that we pray for, give us Thy grace to labor for"

—St. Thomas More

All things considered, St. Thomas More could do worse. Ted Stroie's double garage attached to a split-level house in Brunswick Hills is filled with machinery and tools all covered with a fine patina of plaster and gypsum dust. It's the last place you'd expect to encounter More.

But the 41-year-old Stroie is in there diligently crafting a wooden likeness of the saint. He's using a chisel and other wood-carving tools to bring More to life, back from the 1500s, out of a 300-pound block of basswood.

Stroie doesn't even know this statue's final destination; he's a subcontractor on the job. To shape his work, he has researched More by reading and meditating on his life. Earlier this day, he spent time with Scripture as he does each morning‹asking for strength, guidance and inspiration.

"This is God's work," he says, explaining the contemplative focus this ancient art demands. A devotion to both faith and art has long been a part of Stroie's life.

He grew up in Romania and was raised in his family's Eastern Orthodox religion, which he accepted without question and followed without conviction. He saved his passion for other pursuits: electronics, engineering and carving. "My childhood was beautiful. You have to be older to comprehend what the world is about," he says. "It wasn't until I was in the army, after high school, that I found out I wasn't allowed to leave the country."

At the age of 18, just before entering the army, Stroie visited a

beautiful monastery he had heard a great deal about growing up
in Transylvania in northwest Romania. It was six miles from his
house in the Carpathian Mountains. His hike ended when he approached the monastery grounds through a garden. There sat the
Rev. Teofil Paraian, a blind monk who has since become the country's leading Christian evangelist. He was sitting there on a bench
all white. White hair, white beard, white robe. He looked 100 years
old, but he was only 50. He could speak many languages—English,
French, German. He loved poetry and introduced Stoie to many
poems.

"Even though he was blind, he helped me see God in my heart,"
says Stroie with a joy that makes you think the meeting happened
yesterday. He began to visit the priest each week, and to pass the
time on the hour-and-a-half walk, he began carving small wooden
objects with a pocket knife. "That was how I began carving," he says.
"I didn't know anyone who carved, so I started looking for books on
the subject to teach myself." What began as a hobby would wind up
transforming Stroie's life.

"Ted's a rare bird," says former employer Edward Kotecki III,
manager of Kotecki Monuments in Cleveland, where Stroie worked
for 13 years as a sculptor until the company was sold to Rock of
Ages in 1998. "It's hard to find people with his natural ability. He
marries into his subject," Kotecki says with awe. This year brought
the master sculptor a new challenge. For more than a decade with
Kotecki, he was a salaried employee with benefits. Although the
new owners asked Stroie to move to Vermont with the company,
he chose to stay in the Cleveland area and go off on his own. It was
something he had always wanted to try, and this was his chance.

He made his mark in Cleveland. He sculpted the life-size statue
of Christopher Columbus on Mayfield Road in Little Italy. He
carved the bust of the Polish astronomer Nicolaus Copernicus
that's in the All Nations Garden on East Boulevard. The 12-foot
Jesus with outstretched arms on Lot 31 at Holy Cross Cemetery?
That's his, too. So is the front end of the Chevy S-10 pickup truck
emerging from the 50-ton block of granite at the Chevy dealer at
W. 150th St. and Brookpark Rd. Stroie spent a year on that.

Some weeks later, he is back in his garage studio working on a
new project. He's carving a full-size likeness of Joseph. That would
be Joseph of Mary and Joseph. He will carve a full-size statue of
Mary as well for the Poor Clares' chapel on Riverside Drive in

Cleveland. Each will take roughly a month. "It's different now," says the artisan, one of few in the area, if not the state, who has honed his anachronistic craft.

"Before, I used to go to work every day, come home and not worry. Now I have to be more creative. I have to be a salesman, and an estimator. You have to sell yourself with every job. It has been hard. I need the courage to ask for more money." So far, the work has been steady, but Stroie isn't entirely comfortable with the uncertainty that accompanies being self-employed. Stroie is no stranger to adversity. And he's never been afraid to pursue his dreams.

It was on his third attempt, in 1982, that a 23-year-old Stroie and two college friends escaped from Communist Romania during the repressive and bloody reign of Nicolae Ceaucescu. "Our escape was clearly the work of God," Stroie says now, recounting the events while sitting at a picnic table in his back yard. The third attempt was different from the others. Stroie had visited the local library, where he examined maps of the Romanian-Yugoslavian border. It was forbidden to remove map books from the library, so Stroie surreptitiously memorized the documents. Combined with what he feels was "the grace of God," his research paid off.

"We were walking through the forest at night. It was so dark we didn't know where we were going. There were two rivers we had to cross. At each river there was a fallen tree, which allowed us to cross over the water. We walked all night and finally fell down to sleep. We awoke the next morning by the sound of barking dogs. Soldiers had dogs on leashes on the trail right near us. The dogs could smell us, but the soldiers couldn't see us. We lay very still and the soldiers kept going," he says, eating home-grown grapes in the back yard of his three-acre spread.

The consequences of being caught were dire. Stroie's first two escape attempts were aborted before he and his friends could be caught. Stroie says they were very lucky. "If the soldiers catch you, it is very bad because of the beatings. Jail is easy compared to the beatings. They might beat you to death. They do it in such a way that it rearranges your organs on the inside. Jail is nothing."

As day broke, Stroie and his companions, Radu and Mirceau, faced increasing peril as they crept toward the Yugoslavian border. Hiking through tall grass underneath guard towers, wading though sewage-filled ditches and crawling beneath barbed-wire fences, they edged toward freedom. The closer they got, the more careful they had to be. Near the border there were tripwires in the grass.

"My friends gave me their packs and went ahead with sticks lifting up the grass looking for the alarm wires," says Stroie. "It was like a dream. All my senses got so much bigger. I had some water in my shoes from the ditches and they sounded to me like thunder. It was so loud! I kept saying, 'Quiet! Quiet!' After hours of walking, we came to a stone post in a field. The letters on it were written in Cyrillic. We thought we must have been in Yugoslavia."

Stroie and his friends were in Yugoslavia but not out of danger. The Romanian government would have paid for their return. A sympathetic soul picked them up while hitchhiking and drove them to a town near Belgrade. All they had to trade for their freedom were a couple of Casio and Texas Instrument calculators. Stroie had a few gold coins in his pocket. Bogdan, the driver, refused their offerings, bought them lunch and tickets on a bus bound for the Yugoslavian-Italian border.

His instruction was simple: Speak to no one. Their accents might give them away. They traveled through Zagreb to Ljubljana. That night they slept in the parking lot of a school under construction. Sleeping on concrete was heaven compared to the rugged forests of the Carpathian Mountain they had just traversed. The next day they crossed into Trieste, Italy, without incident and were taken to a Romanian refugee camp.

There Stroie called his parents and informed them of his whereabouts. Fearful of government reprisal, they had opposed his escape. His parents begged him to come back. He had no such plans. "I was willing to eat out of the garbage to get to the U.S. That's how determined I was," Stroie says.

Seventeen years later, Stroie is married to Sorina, a Romanian native from his own village whose family immigrated to Cleveland in 1977 when she was 12. They have three children, Christina, 15; Ted, 11; and Nicole, 10. His parents immigrated to this country in 1986. Stroie's mother died in 1993, but his 72-year-old father, Ted, lives with the family. The entire family speaks fluent Romanian and are all active in the local Buna Vestire Romanian Orthodox Church.

Though Stroie is thousands of miles from his homeland, he's never far from his spiritual mentor, Rev. Teofil. The priest sends cassette tapes of his sermons from Romania, which Stroie plays to keep his faith alive and to remind himself why he came to the United States. During a typical day, Stroie works in the garage studio on his statue with some help from his father. Together they listen to a tape from Teofil. The dog, Sadie, and cat, Peter, also are usually in attendance. Stroie gets much of his work these days from Cleveland's Milano Monuments, for whom he completes an average of two granite sculptures a month.

Ted Stroie's sculpture projects are long, arduous endeavors requiring a combination of skills that draw extensively on the mind, body and soul. His training as both an artist and an engineer (he was an engineering major in college in Romania) come uniquely into play. When he receives a request for a statue, he responds with a sketch or drawing of what he envisions the completed work will look like.

"For me, this is the hardest part, creating the work," Stroie says. When the drawing is approved, he begins molding the statue out of clay. He uses the clay statue to make a plaster mold into which he then pours cement. Once he has carefully chipped away the plaster, the resulting concrete replica serves as his model for the work. He quickly "roughs" (removes the bigger, extemporaneous pieces) from the wood or stone, and then the painstaking carving process begins. "As I get to the parts like the face and the hair, my tools get smaller. I use a v-chisel, and sandpaper with wood.

With stone, sometimes I use power tools like a little die grinder with diamond bits. This is the most time-consuming part of the work, but not the most difficult. Once I've created something on paper it's just a matter of following through," he says.

He also fashions replacement pieces for intricately carved wooden furniture for auction houses and antique shops. Michael Wolf, director of Wolf's Auction House in Cleveland, has hired Stroie for restoration work.

"You've met Ted Stroie? Don't you want to *be* him?" he asks. "The thing I like best about him is that unlike so many artists he appears to have no ego. He's got talent, integrity. There's just nothing about the guy I don't admire."

"Ted does all of our sculpture work," says Jim Milano, president of Milano Monuments, whose employees work on headstones. "His detail work is lifelike. He has a God-given gift that makes his work of a higher quality. I don't know anybody in the area who does what he does. It's not about the money for Ted, it's about the work."

While Stroie must make a living, it's clear that the end result is more important than the paycheck it brings. "I know a guy in Colorado who carves wildlife figures, like eagles," says Stroie. "He'll do a whole bunch of the same eagle fast. He makes about $200,000 a year. I like wildlife figures. I may do those sometime. But right now it's not so much about what's in my pocket, it's also about what's in my heart."

October 24, 1999

POPULAR CULTURE

CRAZY FISTS IN GOLDEN GLOVES

"Unless you've been in the ring when the noise is for you, there's no way you'll ever know what it's like."
—Sugar Ray Robinson

Climbing into the ring, I was crazy with fear and adrenalin. The loser of the previous fight had just been helped out of my corner. The gym was crowded and by the 10th fight the spectators were restless and noisy.

For lack of something better to do I threw a few punches and tried to imitate some little dance I had seen a fighter do on television. In the process I noticed something I hadn't seen before. There was a large smear of dried blood on the lower part of the robe provided me by the Golden Gloves officials.

It was only then that I realized the gravity of my undertaking. There I was standing under the bright lights in front of the howling crowd. It still hadn't had its fill of blood and violence after nine fights. My previous experience was sparring in high school about seven years earlier and a single barroom scuffle, the result of 4 or 5 beers too many.

My training consisted of three days of eating nothing but lettuce, and a second viewing of *Raging Bull*. I couldn't look at my manager, Denis, whom I had recruited several days earlier in a last ditch attempt for moral support. He knew I wasn't a fighter, but he thought that I at least had a grasp of the fundamentals.

My opponent, a tall lanky kid, stood in the opposite corner looking around like he was very bored. I had a feeling that he was no stranger to the ring. I figured my only chance of survival was to clock him early in the first round, preferably with the first punch. The longer it went on the shorter were my chances of escaping bodily harm. I kept telling myself that the whole scene would be over in six minutes and then realized it might be sooner. Gone was the drama of *Raging Bull* and the romance of *Rocky*. I was power driven on cold, black fear.

I guess it's all Robert DeNiro's fault, the broken nose and everything. I mean it was definitely MY fault, but DeNiro was the guy who inspired me. It all started when I went to see *Raging Bull*.

DeNiro's Oscar was well deserved. The fight sequences were beautifully brutal and surreal. Jake LaMotta said that at the time of the shooting, DeNiro was good enough to contend for the middleweight crown. That impressed me enormously.

Not long after seeing the movie, I was paging through the *Daily News* looking for *Doonesbury* when I ran across the entry form for the New York Golden Gloves. I read it through, slowly noting all the qualifications. Jokingly I clipped it, put it in my desk and forgot about it. The following week, returning from lunch I ran across the form, filled it out and mailed it.

A month later I was surprised by a letter informing me that I would be required to undergo a physical examination on Sunday morning several weeks hence at the *Daily News* building.

Arriving at the designated place on time, I saw about 150 teenagers sitting in a long line against the south wall of the lobby. As a group they didn't look especially menacing. Sure there were a few evil looking thugs here and there, but for the most part the crowd was composed of hard-core urban jocks.

I walked down that line feeling somewhat self-conscious, being the one of a small group of white contenders and the only one with shoulder-length hair. Sitting down I began checking out guys who seemed my height and weight, and imagined slugging it out with them.

I wasn't too nervous at the prospect, for I never believed I would follow through.

By the time I got dressed I had been told to buy an AAU (Amateur Athletic Union) card, given a list of gyms where I could work out and told that the date of my first fight would be mailed to me in a month.

I told no one about my Golden Gloves aspirations because of the circuit-breaker system I had installed into the sequence of events leading to the fight. I'd have to lose 10 pounds, something that looked highly unlikely in view of my sybaritic life-style, and also it was probably too late to get my AAU card.

Somewhere along the line I would be prevented from fighting by some technicality beyond my control. So there was no need or reason to rave about my bid for pugilistic glory to anyone, save a friend at work, who, unaware of my failsafe system told me I was nuts.

One day many weeks later I stopped at my mailbox looking for the latest rejection of my novel. Instead I found a letter from the Daily News Charities informing me that my first fight would take place on Feb. 9, the following Monday at 7:30 at Benjamin Franklin High School on Pleasant Avenue in Harlem.

I was stunned. My most dependable reason for not competing had fallen through. Unknown to me was the fact that amateur athletics are rarely well organized and often run beyond given timetables.

I had seven days notice. I thought about my weight and lack of an AAU card. Relying on my lack of discipline, I promised myself that I could enter only if I could lose eight pounds and still hoped that the AAU card was unavailable. I was getting close to the bell.

Tuesday morning at work I began my training. I purposely left my cigarettes at home depending on a woman at work who smokes my brand for a minimal ration of nicotine. I desisted from my usual bag of Pepperidge Farm cookies for breakfast.

I canceled the french fries which usually accompanied my midday repast. I started poring over old copies of Sports Illustrated looking for boxing stories, getting myself mentally prepared. The New York winter still raged and, to my way of thinking, made roadwork in Riverside Park impossible.

To compensate I got hold of a jump rope and spent about 10 minutes of light skipping and tripping in the basement of my building. I then staggered to the elevator and went directly to my apartment where I tore up my bedroom looking for my cigarettes.

Thursday I remembered to call about my AAU card. The man at the other end of the line chastised me about my neglect, which relieved me, thinking that I was too late, and then he told me to come down to his office the next day with $9. It was then that I realized that there was nothing between the ring and me except eight pounds and the primal alternative, flight.

Roadwork was in order and since I needed a pack of cigarettes anyway, I decided to run up Broadway to a little place where they let a pack go for 60 cents. On my way I noticed that *Raging Bull* was playing at the Olympia for two bucks. I got my cigarettes, a ticket to the show, popcorn (without butter) and a Coke.

After the lights went up and I had thrown down the last of a great many butts, I was somewhat disappointed. On second viewing the film seemed not so much about boxing, but about a foolish man who spent his entire life in conflict with himself.

Not really what I had in mind. I rushed from the theater and decided to run full speed down to my apartment on 94th. Halfway there my legs gave out and I walked the rest of the way thinking about victory and wondering about my weight.

Once home I hopped on the scale. By some miracle of God I had lost three pounds. With all of this momentum going for me I went to the kitchen and devoured another bowlful of lettuce. During my post-meal cigarette, a new training regulation, I reviewed some of the pamphlets I had been given after my physical some months back.

I found that I was allowed to bring a manager to the fight. I thought it might be helpful to have someone in my corner to provide moral support and a ride home in case I got knocked out.

I called old college buddy Denis O'Keefe. His first reaction was disbelief but he got excited when he realized I was serious. For the next three nights I received regular phone calls from my "manager" inquiring about my weight and well-being.

I had explained to Denis, very clearly, that if I didn't make the weight I wasn't going through with it. As the day of reckoning drew closer I became more vociferous about making the weight. Denis realized the gravity of my undertaking and was both sympathetic and reassuring.

Friday I got my AAU card and stocked up on lettuce and low cal dressing. It was one of the longer weekends of my life. There was to be very little eating and absolutely no drinking. What I needed was exercise and lots of it. I wrote letters, watched old movies, and munched on celery between situps and jumping rope.

By Sunday I was down to 134 pounds and even braved the cold of Riverside Park for a three-mile jaunt. I completed the course without stopping. I had come to accept this fight as something that actually might happen.

Denis arrived at my office at six sharp on Monday night and had brought along his brother, David a New York City fireman. I had

specifically asked Denis not to bring anyone. As I had put it the
night before, "Look Denis, you already know I'm an idiot. If I dis-
grace myself tomorrow night you won't have found out anything
you don't already know!"

"I getcha," he said.

It was a good thing that David came along. Neither Denis nor I
knew how to tape my hands or tie on my gloves. David had some
experience and we immediately made him the trainer. As we approached the gym and I was thinking rather seriously about the
mindless zeal with which I approach so many things in my life,
Denis and David gave me advice. The one tip that comes to mind
was "If we tell you to stay down, stay down." I hinted that if it was
obvious to them, I might already be in on the secret.

I was surprised by the number of people in the crowded gym. I
flashed my AAU card to the man at the door. My entourage and I
were shown through the gate.

The locker room turned out to be a history classroom. Rows of
tiny desk lines the room full of fighters and managers exchanging
words of advice and encouragement. After weighing in and being
taped I found that I was fighting one Reynold Lewis in the 10th
bout. Not knowing who he was intensified my fear as I scanned
the room.

It turned out Reynold wasn't even there. I practiced my punch-
ing and dancing to relieve the almost crippling tension. After no-
ticing my enthusiastic warm-up, David told me to save something
for the fight.

I watched the first nine fights in order to glean some technique
from the other fighters. Some of the fights were brutally one sided,
and while the ref stopped them when this became apparent, the
battering and bleeding did nothing to calm my nerves.

During the eighth fight I went back to the vestibule to put on
my gloves, headgear and get my robe. There I saw Reynold. He
was everything I was hoping I wouldn't have to face. Tall, slender
and rangy, he looked like he had the moves of a cat. He had a light
brown complexion and jet black hair topping off a look of dead cool
which gave nothing away. His manager, a huge black man wearing
a coat from some obscure boxing organization, noticed me staring
in their direction.

"You Heaton?" he asked.

"Yeah."

"Reynold, this the guy you gonna fight!" Reynold looked over at me slowly before he walked out into the gym.

"We'll do just fine," he said over his shoulder.

I stayed about 20 feet behind Reynold during the ninth fight. While I was jittery, jumpy and chewing the hell out of my mouth-piece, he sat there cool as dew with his long arms dangling at his sides, occasionally making comments to his manager.

After the introduction but before the bell I stood in the corner ready to explode with nervous anxiety. Denis was all "go gettum kid!" while I was finishing a silent act of contrition.

At the sound of the bell I shot out of my corner like an amphet-amine crazed orangutan, crossing the ring before Reynold had even taken two steps. Stopping three feet short of my opponent I leaped toward him with both arms extended, like I was diving into a swimming pool.

I saw his eyes widen as I sailed towards him. The look on his face was something between confusion and disbelief. In his state of shock he did nothing but raise his gloves to fend off my missile like attack. I hit him squarely on the nose, though I had lost almost all velocity which negated any power the punch may have had .

The crowd roared with approval at my unorthodox style as we both fell into the ropes. After the ref separated us the look on his face indicated to me that he hadn't seen anything like it either.

We began to trade roundhouses and after about 20 seconds of futile swinging I was completely winded. I felt I couldn't go on.

The worst part of it was that my arms were too short to connect from the outside. The only way I could do any damage was toe-to-toe, from the inside. This required taking two or three good shots to the head before letting fly with my one punch, a looping right hand roundhouse.

I remedied this imbalance of power simply by lowering my head before aggressing. The main disadvantage of this technique is that all you can see is your opponent's shoes. I buried my head in his solar plexus and pushed him back into his corner where I began to flail away at his stomach and ribs. The ref broke it up again and said something to me that he would repeat many times throughout the fight.

"Keep your head up."

We squared off again at ring-center and I gave him another of my two fisted leapers and the crowd howled again with laughter and excitement. By now Reynold had learned to deal with this ludicrous attack by merely deflecting my gloves to the right or the left depending on what corner he wanted to see me sail into.

As I returned from one of the corners, I looked over and saw Reynold's manager grinning from ear to ear. This was the first time since the fight started that I realized I was making an ass of myself. Earlier I was thinking only of survival and maybe one lucky punch. I quickly filled with embarrassment and anger.

I stalked over to Reynold and ripped loose with a wild right that somehow connected. His mouthpiece flew into the fourth row while his eyes rolled in his head. The fight had to be stopped, lucky for me, while the mouthpiece was found and retrieved. Falling off the ropes I hung there lifeless, gasping for breath while the crowd carried on in its usual delighted manner.

I glanced over to my corner and saw Denis shouting instructions frantically, but could not see David. Later I learned that he was on the floor laughing throughout most of the fight. Denis told me that occasionally he would rise, watch for a minute, and say, "he can't fight!" and resume his position on the floor. Seconds after Lewis got his mouthpiece back, the round ended.

Sitting on the stool, all I could think about was how I would get through the next two rounds. Three days of lettuce had left me with a scant energy reserve. Denis crouched behind me and by the tone of his voice I could tell that he was angry. Not that I cared, my primal instincts had carried me through the first round without serious damage and I was satisfied.

"Mike, ya got nothin'! Nothin'' at all! No stance, no jab, no nothin'. I'm gonna tell you two things, just two things," he put the water bottle up to my mouth and squeezed some in, "stance, and jab, stance and jab. You're lucky he hasn't killed you! Now just remember two things. Spit," he said holding up the bucket. I hadn't the strength to expel the water and it ran down my chest into my shorts. This got a laugh from the spectators near my corner. "Two things Mike, stance and jab. Stance and Jab, stance and jab. What are you going to remember?"

"I don't know."

"STANCE AND JAB!!"

"Right," I said as the bell rang and Denis pushed me out into the ring.

As we squared off again I thought momentarily about stance and jab before reverting to my search and destroy mission. Ignoring the ref's pleas to keep my head up, I staggered about the ring trying to find the mythical knockout button on Reynold's chin. Why he never threw an uppercut to end the comedy I'll never know. Maybe he felt it would be too easy.

Halfway through the second round I was too tired to continue the chase and attempted some semblance of a boxer. Reynolds quickly snapped a left which missed and a right which broke my nose. I fell back against the ropes as he came in for the kill. As I bounced back I grabbed him, pinning his arms to his sides. We waltzed awhile before the ref broke it up. So much for stance and jab, I thought as we squared off again.

I returned to my favorite attack, which now has several names including, the two-fisted leaper, the double whammy and the kangaroo.

So the fight was on once again in its original hilarious form as I staggered, fat-faced and fuzzy-brained, after Reynold with my head down and my arms flying while the crowd cried for more.

I landed a couple of good punches for every two or three I got. I rocked him a couple of times but I never had enough steam to follow through. When the second ended I felt I had been fighting all that day and half the night. My legs were rubber and my lungs were full of napalm. I sat in my corner glassy-eyed and numb, while Denis, who had given up on coaching, assured me that this was the third and final round. I had lost count.

The beginning of the third round was pretty uneventful; Reynold had finally reached my level of exhaustion. Realizing this, I summoned up all the cellulose in my body and let fly with another right-handed sidewinder, removing Reynold's mouthpiece again. This buoyed my spirits and bought me breathing time. By now the right side of my nose was swollen and full of blood, making it hard to draw air. Reynold's nose was bleeding, too, but that was just a sign that his nasal passages were clear.

I couldn't get enough air. I threw a wild right that missed and it brought me off balance and crashing to the canvas. I quickly recovered and the ref asked me if I was all right. I said, "Yes, considering the circumstances," not easy to say while wearing a mouthpiece, and we continued to pummel each other, my fall being ruled a slip.

I figured that at this point neither one of us had enough strength to do much damage, but I was wrong. Our weakened status provided for extreme vulnerability. We exchanged some devastating blows between hugging each other and dragging around the ring in each other arms.

The final bell rang just when I decided it was broken. I staggered to my corner imploring Denis to remove my headgear and mouthpiece, which we found, by trail and error, has to be done in just that order. Meanwhile I nearly suffocated while Denis figured this out.

Once freed of my equipment and filled with the chagrin of my comical performance, I asked Denis if I had even the slightest chance of winning. He lied, saying, "Sure you do."

The moments in the ring waiting for the decision were filled with scrambled emotions. I was all at once elated for having gone the distance and humiliated by my antics. People had hooted throughout the fight, including my own manager and trainer. I wanted to hide.

Reynold got the decision as he should have. He should have gotten an award for remaining a gentleman during a brawl. I gave him a hug and headed for the locker room. I was dizzy and aching from my ribs to the top of my head as I stepped through the ropes.

To my surprise, the crowd near my corner was looking at me and grinning, shouting, "nice fight kid," and a couple of brothers flashed the power salute and smiled showing their satisfaction.

"Lots of laughs, huh?" I said, sure the joke was on me.

"Mike, that was the kind of fight they came to see," David said. I mulled this over as I walked around that classroom trying to get my breath while looking at pictures of Bobby Kennedy and Martin Luther King on the wall. Only now did I feel the pain of every punch that was thrown and had connected. My face felt like mush as I heard the crowd howl at the next lucky couple in the gym.

Denis and David helped me out of my fighting gear and into my clothes but couldn't help telling me how funny the fight was and how amazed they were when they realized I possessed none of the necessary boxing skills. I felt bad and went to the men's room.

When I got there, Reynold was standing around fooling with his gym bag. We shook hands and I mumbled something about being sorry for being such a wildman. He pulled a pint of Crown Royal from his bag and offered me a swig. I took it gratefully and didn't feel so sick. He told me I had a nasty right and I wished him luck in his next fight.

As we strolled through the cool Harlem night headed for a friendly bar, David's laugh rang clear through the burnt out streets. He clapped Denis on the back in a gesture of thanks for including him on the evening.

"It was definitely worth it, Denis, definitely worth it."

Despite my new profile and the ringing in my ears, I had to smile. I thought so, too.

February 13, 1983

IN PRAISE OF ANGELS

Winged wonders are on the rise

They're everywhere.

They inhabit every level of our culture. They figure heavily in music, art, literature and science. They populate common lore across all ethnic boundaries. They are especially prized by the very young and very old. They can be found in food, flowers, furniture and films. They have been written about by Shakespeare, St. Thomas Aquinas, Disraeli and Greg Allman. That's not to mention the Bible, Old Testament and New, the Koran and all Persian and Islamic theologies. They save lives; they've taken lives; they are scary; they are kind. And thanks in part to Sophy Burnham (more on her later), they are about to make a comeback that would impress even Frank Sinatra.

They are angels. Think about it. Leonard Maltin's movie and video guide lists no less than 35 films with angel or angels in the title. And that doesn't count Frank Capra's *It's a Wonderful Life* or Wim Wender's *Wings of Desire*. There's angel hair pasta, angel food cake, angel pie (meringue shell filled with strawberries and whipped cream, a bit on the sweet side), angels on horseback (oysters wrapped in bacon broiled and served on toast), angel's kiss (brandy with crème de cocoa and cream), *Look Homeward, Angel*, Angel Cordero, Hell's Angels, those angels kids make in the snow and the angel bed.

Don't forget Curtis and Lisa Sliwa, founders of the Guardian Angel street-vigilante organization; Los Angeles—the alleged city, with its alleged inhabitants, *angelinos*; angelfish and angel sharks; angel-wing begonias and angel's trumpet; angelica the herb that gives rise to angelic acid and angelic oil. And the songs, forget it. "Angel of Harlem" (U2), "The Angels Want to Wear My Red Shoes" (Elvis Costello), all the way back to "Johnny Angel" (Shelley Fabares). And that's only rock and roll, as Mick Jagger might say, who wrote "Sympathy for the Devil," who *used* to be an angel.

We're saturated with these winged wonders and yet they generally get little more respect than say, the Easter Bunny. Maybe it's a forest-for-the-trees situation. Maybe they're just not getting proper PR.

The odd thing is that there's no lack of interest in the supernatural. It's just that people today seem more drawn to the dark side. Book racks are overflowing with shiny corrugated covers of horror novels. Possessed children, pets and plants; evil houses, bad Buicks and corrupt clowns populate popular literature. The stuff of Stephen King, Dean R. Koontz and Clive Barker haunts our televisions, movie screens and bedroom night stands. King is a veritable factory of evil that pumps round the clock every day of the year. Why? Because it sells. He just finished his 29th novel. There seems to be no end to our appetite for the macabre, the horrible, the unthinkable evil that plagues the planet. A whole generation of children is in thrall to the likes of the razor-clawed Freddy, and the hockey-masked, ax-wielding Jason. We've even bred the friendly tortoise, formerly known as a paragon of plodding patience and dogged determination, into a super-race of mutant death experts. We're a culture in love with the bad, the worse and the ugly.

But what about the good guys? Those beings of virtue and light, put upon this earth to help us fight the malefactoring forces of evil? What good is that guy on top of the Christmas tree if he's nothing more than a paper cup and wad of cotton?

Dennis Lippmann, pastor at the Cleveland Family Worship Center, a non-denominational Pentecostal church on the city's East Side, says this lack of appreciation and understanding about angels is in part the fault of the Christian church.

"Maybe it's felt that people won't tolerate something so science fictiony," he says. "Well, if they won't tolerate the creator, they certainly won't tolerate one of his creations, which is what the angels are. They're supernatural beings created by God to perform supernatural functions for God, and his church. It says in the Bible, 'We walk by faith not by sight.' The angels are part of that."

In Billy Graham's book, *Angels: God's Secret Agents*, he says that angels are mentioned 300 times in the Bible and have a far more important place than the devil and his demons. "I believe in angels because the Bible says there are angels, and I believe the Bible to be the true word of God," Graham writes. "I also believe in angels because I have sensed their presence in my life on special occasions."

But angel stories are not limited to Bible-Belt Baptists and Pentecostal preachers. Most of us are familiar with an angel story or two. Like the one about the angels who destroyed Sodom and Gomorrah, or the angels who appeared to the shepherds to announce the birth of Jesus. In the Old Testament, Jacob wrestled with an angel and the Angel of Death passed over the doors of the Israelites who had sprinkled lamb's blood over them.

Not all angel stories come from the Bible. Graham tells of missionary John G. Paton and his wife, who were in the New Hebrides Islands west of Fiji spreading the Gospel. One night a hostile native tribe surrounded his headquarters and threatened to burn the place down and kill the couple. They prayed all night and went unharmed.

A year later, when the tribe had been converted, Paton's wife asked the chief what had kept the natives from killing them. The chief insisted that their hut had been surrounded by big men in glowing gowns with drawn swords that scared the warriors away.

Sophy Burnham's recently published *A Book of Angels* lists numerous modern-day encounters with celestial spirits. Professor Ralph S. Harlow, who has a B.A. from Harvard, and M.A. from Columbia and a Ph.D. from Hartford Theological Seminary, recounts a walk he took with his wife one spring day.

Hearing a noise, they looked behind them and saw 10 feet in the sky "six of them, young beautiful women dressed in flowing white garments and engaged in earnest conversation. They seemed to float past us, their graceful motion seemed natural, as gentle and peaceful as the morning itself."

A New York cab driver told Burnham that, as a child in Greece, he had once seem three "baby angels" playing on the stairway of a saintly woman who had just died. Country singer Johnny Cash claims he was visited by angels twice to tell him of the deaths of relatives.

In 1985, a report surfaced about six cosmonauts aboard the Soviet space station Soyuz 7, who saw "seven giant figures in the form of humans but with wings and mistlike halos. . . . They appeared hundreds of feet tall with a wingspan as great as a jetliner." This sighting was witnessed by only three of the cosmonauts, but 12 days later the seven angels returned and the other three scientists saw them, too. "We were truly overwhelmed," said Svetlana Savistskaya, the woman in the group. "They were smiling as though they shared a glorious secret."

Angels don't always appear in winged glory. Many of the eyewitness accounts in *A Book of Angels* credit voices, dreams and invisible forces for saving lives. Angels seem to favor children and often do nothing more than let their presence be seen. Vicki Israel of Somerset, N.J., wrote to Burnham about one such incident that occurred when she was 6. "I woke up and saw two angels standing in front of my closet. I didn't really feel scared but of what I remember they didn't have wings like what we think of angels. They were two men, tall men and they were talking softly."

So who are these guys anyway? Where did they come from, why are they here and what are they supposed to do?

The word *angelos* is Greek for messenger. And there are lots of them. In the Old Testament, David saw 20,000 riding chariots in the sky. Moses saw 10,000 angels when he received the law of God on Mount Sinai. Except for specific instances, stories where angels are on missions from God, they usually appear in tremendous numbers. They're described as armies, and legions. The Jewish Kabbalah says there are 49 million. Daniel, whose life was saved by an angel when it shut the mouth of a hungry lion, once had a vision in which he saw "thousands and thousands ... and 10,000 times a hundred thousand." If everybody gets at least one guardian angel— some believe each person gets two—they'd be increasing with the population. It's also been said that there's an angel to watch over every blade of grass. Let's just say there's a bunch of them.

Depending upon who you believe, there are all kinds of angels. And they have very distinct ranks and duties. St. Theresa of Avila, who saw angels with amazing frequency, wrote that they "do not tell me their names, but I am well aware that there is a great difference between certain angels and others, and between these and others still of a kind I could not possibly explain."

St. Thomas Aquinas suggested that there were three angel triads, a theory retold in another recently published angel book—Malcom Godwin's *Angels: An Endangered Species*. The first and highest of Aquinas' triads consists of Seraphim, Cherubim and Thrones. The second contains Dominations, Virtues and Powers. The lowest triad holds Principalities, Archangels and Angels.

The Seraphim are the fiery lovers of God who chant "*kadosh, kadosh, kadosh*," which is angelese for "holy, holy, holy" around the throne of God. They do this non-stop so that there is endless song and celebration of love in heaven.

Next are the Cherubs, who are commonly thought to be those fat little babies you see dancing around so much Renaissance art. They are said to be the angels of knowledge. Ezekiel from the Old Testament got an eyeful of four cherubs and said they had four faces and four wings. That doesn't sound like the little cupids they're so commonly depicted as.

The Thrones are also called "wheels," and they don't adhere to any kind of human form at all. They're burning rings of fire with rims full of eyes like windows.

Which is why, Godwin says, UFO people have tried to pass off flying saucers as thrones. And vice versa.

The second triad has the Dominations, which are called angels of mercy. The Virtues, angels of grace, and the Powers patrol the DMZ between heaven and hell keeping the fallen followers of Satan from crashing the gates of Paradise. The bottom rung houses the Principalities, who are in charge of and care for various cities and regions on earth, and includes the Archangels, your basic messengers and couriers. The three most commonly known and the only ones mentioned by name in the Bible are Michael, Gabriel and Raphael.

But these designations and titles are only for the most hard-core angelologists. The current literature on angels spans a gamut of approaches. Godwin's *Angels: An Endangered Species* is thorough but clinical, leaning toward the tone of Time-Life books on mysteries of the occult. Billy Graham's *Angels: God's Secret Agent"* is passionate but tightly tied to his evangelical work, leaving little room for anyone outside the Christian faith.

Far and away the most engaging book out this season is Sophy Burnham's *Book of Angels*. Burnham is part research, part soul search. She doesn't limit her writing to the Judeo-Christian angels of the bible. The book includes several contemporary angel visitations experienced by Burnham and others she has known or sought out.

Burnham, who lives in Washington, D.C., says that her own spirituality has deepened since the publication of *Angels*. "I pray every day. I pray in the morning and evening before I go to bed. Very ritualized prayer. Prayers of surrender. I have more of a need for a form. I was raised in the Episcopal Church and went through periods of Buddhism and Hinduism, but I find myself returning to that Episcopal Church. Even more, I feel like I'm turning into a 12th-century Catholic. I'm getting this greater understanding of who Christ is.

"Searching for God is a one-on-one experience and yet we find Him so often through other people. It's all opposites and contradictions that make perfect sense. ... I've gotten more satisfaction from this book than from any other and it's the one I feel I've had the least to do with."

Burnham's fervent belief is genuine but lacks a certain clerical cache.

Rabbi Bruce Abrams, from Temple Ner Tamid in Euclid, shares Burnham's enthusiasm for angels if not her scope. "They're great, yes absolutely," he says. "I just left a widow whose husband had Parkinson's disease and was paralyzed for 30 years. I was talking to her about this very thing. She wanted to know how to reach her husband, this man whose side she never left.

"Our soul is like this line that extends from our physical selves to higher thoughts, words, emotions, to creative thought and on up to God. The angels bring messages from the widow to the widowed. It's a beautiful idea. You can't see angels, but you can't see love either, although you know when it's there.

"They're totally unprovable. It's not a physical concept. It's like Jacob's ladder, up and down with the messages. I've never seen an angel, but I'm young. Maybe when I get a few more lines on my face. But I believe in them. Seeing them isn't what it's about for me. When somebody tells me they have an angel in their pocket, I turn and run the other way. I don't want angels becoming another roadside attraction."

Over in the Roman Catholic camp, Father David Novak, the associate pastor at St. Francis of Assisi Church in Gates Mills, believes angels are considered anti-cultural and unfashionable in some theological circles. "They're intermediate beings and ministering spirits," he says. "We're constantly surrounded by messages from God. Maybe we should take a hint and use all God gave us. . . ."

"The living faith of the Church is kept more places than the church. I'm sure I've seen one, I just didn't know it. They're not like traffic police. A lot of people have seen me and didn't know they saw a priest. Seeing angels unawares is a great sub-theme in literature and liturgy."

But why are the wondrous spiritual occurrences of the Bible seemingly in such short supply today? Is it us or them?

"Maybe we've grown too dim to see them," says Novak. "In a culture of edible underwear, Bart Simpson and snowmobiles, maybe we've forgotten how to look.

December 23, 1990

CADILLAC CRUNCH

Doom drivers in the demolition derby

I said "yes" so quickly when Tom Lowe called from Barberton Speedway, that the surprise in his voice could have been measured on the Richter scale.

"You will?" He sounded flabbergasted.

"Yeah," I said. "When is it?"

He had asked me to participate in the Barberton Speedway Demolition Derby. All Cadillacs. Twelve—count 'em, a dozen—Cadillacs. All I could think of was a skit from an early David Letterman program in which all the new, stupid cable networks were lampooned. There was the Aquarium Channel, the Fireplace Channel, you get the idea. My favorite was the Eighth-Grade Boys Channel. It was a series of car-crash segments edited together. On the money. Very funny.

In the heart of every man there is an eighth-grade boy longing to blow up something, demolish some huge piece of machinery or just generally wreak havoc on some man-made thing. Don't ask me why. It's like women and shoes. A gender-genetic-hormone thing.

Perhaps it starts with the dodgem cars at amusement parks. Or maybe it's caused by watching too many cop movies. All I know is that it's a reflex action. When somebody calls and asks if you want to reduce a Cadillac to iron filings, you just say, "Yes." Then you hang up, get on with your life.

Eventually the day approaches. As do second thoughts. I spoke with Chris Jensen, *The Plain Dealer*'s auto writer. Now here's a guy who likes to fool around in cars. He's raced across deserts, driven up the side of mountains and had the opportunity to test-drive many new and strange vehicles.

Here, I thought, I'll get encouragement, good driving advice and perhaps a crash helmet.

"You're nuts," he said immediately. "You couldn't get me involved in one of those things for all the money in the world. You could get really hurt."

"Yeah," I said, swallowing hard. "It would be a drag to spend the rest of the summer with a broken leg."

"A broken leg I could handle," he said. "What I'd be afraid of is having back problems for the rest of my life. Or a spine injury. Or having a gas tank go and being burned beyond human recognition. That's the stuff I think about."

Anyway, he did have a helmet for me to wear. And a racing suit he told me was "fire resistant" but not fireproof. "What it does," he told me, "is give you maybe 10 extra seconds to live before you're completely consumed by fire."

To prepare for the race, I rented the Tom Cruise movie *Days of Thunder*, which was basically *Top Gun* on the ground. Robert Duvall, of course, was excellent as the pit boss. But it got me a little psyched. Plus the racing suit Jensen lent me looked cool. The helmet looked like something designed by NASA, or Jules Verne. I couldn't decide which.

By the time race day rolled around I was pretty nervous. I was walking around the house muttering things like, "How do I get myself into these situations?" The eighth-grade-boy enthusiasm was replaced with "I'm too old for this crazy stuff."

My sister Fran was kind enough to drive me down to Barberton and be there for moral support. "If anything happens to you out there tonight," Fran asked solicitously, "can I have your Jeep?"

It was just getting dark when we got to the speedway at 8. I ran into Bob Dyer, a writer with the *Beacon Journal* in Akron. He and three or four other media people, including Mike DiPasquale from WJW Channel 8, had agreed to participate.

"It sounded like so much fun when I agreed to do this," Dyer told me. "But all I've heard ever since is horror stories about guys who had major brain damage and walked sideways for three years after the event. I've got two kids. What am I, nuts?"

We then found out that two guys, one from an Akron radio station and another from Akron TV, had pulled out at the last minute. We couldn't decide whether we hated them for their cowardice or wisdom. In any case, it gave us a tempting option. We discussed making a pact wherein we'd both slink away quietly and vow that not a word would be written. As though it never happened.

We went up to the press box for a beer. There was some question about drinking and driving, but I thought the reason you don't drink and drive is to avoid smashing up your car. Which, of course, was the whole point of this evening. We watched two races in which there were back-to-back accidents. The first was a violent two-car collision that took out part of the wall. The second involved a car's engine blowing up and bursting into flames. Nobody got hurt. The crowd, of course, went wild. Dyer and I looked at each other, then at the full moon, which was high above the racetrack.

"All doom drivers please report to the race tower," said the announcer. "What's a doom driver?" I asked. Somebody said, "That's for the demolition derby." Great, I thought. I'm a doom driver.

We gathered around a race official, who explained the rules. No direct hits on the driver's side (or T-boning, as it is called). No hitting a stationary vehicle. Any vehicle stationary for more than 60 seconds will be disqualified. We headed to our cars—after signing our lives away.

We lined up our cars in the infield, six cars on one side, six on the other, backs facing each other. We had been informed that the key to staying alive in a demolition derby was backing into people. Once you smash your radiator, you're pretty much history. I was directly across the field from Dyer. Somebody gave a signal and we both gunned our cars in reverse.

It was a weird thing to overcome. You spend your whole driving life trying to avoid hitting people and now you have to lose all those instincts. Dyer and I zoomed toward one another. Just before impact, we both slammed on the brakes and the Caddies met at midfield with a resounding "dink." The crowd laughed.

The next thing I knew, one of the professional drivers was barreling at me backwards and broadside. WHAM! That meant war. The next 20 minutes was a blur of smoke, broken glass and astounding vehicular violence. It had the fury and confusion of war with the crowd supplying a Roman circus atmosphere in its cries for blood.

Dyer and I collided once more, this time with a bit more velocity. There was smoke everywhere. Three cars had already been abandoned. I remember driving backwards very fast through a cloud of smoke and looking over to find myself trading paint with DiPasquale's car. We were locked at the car door handles until somebody hit him, which spun me off.

My most vivid impression was the turbocharged, violent atmosphere. There was pounding, screeching, burning and bending going on around me. And yet there was also that crazy nervous laughter that always followed a direct hit. Once you knew you were all right. We were nuts.

At some point my engine died and I couldn't get it to turn over. I decided to get the hell out of there. The rules had turned out to be merely suggestions. Suggestions ignored by one and all. I didn't feel safe just because I was sitting still. I got out the window and high-tailed it for the track where a crew waited with fire extinguishers. Dyer soon joined me.

The derby had wound down to DiPasquale, a girl in a pink Caddy and one of the professionals. DiPasquale was a madman, tearing up the field on two rims and a prayer. "It just confirms my theory," Dyer said. "All television people are psychopaths."

It was amazing to see how much abuse these big old American cars could take. Eventually, the pro took first, DiPasquale second and the girl in the pink Caddy third. Nobody got hurt.

A week later I got a call from Tom Lowe. We talked about the evening and had a lot of laughs recalling all that had transpired.

"You know," said Lowe, "we're going to have another one of these . . . I'd love to have you back to do it again if you're interested."

"I'd love to," said the eighth-grade boy within. Then I caught myself. "But only if Dyer does it, too."

August 18, 1991

BIG HAIR: A STYLE, AN ATTITUDE, A WAY OF LIFE

JO ANN WATKINS—A GIRL AND HER HAIR

Let's face it. Other than being a student of the phenomenon of Big Hair, what do I really know about it? Nothing, right? Right. So I began my investigation. I had to find a woman who embodied the Big-Hair ethic, whatever that was.

After days and nights of combing bars and clubs looking for Ms. Big Hair, I found Jo Ann Watkins waitressing at the Flat Iron Cafe in the Flats. Jo Ann, though small in stature, not only has Big Hair, but a big personality as well. Several women I approached on the subject recoiled in horror, believing that I was up to no good. That I would ridicule and make mock of them. Jo Ann had no such fears. She loves her Big Hair. And she isn't afraid to tell you so.

We met for drinks before Jo Ann was off to an audition for a band at the Agora. She has a beautiful voice. Her hair that night was not only big, it was a work of art. Imagine a blond crashing surf on top and a woven wheat waterfall cascading down her back. It's not surprising that guys notice Jo Ann, but I saw women checking her out, too. Big-Hair envy.

Jo Ann began her Big-Hair ways back in the late '70s at Midpark High School in Middleburg Heights. "I had a mane back then," she says. "The Farrah Fawcett feathered look was very big then, too. But I loved the Big Hair. It's uninhibited. It's 'Ta Da!', if you know what I mean. You go to clubs and bars where there's Big Hair and it's easier to get to the john than it is to get in front of the mirror. I can't tell you how many times I've been zapped in the eye by some girl doing her hair. Big Hair says something about the way you feel. It's how you want to present yourself."

Big-hair trauma

Big Hair is not without its hazards. Something so carefully crafted is vulnerable to a myriad of potential disasters. Big-Hair wearers dread several natural and unnatural occurrences to their do's, which, Jo Ann informed me, have an average shelf life of a day and a half. "That is, unless you get a bad case of Bed Head," she tells me. "Bed Head can be traumatic and results in your hair being completely flat on one side. There's also Hat Hair. I was working the restaurant one night and a guy put his cowboy hat on my head. So I just wore it as I was working my tables. When he left, he came by and just took it away from me and I had this big cone-shaped thing on my head.

"Big Hair done right should withstand a lot of things, but sometimes you've got nature to deal with. Wind, rain and snow are the big three. Snow you can shake off. Real good Big Hair should stand up to wind. I've even ridden on a motorcycle without any real damage. But a lot of that had to do with ducking down behind the guy driving the bike. There's a skill to that, too. But even when you do run into problems, you have to be ready. You've got to be skilled at Big-Hair Repair."

Aqua Net is a girl's best friend

"I keep a can in my purse and a can in my car," says Jo Ann. "If you're at a party or a club, you'll notice that women with Big Hair are friendly toward one another. That's a law of Big Hair. Big Hair gravitates toward Big Hair. That's because you know if you need Big-Hair Repair, another woman with Big Hair will have it.

"The basic tool of Big-Hair maintenance is hair spray. What we call 'Do-Glue.' Aqua Net is definitely the best. It's been around forever. There are so many kinds, you can't believe. I use Aqua Net Unscented Ultra Super Hold. In the purple can. My grandmother probably used Aqua Net. Aussie also has something called Mega-Spray. That's good, too. We also call hair spray 'Coif-In-A-Can.' Mousse and gel are pretty much out. They tend to weigh hair down. With Big Hair, you're looking for uplift.'

All-purpose do-glue

"Aqua Net is great because it has so many uses," Jo Ann says. "You can dry your nail polish with it. Just a couple sprays. You can stop a run in your stocking with it. It'll take the stains out of clothing, not your silks but anything cotton. And you can kill spiders with it. Say you're in the bathroom and you got some creepy bug climbing up the wall. You just give him a shot, which freezes him; that gives you time to get a tissue and throw it in the john."

Where, oh where, big hair?

"Parma is really the home of Big Hair. I grew up on the outskirts and was probably influenced by it. Parmatown Mall is a great place to watch the Parade of Big Hair. Another good spot is the McDonald's on Day Drive Friday night after the football game. You'll see all kinds of Big Hair there.

"Outside of Parma, the next real Mecca for Big Hair is the Flats. Shooters and Coconuts both attract Big-Hair crowds."

The tools of big-hair repair

Sudden changes in weather, rides on motorcycles or in convertibles, the occasional flying drink in a bar all pose serious problems for wearers of Big Hair. Any Big-Hair repair kit, says Jo Ann, must contain five tools:

"You need your hair spray, of course. That you use all over for hold. Your spritz you need for the poufing up of the little tufts. It's for special effects really. Then you need a curling iron, a blow dryer and a pick. But really, the most important thing you need is talent. You have to have a gift for Big Hair. Some people are naturals, others just don't have it. I'm good because I've been doing it for 10 years. Practice makes perfect."

Big-hair personality

"Not everyone can wear Big Hair," Jo Ann says. "Some people just don't have the personality for it. It takes a certain kind of person. You can't be shy or withdrawn. Big Hair announces you when you walk in a room. If you can't handle that, you can't wear it. Big-Hair people are 1) outgoing; 2) bubbly; 3) fun-loving; 4) performers, and 5) confident. It pumps you up," she says. "I'm 5-foot-2 before I do my hair. Afterwards, I'm 5-6. I can get on every ride at Cedar Point."

HAIR EXPERT ROY BLOUNT JR. ON ALL THINGS BIG AND HAIRY

Roy Blount Jr., essayist in *Spy*, *The Atlantic* and *Rolling Stone*, and occasional *Tonight Show* chair warmer, is the distinguished author of 11 books, including *It Grows On You: A Hair-Raising Survey of Human Plumage*. Mr. Blount was kind enough to take time from his busy schedule lecturing and discussing his new book, *Camels Are Easy, Comedy's Hard* (Villard) to share his vast knowledge on the subject of hair.

What compelled you to write a book on hair?

"I've always tried to write about the little, seemingly inconsequential things people think about when they're talking about the big things. People may talk about the search for truth, but in fact while they're doing it they're probably playing with their hair. There are things, like hair, which concern people on a day-to-day basis. They may not like to admit it, but people give an awful lot of thought to their hair. After all, it is one of the few things in your life you can do something about."

In your book, you proposed a radical theory on hair and evolution. Could you summarize that for our readers?

"Human hair fascinated me because it grows to preposterous lengths and only on top of our heads. I came across a picture of hair as it grows on someone in its natural state and noticed that it completely covers the face. Now, almost all research agrees that man evolved when he began to walk upright. It occurred to me that he learned to walk upright by using his front 'feet' to knock his or her hair out of his or her eyes. Eventually, man had to be upright all the time to keep his hair out of his face so he could see.'

You said that the research for your book allowed you to do two of your favorite things, drink and talk to women.

"Often at the same time."

What did you learn?

"For one thing, I discovered how completely women's hair affects their lives. For most men, the only worry about hair is losing it. But for women, it can, in many cases, completely define them— their mood, their attitude. I also found that many women seem to lose their will upon entering a hair salon. Perfectly intelligent women become subservient to their hairdressers. Most of the stories I heard were about disaster perpetrated on women by hairdressers. Every woman seems to have one."

Did you see a lot of Big Hair growing up in the South?

"The current trend in Big Hair is, at the very least, free from the stories I heard as a kid about spiders and bugs making nests in the big bouffants. I haven't heard any rumors about insects in the Big Hair of today. They've got that going for them."

Do you see any social significance in today's Big Hair?

"It could be any number of things. It could be a symbol of someone not having anything IN their head having a lot ON their head.

There may be some link to the Gulf War, wearing our hair tall and proud for America. The '80s were a very inflated time, that may tie in."

How many American hairstyles have been reflected in our cultural life?

"The movie about the '50s was *Grease*, the play about the '60s was *Hair*, the movie of the '70s was *Shampoo*, and I always wanted to write a movie about the '80s called *Mousse* but I never got around to it.'

What do you think will characterize the hair of the '90s?

"Cheap haircuts."

Any other thoughts on Big Hair?

"I wrote a song about Big Hair once."

Well?

"It goes like this (singing softly with a lilting Georgia accent):
You got big ol' hair
But a little bitty heart.
I should have known about you from the start.
Your pompadour is a work of art.
You got big ol' hair
And a little bitty heart."

CARTOONIST TOM BATIUK ON BIG HAIR AND CINDY SUMMERS

Funky Winkerbean cartoonist Tom Batiuk didn't invent Big Hair, but he's gone a long way toward identifying and chronicling its growth as a hairstyle movement in America. Batiuk, whose comic strip runs in 384 newspapers nationwide, transformed character Cindy Summers in summer 1987 with a few broad strokes of his pen.

"I was sitting in an art class at Midview High School [in Grafton], where I get a lot of my ideas. I saw a girl with the Big-Hair look and I got the idea to give it to Cindy. I've always made it a point to avoid high-school fads and fashions in the strip. They change so quickly and I didn't want the strip to be dated. I've tried to avoid the teenage cliches like kids talking on the phone, things like that. Previous to this time Cindy was only identified as the most popular girl in school. But when I gave Cindy the Big Hair, I couldn't believe how it absolutely transformed her. Suddenly she was just jumping off the page with all this attitude," he says.

"Cindy's the most popular girl in the school. She's the head of the really mean clique and the Big Hair is the perfect finishing touch for that. Her hair is her social power," he adds.

Batiuk sees Big Hair among high-school girls as a badge of honor. "Kids are always trying to do two things: They want to set themselves apart from society at large, and they want to conform to their peers. The Big-Hair look in all its various forms allows them to do both things," he says.

In a related item, Batiuk sent along two newspaper clippings, one from the Newport (R.I.) *Daily News* and the other from the Wichita (Kan.) *Eagle*. Both had to do with banning hair spray from girls' restrooms. Students were complaining about breathing problems, and an explosion had occurred when one student lit a cigarette in a fog of hair spray. The Big-Hair trend is trickling down from high school to junior high school. As usual, Batiuk's on top of the development.

Recently, Cindy Summer's little sister Mercedes has appeared in *Funky Winkerbean*. Mercedes, although smaller than Cindy, is no less evil, from her designer T-shirts to her pointy and poufy helmet of Little Big Hair.

There's going to be some changes and surprises in the strip this year, according to Batiuk. "All I can say right now is keep your eye on Mercedes."

PILGRIMAGE TO PARMATOWN: BIG-HAIR HEAVEN

When you ask people about Big Hair, if they see it, where they see it, one after another they will come up with the same answer. Where Big Hair is concerned, all roads lead to Parmatown Mall.

So I set out for Big-Hair Mecca and was not disappointed. Not only was I able to romp in a veritable forest of Big Hair hanging from women of all ages, I even found a place that serviced those without the slightest hope of having Big Hair. . . .

Sharon Mytrosevich works at Paris Connection, an outlet that actually sells Big Hair. No kidding. Big Hair to-go. Wigs of all shapes and colors hang from racks on either side of the cart. Paris Connection originally had carts in other malls around Cleveland, but the Parmatown location has been the only really successful big-seller. Paris Connection was even the recent recipient of the red ribbon for top sales in Parmatown Mall among carts.

"Wigs and pieces, as we call them, were very big back in the '60s and '70s," says Mytrosevich. "The '80s were a down time for wigs. But they're back now in the '90s and they're going to be bigger than ever."

The Paris Connection sells an average of 10 to 12 wigs a week, ranging in price from $49 to $179.

"They're all synthetic," she says, "and we sell a special kind of hair spray for them, too. The pieces are even more popular. We sell 150 to 200 of those a month."

Mytrosevich says the store hopes to expand on its Parmatown success by opening four stores in malls in the Tampa, Fla., area. I asked Sharon T., another Paris Connection employee, what she likes about Big Hair. "I change my hair three times a week. I come home at night and my husband doesn't know who he's married to."

There you have it. Big Hair Saved My Marriage. Yet another Big-Hair success story.

BH GLOSSARY

Big-Hair expert Jo Ann Watkins offers the lowdown on BH terminology. "I have what I call standard Big Hair," she says. "It's a two-part deal. It's big and tall on top and long in the back. But there are lots of other kinds." For example:

Heavy Metal Big Hair. "That's more teased and scarier. Mascara plays a big part in that look. You want to see Heavy Metal Big Hair, you go to the Cleveland Cafe, or Flash Gordon's on certain nights."

Little Big Hair. "You see that in Junior High. It's a reduced Big-Hair look. They have the style without the volume. Those are Big Hair girls-in-training. They're the Big Hair junior varsity."

Country Western Big Hair. "Dolly Parton is the queen of that, but Reba McEntire and the Judds are new Big-Hair ladies. Country Western Big Hair is big all over. It's not the two-part deal. It's all maximum bigness."

Cher Hair. "There are women who use extensions and make them big. Women who can't wear Big Hair to work. I call that Cher Hair. Cher is very big on extensions."

Attempted Big Hair. "Those are women who use banana clips to pull it up but none of the gunk. As soon as the clips are out it just falls down. It's cheating in a way."

Hangover Big Hair. "When you're beat, the hair just won't respond. It's like your hair is sad."

Old-Fashioned Big Hair. "That's what they're talking about when they say 'fried and dyed.' It's the platinum-blond thing done to a frazzle."

Fire-Hazard Hair. "Big Hair badly done I call Fire Hazard. You're talking worst-case scenario there, but you see it a lot."

November 17, 1991

CLOTHES MAKE THE MAN
(FEEL LIKE A TOTAL DORK)

Maybe clothes-shopping isn't all that dramatic, traumatic and Orwellian to you, but I'd rather do almost anything else than go to a store and buy clothes. I'd rather do my taxes than shop. Is it a guy/girl thing? Is it a women's conspiracy? Or is it just me? You make the call.

My first ugly shopping experience occurs when I am in the fifth grade. My mom is driving me to Westgate in the Corvair. I should be out with my friends vandalizing something, but no. We're shopping for trousers. The mere mention of the phrase "Back to School Shopping" makes me vaguely nauseous to this day. There's a sale on boys slacks at Halle's. Used to be she could just buy me stuff, bring it home and I'd wear it.

But now, she tells me I'm getting to be a man. As if she thinks I'll fall for that line. Any time she's trying to get me to do something I don't want to do, it invariably has something to do with me becoming a man. I'm thinking, if I'm a man, how about the keys to the car and make me a bourbon old-fashioned while you're at it. But of course I keep those thoughts to myself. Otherwise I wouldn't be allowed to watch *Johnny Quest* on Friday night.

We get there, find the boys department and are greeted by the saleslady. She's a rotund 50-year-old with badly dyed gray hair, rhinestone glasses and a dress that looks as if it was made out of somebody's drapes. She looks like a cross between Ethel Merman and Divine. One look and I'm thinking, I'm dyn' to have this broad deck me out.

She and my mother begin talking about me as if I'm not there. They're plowing through a stack of plaid rags, saying, "These would look nice on him." And, "They're quite sturdy and durable." "Very sharp."

Sensing my sullen disapproval, Ethel Merman throws me a bone of recognition. "These are very popular with the young men today." (The manly ploy again.) As if this bat would have the slightest clue about popularity. I want to say, "Popular? I'll tell you what's popular. Any girl in my class with a training bra. That's popular."

Then we move into the next phase of humiliation. The Dressing Room. First they give you all this malarkey about what a big man you are, then they follow you into the dressing room and practically pants you. I'm thinking, isn't it a little crowded with all three of us in here? Why don't we invite the whole store in and go for the Guinness record? Ethel Merman pipes up with, "Now don't be embarrassed, this is nothing I haven't seen before." I'm thinking, "Excuse me, but you haven't seen THIS before and I'd prefer we keep it that way. And hey! Watch the zipper, would you?"

The next circle of hell is the Hall of Mirrors. I'm forced to leave the dressing room and parade around the store in these checkered pantaloons that have obviously been ordered by the gross from Omar the Tentmaker. Once they get me in front of the mirror, Ethel Merman steps up and grabs the pants by the waistband and with all her considerable might heaves them up to my armpits giving me a splendid wedgie. The next move, lightning fast and right out of left field, is the crotch grab and downward yank. This indignity was always brought to a close with the statement, "He'll grow into them."

So we repeat this procedure endlessly until my spirit is broken and I'm this human mannequin brainwashed to obey any and all perverse commands. Walk this way. Walk that way. Hold your arms up. Then Ethel starts talking to my Mom again as if I'm not there, and she drops this gem. "He has large hips for a boy." The final insult. First, they call me a man, then treat me like a eunuch, and now I'm a hermaphrodite. I have large hips for a boy? Lady, you have large hips for whatever oversize prehistoric species claims you.

OK, so I'm not bitter and there's no resentment. Right? Now fast-forward to the present. It's 25 years later and I'm back at Westgate. Halle's is gone and so is Ethel. Now I am a man. A man in control of his life. A man unashamed of his body. A man with a mind of his own who knows what he wants. A man with a credit card. A man in search of trousers. Where do I go? The Gap.

Ethel Merman has been replaced by a lithe, wispy, blond teenage girl who recalls Uma Thurman.

In 25 years, I've gone from Merman to Thurman. The result? I'm still embarrassed to buy a pair of pants. Even though Uma doesn't follow me into the dressing room, yank the crotch out of my duds or denigrate my physical appearance, I still feel like some weirdo on parade. The fact is, I don't really need her there observing my purchase. I know she's just doing her job, I just wish she wouldn't. She makes me feel old and misshapen.

When several years pass between shopping sprees, you tend to forget all the vital information necessary to buy clothes. Your waist size, collar size, inseam, are not only difficult to remember, but they also tend to change. It's embarrassing to have a teenage girl running a tape-measure up the inside of your thigh or telling you while you're bursting a blood vessel trying to button your pants, that perhaps you should try on a pair of 38's.

Then there are those mirrors. You know, the ones that have three panels so you can see yourself at every possible bad angle. The bald spot, the paunch, the wide-body rearview. The great thing about looking straight at a regular mirror is a phenomenon called the "ego hallucination." The ego hallucination is a psychological self-esteem device through which every adult looking in a mirror still sees themselves as he or she was at 23. The three-paneled mirror destroys that effect. You see yourself as you really are and discover how cruel nature can be. All under the helpful gaze of Uma Thurman.

Thurman-Merman. Merman-Thurman. That reminds me. I've got taxes to do.

March 22, 1992

BALD, BALDING, BALDEST

Next to famine, the economy and ecology, women worry about their weight. The men, about going bald. It doesn't seem fair. Does it, guys?

You can lose weight with willpower. Just lay off the doughnuts and Zima for a half-hour. But you can't grow hair at will. Except in places where you don't want it. Like the inside of your ears. Is it any wonder women complain that guys don't listen? What? A little louder, please.

Vanity in the '90s is a transsexual and transparent obsession. And hair, from the male view, is involved in a big way. Yul Brynner aside, being bald is usually reserved for old tires, lies and billiard balls. You may have them, tell them or own them, but you wouldn't want them on your head.

Yet 30 million American men are experiencing some baldness, according to Sy Sperling of the Hair Club For Men. You know, he's not just the president . . .

But has any generation been more obsessed with hair than baby boomers? How's this for a milestone: The Broadway show *Hair* just celebrated its 25th anniversary.

The play defined a generation; those hedonistic social anarchists who are currently paying mortgages, car insurance and other people to raise their children. People who on the weekends worry about their lawns and talk nervously about not seeing one penny of what they might have paid into Social Security. They thought the idea of nuclear destruction was scary. Ha! That's nothing compared to waking up in the morning and seeing Bozo the Clown in the mirror.

Elvis was the first American icon with "long" hair. That greasy ducktail, which eventually grew into a socially acceptable Las Vegas bouffant. Then the Beatles, or the "mop tops" as the press called them. Then really long hair became the thing. And it's back again. Unless, of course, you don't have any.

What's so funny about a bald man? Chrome dome, skinhead,

forehead forever, fringe-face, baldy or solar panel for a sex machine. I could go on. You have a wave in your hair and it's waving
goodbye. Hey, it happens. You're not alone. But it still bugs you. Or
does it? And how much hair do you have to lose to be considered
bald? Losing hair is not life-threatening, so what's the big deal?

Here's the deal. It's a sign of mortality. You're getting older, and
one breath closer to death as Pink Floyd, that long-haired British rock band, sang. But some guys lose their hair in high school.
They're not worried about death. (A dearth of dates perhaps.) It's
really a genetic thing, passed on from your mother's father. And,
according to scientific research, irreversible. Bummer, man.

We can put a man on the moon but . . . where are our priorities?
Our dads invented the comb-over, the hairstyle with the part just
above the ear. It works except for one thing: wind.

But the boomers would not be outdone. We have a simpler, less
deceptive solution. It's called Bald Guys With Ponytails. I am a
member in good standing of this august group. We don't have annual meetings or anything. But some bald guys do.

John T. Capps III founded Bald-Headed Men of America (in
Morehead City, N.C.) after he claimed he was refused employment
because he lacked hair. BHMA is the oldest bald-rights organization with 25,000 members in 50 states and 39 foreign countries.
They hold annual conventions. The group's motto: "If you don't
have it, flaunt it."

But, like most civil-rights groups, bald men have a radical, ex-
tremist branch founded by Ed Leibowitz in 1991. Leibowitz fronts
the Bald Urban Liberation Brigade (BULB) in New York City, and
was responsible for the distribution of fliers around Manhattan
which "outed" or "scalped" toupee-wearing celebrities such as William Shatner, Ted Danson and even John Wayne with computer-
generated images of how the men would look without their rugs.

And, like most liberation movements, the bald-rights uprising
has spawned literature, or at least its own book. *Bald Like Me—The
Hair-Raising Adventures of Baldman*, written by Richard San-
domir, in 1990, may be the bald man's bible. The New York author
even wrote President Bush in 1991 requesting a Bald Man's Bill of
Rights. There's no word on whether he has contacted the Clinton
administration.

All three men promote a "bald is beautiful" philosophy, which emphasizes what's in a man's head rather than what's on it. Capps' group even has a prayer: "The Lord is just. The Lord is fair. He gave some brains and others hair."

Amen, Brother Capps.

I n the other corner of the bald battle is Sy Sperling, founder and president of the Hair Club For Men. In case you don't own a television or don't get cable, he's also a client.

The Hair Club is an $80 million-a-year business with offices in 55 cities nationwide, including two offices in the Cleveland area. More than 100,000 customers have been served since 1968.

Sperling, a droll 51-year-old with a soft South Bronx honk, speaks from his Manhattan office about the Hair Club, himself and his views on baldness. He also admits to some enjoyment of the strange cult of personality his ubiquitous infomercials have created. He's become a Faux Hair Celebrity, whatever that is. But he's not complaining.

"Jay Leno mentions me once a week in his monologue," he says. "I've been asked to do stand-up comedy, there's street recognition. It's amazing what the media can do for you."

Sperling then tells the story of a divorced, 27-year-old swimming-pool salesman whose hair was thinning rapidly. He originally had a weave done using his remaining hair as anchors for the artificial strands. When the anchors gave way, so did the weave.

"It was terrible," says Sperling. "I went from thin to full to total baldness."

Then he met Walter Tucciaroni, who has developed what he calls the Tucci Original (later known as the Polyfuse Method). Cornrows are attached around the fringe area and a nylon mesh is stretched across the scalp into which the new hair is woven strand by strand. The initial fitting costs $2,000 to $3,500. It must be retightened and styled every six weeks, which costs $60. Every three to five years later, the initial fitting must be replaced, which is $1,000 to $1,500. And that ain't hay. In fact, the hair, which is real, comes from India. A great place to buy a rug.

Sperling admits to some problems with the system. For example, a man must wash his woven hair with more care than if washing his own hair. But he believes in his product and understands its success.

"This is my pitch," he says. "When you meet a woman for the first time, you have a split second for her to decide whether she likes you or not. Once you're past that, she's going to decide on the basis of who you are. You get past that and she's accepted it. She may even say you don't need it as far as she's concerned. We live in a superficial society. We're very image-conscious. Your looks are important."

Sperling admits that what his product is largely about is self-esteem. And that the Hair Club isn't for everyone.

"Bald is OK if you feel OK. Michael Jordan doesn't need hair. He's good-looking, he's rich, he's successful. He feels good about himself. Some guys just don't look as attractive as they would with hair. It lengthens your face when you're bald. Hair gives you more proportion. It's about how you look and how that makes you feel."

Summing it up, Sperling sounds more like the streets of South Bronx than he does a men's movement guru. But the message remains the same, if more direct. "Hey, ya gotta do what ya gotta do," he says.

Leaving out the Hair Club, covering your head these days can be reduced to this mantra: rugs, plugs, drugs and hair in a can. So it doesn't work that well as a mantra. Let's examine the options.

Toupees. Forget it. They're silly. And if Burt Reynolds can't find a good one, it doesn't exist. It's been said that every man looks funny chasing his hat down a street. Take it a step further.

Plugs. This is a medical procedure in which hair from the back of the head is implanted in the top of the scalp. It is painful, time-consuming and expensive. It doesn't look that great either.

Drugs. Rogaine (minoxidil 2%). FDA approved. Hypertension medicine that has the side effect of growing hair. Finally, a desirable side effect. However, *The Consumer Affairs Letter* and *Consumer Reports* magazine say that the drug results in a full head of hair in only 8% to 10% of cases, with another 11% to 13% producing only peach fuzz. You also have to take it every day until you die (at a cost of $50 to $60 a month). Think of it as scalp methadone.

Hair in a can. From Ron Popeil, the man who brought us Veg-O-Matic and the Pocket Fisherman, among other life-changing devices, comes GLH Formula Number 9 Hair System. It is an aerosol-based dye that covers open patches of scalp in your hair color.

There's also scalp reduction (letting your eyebrows grow and combing them back), wearing a hat and cutting off your head. I mean, if it bugs you that much, why go on?

What's funniest about a bald man? A sense of humor, I think.

My favorite bald joke comes from my father (a man with a healthy head of hair, by the way). He tells this story about former Cleveland Browns lineman Bob Gaine. During training camp at Hiram College, Gaine would get his classic male-pattern-baldness fringe trimmed in nearby Garrettsville.

One day, the barber patted the top of Gaine's head and proclaimed, "As soft as my wife's behind." Gaine reached up and patted it himself. "Yeah, you're right," he said.

July 18, 1993

AT GROUND ZERO, FATIGUE AND FRAYED NERVES

TERROR HITS HOME

Three days after the Word Trade Center attack, Edgar Rojas, the executive chef at Oro Blu Ristorante Italiano, is open, but not for business. While it pours rain outside, he's cooking food: fried chicken, steamed vegetables, salad and fruit, enough for the rescue workers at ground zero in Manhattan's financial district.

"My cousin, Telmo, he was a busboy on the 106th floor of the Trade Center," Rojas says. "He was 23 and married with a little boy. We are so sad for him. And the men down there, they are doing a great thing."

There is a problem, though.

"I have no car to get it down there," Rojas says.

The word gets out, and an hour later a camouflage Humvee arrives at the restaurant at 333 Hudson St. A sergeant from the Brooklyn National Guard steps from the vehicle and walks into Oro Blu.

The sergeant and two of his men load enough food for 100 people in the back of the Humvee and head back downtown to 345 Chambers St., where Stuyvesant High School has been transformed into a bustling relief center.

The center provides food, medical care, clothing, beds and bathrooms for the thousands of rescue workers who have been sifting and removing a mountain of twisted steel and broken cement six stories high.

A GUARDED ZONE

The ride to ground zero is slow under a wet, slate-gray sky. Every few blocks there are police barricades where officers scrutinize every individual and vehicle looking to gain access.

No one gets through without an official vehicle or picture identification with proof of residence. New York's Finest have turned back wave after wave of media people and curiosity seekers.

The Humvee has no problem.

As the vehicle descends into lower Manhattan on Broadway it passes the popular Odeon restaurant on the left. Across the street are two once-luxurious automobiles, stacked like crushed tin cans.

A man walking a small dog, a SoHo resident, passes a group of soldiers, a camera crew and two firemen before bending to clean up after the pooch with a plastic baggie. Ten blocks to the south, a mess beyond comprehension sits smoking.

At the final barricade, the one that opens into the grim city within a city that is ground zero, cameras and producers from all the major television networks are camped under umbrellas.

A woman from ABC approaches the Humvee, signaling the sergeant to roll down his window.

"Any news?" she asks.

"Just delivering food," he replies before driving on.

On the left is a big red McDonald's truck. A worker offers the guardsmen quarter-pounders.

"We're gonna get fat if we don't watch it," the sergeant says. "People give you everything you can imagine."

The day's rain helps control the dust from the 75-foot mound of rubble that construction workers and firefighters are attacking. Five soldiers guard the gate to the entrance of the wreckage.

The guardsmen pass the smoking heap without comment. Emergency vehicles line the streets in all directions. NYPD squad cars and vans are next to Chicago Fire Department engines and utility vans from New Jersey, Long Island and Connecticut. The Humvee parks in front of Stuyvesant High School.

A PLACE TO TAKE A BREATHER

Inside, police officers, firefighters and constructions workers are in various states of temporary repose. Workers wearing yellow T-shirts with Scientology Volunteer Ministry on the back staff a registration desk. Behind that a temporary M*A*S*H unit is set up.

To the left there are stacks of 50-pound bags of dog food for the K-9 unit. Twenty dogs are working in shifts, helping workers search for the missing. A handwritten note taped to a pillar says "Asbestos Levels Are Very High—Wear Your Mask at All Times." Almost no one is wearing a mask.

The sergeant and his men take the food up the stairs past the second-floor landing, where massage therapists are working on a half-dozen firefighters.

Up the next flight of steps, in the back room, a woman named Candy oversees the feeding and care of the rescue workers. "Thank you, baby" she says to the sergeant.

The food from Oro Blu has arrived just as the previous meal in the steam trays has been finished. The timing couldn't have been better. Across from the steam trays are tables full of fruit, cookies, candy bars, crackers, snacks and every imaginable form of packaged food.

Behind that are cafeteria tables where firefighters discuss Israel. At another table, two New York City policemen sit upright and asleep with two full plates of food in front of them.

Off the food room is a grief counseling area where mental health professionals are sitting with stricken colleagues of the missing.

With all the activity, all the men in uniform, supplies stacked to the ceiling in several corners and the noise of gas generators humming outside, it's hard to imagine this place is a high school. But next to the food area is a glass case with pictures of students posing with Mario Cuomo, Tim Robbins, Frank McCourt and other celebrities.

One entire hallway is full of boxes of clothes. A firefighter is in there changing his soot-covered shirt. The volunteer asks him if he's very attached to it.

"The reason I ask is that because of all the stuff in the air, we throw the used clothes away," she says.

He looks exhausted and doesn't argue.

Back downstairs there's talk that President Bush will be paying a visit. The other celebrity du jour is *The Sopranos* actor Michael Imperioli, who is acting as security and goes virtually unrecognized.

SHORT FUSES, AMPLE HELP

Closer to the front doors, policemen are trying to calm an upset colleague.

"I don't care what his rank is, there is no reason for him to talk to me that way!"

An officer escorts the angry man outside as the other officers argue about the breach of respect. Everyone seems tired and tense.

Every half-hour truckloads of food, clothing and medical supplies arrive and must be organized and stored. Volunteers stand outside in groups, trading information while waiting for the next truck.

Across the street several hundred construction workers stand in a long line waiting to be authorized to work on the collapse site. Two guys from New Jersey unloading the trucks talk about what brought them here.

"I couldn't stand watching it on television any more," one said. "I had to come down here and do something."

Outside, there's a flurry of activity as Secret Service agents and New York City police brass patrol the area in anticipation of the president's arrival. Workers leave the building to staff new barricades erected to give the president some space and security. The streets are being cleared. Somebody or something's coming.

There's the sound of a truck coming down the West Side Highway. More people gather to see what the excitement is.

A large silver truck spattered with graffiti enters the barricaded area. People strain to look and then sigh and look away. On the side of the truck in big black letters it reads: Bellevue Morgue.

The truck groans on into the site.

September 15, 2001

ABOUT THE AUTHOR

MICHAEL HEATON is an award-winning columnist and reporter. His byline has appeared regularly in *The Plain Dealer* since 1987. Prior to that he was a critic and columnist for the *San Francisco Examiner* and a reporter for *People* magaine. He is a graduate of Kent State University. He is co-author of the *New York Times* bestseller *Motherhood and Hollywood* by his sister, actress Patricia Heaton, and co-author of *I'll Be Right Back*, the autobiography of TV host Mike Douglas. A book collecting his *Plain Dealer* columns, titled *Best of the Minister of Culture*, was published in 1992. The son of legendary *Plain Dealer* sportswriter Chuck Heaton, he lives in Bay Village, Ohio.